Values and Ethics in Social Work Practice

LESTER PARROTT

Series Editors: Jonathan Parker and Greta Bradley

LearningMatters

First published in 2006 by Learning Matters Ltd.
Reprinted in 2007 (twice)
Reprinted in 2008
Reprinted in 2009

British Library Cataloguing in Publication Data
A CIP record for this book is available from the British Library.

ISBN: 978 1 84445 067 1

The right of Lester Parrott to be identified as the Author of this Work has been asserted by him in accordance with the Copyright, Designs and Patents Act 1988

Cover and text design by Code 5 Design Associates Ltd
Project management by Deer Park Productions, Tavistock, Devon
Typeset by Pantek Arts Ltd, Maidstone, Kent
Printed and bound in Great Britain by Cromwell Press Group, Trowbridge, Wiltshire

Learning Matters Ltd
33 Southernhay East
Exeter EX1 1NX
Tel: 01392 215560
info@learningmatters.co.uk
www.learningmatters.co.uk

BT2   02/10

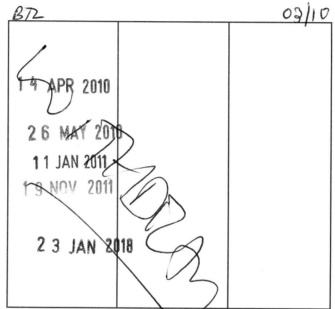

14 APR 2010

26 MAY 2010

11 JAN 2011

19 NOV 2011

2 3 JAN 2018

This book should be returned/renewed by
the latest date shown above. Overdue items
incur charges which prevent self-service
renewals. Please contact the library.

Wandsworth Libraries
24 hour Renewal Hotline
01159 293388
www.wandsworth.gov.uk Wandsworth

L.749A (2.07)

Contents

Acknowledgements   vii

Introduction   xi

1   Preparing for social work   1

2   Anti-oppressive practice   23

3   Principles and consequences   44

4   Being accountable   65

5   Managing risk   83

6   Advocacy and social work organisations   98

7   The ethics of partnership working   119

8   Ethics in social work organisations   135

References   153

Index   161

Acknowledgements

I have many people to thank for helping me to write this book. First my partner Bernadette and our children Frances, Zoe and Joseph.

All the students at North East Wales Institute (NEWI) who have helped me with feedback on different aspects of the book; my colleagues at NEWI, in particular Jonquil Ifans who read a number of the chapters and gave me some sound advice; Jenny Lloyd who took many calls on my behalf when I was away researching different topics for the book; Josephine Norward, Assistant Professor, Keane University, USA, for graciously allowing the use of her article on social work in Apartheid South Africa; Professor John Harris, University of Warwick, for the use of his article on management-speak in social work.

Finally, I would like to thank Learning Matters for their help and support, in particular Jonathan Parker and Greta Bradley for their encouraging and helpful readers' comments and editorship, and Di Page and Kate Lodge for treating some of my more improbable enquiries and questions with more politeness than they deserved.

This book is dedicated to:

Ada Mary Elizabeth Parrott born 7 September 1917, died
13 December 2005

Introduction

This book is written for student social workers who are beginning to develop their understanding of values and ethics in social work. While it is primarily aimed at students in their first-year level of study, it will be useful for subsequent years depending on how your programme is designed, what you are studying and especially as you move into practice learning. The book will also appeal to people considering a career in social work or social care but not yet studying for a social work degree. It will assist students undertaking a range of social and health care courses in further education. Nurses, occupational therapists and other health and social care professionals will be able to gain an insight into the new requirements demanded of social workers. Experienced and qualified social workers, especially those contributing to practice learning, will also be able to use this book for consultation, teaching and revision and to gain an insight into the expectations raised by the qualifying degree in social work.

Requirements for social work education

Social work education has undergone a major transformation to ensure that qualified social workers are educated to honours degree level, and develop knowledge, skills and values which are common and shared. A vision for social work operating in complex human situations has been adopted. This is reflected in the following definition from the International Association of Schools of Social Work and International Federation of Social Workers (2001):

> The social work profession promotes social change, problem solving in human relationships and the empowerment and liberation of people to enhance well-being.
>
> Utilising theories of human behaviour and social systems, social work intervenes at the points where people interact with their environments. Principles of human rights and social justice are fundamental to social work.

While there is a great deal packed into this short and pithy definition, it encapsulates the notion that social work concerns individual people and wider society. Social workers practise with people who are vulnerable, who are struggling in some way to participate fully in society. Social workers walk that tightrope between the marginalised individual and the social and political environment that may have contributed to their marginalisation.

Social workers need to be highly skilled and knowledgeable to work effectively in this context. The current government is keen for social work education and practice to improve. In order to improve the quality of both these aspects of professional social work, it is crucial that you, as a student social worker, develop a rigorous grounding in and understanding of the underpinning values and practice ethics of the discipline. Such knowledge enables practitioners to understand the basic practice principles upon which social work is based and enables service users to know what to expect from the social workers who work with them.

Department of Health and Quality Assurance Agency

The book aims to meet the learning needs outlined in the Department of Health's pre-scribed curriculum for the development of values and ethics in social work. In addition it will list subject skills identified in the Quality Assurance Agency academic benchmark criteria for social work. These include understanding the nature of social work values and ethics in practice and include:

2.4 *Social work is a moral activity that requires practitioners to make and implement difficult decisions about human situations that involve the potential for benefit or harm. Social work honours degree programmes, therefore, involve the study, application of and reflection upon ethical principles. Although social work values have been expressed at different times in a variety of ways, at their core they involve showing respect for persons, honouring the diverse and distinctive organisations and communities that make up contemporary society and combating processes that lead to discrimination, marginalisation and social exclusion. This means that honours undergraduates must learn to:*

- *recognise and work with the powerful links between intra-personal and inter-personal factors and the wider social, legal, economic, political and cultural context of people's lives;*

- *understand the impact of injustice, social inequalities and oppressive social relations;*

- *challenge constructively individual, institutional and structural discrimination;*

- *practise in ways that maximise safety and effectiveness in situations of uncertainty and incomplete information;*

- *help people to gain, regain or maintain control of their own affairs, insofar as this is compatible with their own or others' safety, well-being and rights.*

2.5 *The expectation that social workers will be able to act effectively in such complex circumstances requires that honours degree programmes in social work should be designed to help students learn to become accountable, reflective and self-critical. This involves learning to:*

- *think critically about the complex social, economic, political and cultural contexts in which social work practice is located;*

- *work in a transparent and responsible way, balancing autonomy with complex, multiple and sometimes contradictory accountabilities (for example, to different service users, employing agencies, professional bodies and the wider society);*

- *exercise authority within complex frameworks of accountability and ethical and legal boundaries; and*

- *acquire and apply the habits of critical reflection, self-evaluation and consultation, and make appropriate use of research in the evaluation of practice outcomes.*

3.1.3 Values and ethics

- *The nature, historical evolution and application of social work values.*

- *The moral concepts of rights, responsibility, freedom, authority and power inherent in the practice of social workers as moral and statutory agents.*

- *The complex relationships between justice, care and control in social welfare and the practical and ethical implications of these, including roles as statutory agents and in upholding the law in respect of discrimination.*

- *Aspects of philosophical ethics relevant to the understanding and resolution of value dilemmas and conflicts in both inter-personal and professional contexts.*

- *The conceptual links between codes defining ethical practice, the regulation of professional conduct and the management of potential conflicts generated by the codes held by different professional groups.*

(**www.qaa.ac.uk/academicinfrastructure/benchmark/honours/socialpolicy.asp#13**)

The approach developed in this book requires you to actively engage with the material and requires you to reflect upon the core practice issues which values and ethics in social work address.

National Occupational Standards and General Social Care Council

The book will also meet the National Occupational Standards (NOS) set for social workers. The Standards state clearly that values and ethics are central to competence. In addition the General Social Care Council (GSCC) has set down codes of practice for what they term social care workers and social care employers.

Social care workers must:

1 protect the rights and promote the interests of service users and carers;

2 strive to establish and maintain the trust and confidence of service users and carers;

3 promote the independence of service users while protecting them as far as possible from danger or harm;

4 respect the rights of service users whilst seeking to ensure that their behaviour does not harm themselves or other people;

5 uphold public trust and confidence in social care services;

6 be accountable for the quality of their work and take responsibility for maintaining and improving their knowledge and skills.

In respect of the National Occupational Standards for social work, all the identified key roles below are underpinned by the need to apply values and ethics. To this end, at the beginning of each chapter the relevant NOS will be identified along with the respective links with the codes of practice for social care workers and employers where appropriate. Social workers must:

- prepare for work with people and assess their needs and circumstances;

- plan, carry out, review and evaluate in social work;

- support individuals to represent needs, views and circumstances;

- manage risk;

- be accountable with supervision and support for own practice;

- demonstrate professional competence in social work practice.

Values and ethics underpinning the key roles:

- Awareness of your own values, prejudices, ethical dilemmas and conflicts of interest and their implications on your practice.

- Respect for, and the promotion of:

  – each person as an individual;
  – independence and quality of life for individuals, while protecting them from harm;
  – dignity and privacy of individuals, families, carers, groups and communities.

- Recognise and facilitate each person's use of the language and form of communication of their choice.

- Value, recognise and respect the diversity, expertise and experience of individuals, families, carers, groups and communities.

- Maintain the trust and confidence of individuals, families, carers, groups and communities by communicating in an open, accurate and understandable way.

- Understand, and make use of, strategies to challenge discrimination, disadvantage and other forms of inequality and injustice.

As important as the codes of practice and NOS are, it is also important to recognise that the GSCC has engaged in a lengthy process of consultation with service users. This book has also been written to include the expectations that service users have of social workers and social care workers in respect of values and ethics. The full list of headings is included below; those of relevance to this book are included in more detail underneath the general list.

5.1 Communication skills and information sharing

5.2 Good social work practice

5.3 Advocacy

5.4 Working with other professionals

5.5 Knowledge

5.6 Values

5.3 Advocacy

Social workers must:

(a) Be able to:

  – *lobby on behalf of users and carers to access services;*
  – *challenge their own organisations on behalf of users and carers;*
  – *challenge injustice and lack of access to services;*
  – *challenge poor practice;*
  – *advise users and carers about independent advocacy that can best meet their needs.*

(b) Enable users and carers to be empowered to represent their views.

(c) Help users and carers to represent their views in all meetings affecting them.

(d) Involve independent advocates, where appropriate.

5.4 Working with other professionals

Social workers must:

(a) *Be honest, clear and make sure all involved understand:*

– *what happens to the information users and carers give to the social worker;*
– *how it is kept;*
– *who it is shared with, and why;*
– *how it might be used.*

(b) *Understand what information other organisations can offer and share with users and carers.*

(c) *Work effectively with others to improve services offered to users and carers*

5.6 Values

Social workers must:

(a) *Have respect for:*

– *users and carers, regardless of their age, ethnicity, culture, level of understanding and need;*
– *for the expertise and knowledge users and carers have about their own situation.*

(b) *Empower users and carers in decisions affecting them.*

(c) *Be honest about:*

– *the power invested in them, including legal powers;*
– *their role and resources available to meet need.*

(d) *Respect confidentiality, and inform users and carers when information needs to be shared with others.*

(e) *Be able to:*

– *challenge discriminatory images and practices affecting users and carers*
– *put users and carers first.*

To conclude, the book takes an action-oriented approach to the acquisition of knowledge of social work values and ethics and their application in practice. However this book does not uncritically replicate the requirements of the NOS or the codes of practice for social care workers and their employers. It will therefore identify any problematic areas which you will need to reflect upon when assessing the validity of the standards and codes in the belief that constant critical reflection upon such matters will enable their further development. In particular this book takes as its central theme the importance of a commitment to social justice through anti-oppressive practice as the bedrock upon which social work values and ethics are set.

Book structure

Changes to social work education and the implementation of new degree courses mean that there is a need for new, practical learning support material to help you achieve the qualification. This book is designed to help you gain theoretical and practical knowledge concerning values and ethics in social work. It expects that you will reflect on the arguments and case studies presented here and test the value of the knowledge gained in practice. The emphasis is on you achieving the requirements of the curriculum and developing knowledge that will assist you in meeting the Occupational Standards for social work.

The book has eight main chapters. These examine social work values: the political and social context, anti-oppressive practice, principles and consequences, being accountable, risk, advocacy and social work organisations, the ethics of partnership working and the codes of practice: employers and social workers.

In Chapter 1 you will be asked to reflect upon the nature of social work values, placing them within the changing political and social context of social work. In particular this chapter outlines the changes to social work practice that have pushed social work into becoming more business-like and managerial in its orientation. It will ask you to reflect upon the challenges that these rational technical approaches make to social work values. You will be asked to think about the reasons why you want to become a social worker and it will ask you to reflect upon why you should act ethically. From this you will be asked to identify the influences that encourage you to behave in an ethical way and the justification you bring to acting in an ethical manner.

Chapter 2 then presents the arguments for working in an anti-oppressive way by considering some of the different meanings of anti-oppressive social work (AOP). It then outlines the basic principles of AOP and differentiates between a general orientation to social justice through AOP and specific values and ethics associated with AOP, i.e. empowerment, partnership and minimal intervention. It then asks you to consider approaches to difference and diversity, and analyses the difference between an uncritical approach to difference, outlined as a cultural relativist approach and one which looks at how we can evaluate different cultural practices from the point of view of a social justice approach. A number of case studies is used to highlight some of the conflicts and dilemmas that this involves social workers in when, on the one hand wishing to appreciate different persons' cultures, while on the other hand ensuring that individuals within them receive justice.

In Chapter 3 different philosophical approaches to ethics are considered and you will be asked to evaluate these in turn. Starting with Kantian and Utilitarian approaches which still underpin much ethical social work practice, you will consider both from a critical standpoint using appropriate case studies. From these more embedded approaches you will then investigate virtue ethics which is experiencing a revival within social work and which looks towards the development of the character of social workers to develop ethical practice. Finally you will give consideration to a feminist ethic of care which has sought to reconcile the competing imperatives of universal principles of justice with a specific concern for care and the network of caring relationships which are considered so vital to service users' needs and interests.

Chapter 4 identifies the importance of accountability for social workers and looks at the challenges faced by social workers in being accountable to a number of competing interests. The problems then are identified when faced with the competing accountabilities between the service user and the wider community and between the employing organisation and the service user, all of which place significant strains upon individual social workers wishing to practise in an ethical way. The chapter concludes with a discussion on the importance of critical reflective practice for accountability and looks at the role of critical reflection in developing practice which reflects an anti-oppressive stance. In particular it looks at the influence of oppressive discourses in social work and how they can be transformed through their deconstruction and critical reflection.

Chapter 5 deals with the specific challenges of risk within social work. Increasingly as social work organisations ration and prioritise their services towards those service users seemed in most need, then social workers will progressively be working in situations which present more risk. This chapter outlines the context within which risk has become an important ethical challenge for social workers. It argues that in assessing risk we are practising values in deeming some behaviours and situations as more risky than others. It suggests that social workers need to be aware of risk but not let this consume their practice. It argues for a more positive orientation which looks at opportunities for progressive practice within risk situations. In particular it argues for more empowering practice by considering ways in which service users can be involved in their own risk management so that social workers' risk assessments are done *with* service users and not *to* them.

Chapter 6 takes up the theme of empowering practice and looks at the role of social workers as advocates for service users. It explores the role of the professional advocate and highlights the importance of seeing professional advocacy as necessary but not sufficient for empowering service users. The use of professional empowerment should be used only under specific circumstances and should have as its ultimate goal the acquiring of skills by service users to advocate for themselves either individually or collectively. The chapter concludes by arguing that advocacy for self is also important and discusses the importance of social workers being assertive in their own organisations. It explores this in relation to supervision and uses the Climbié Inquiry as a case study of how a lack of assertion can lead to poor outcomes for social workers and service users alike. In considering self-advocacy it argues that more collective methods may also be appropriate and looks at the ethical arguments for joining trade unions and for engaging in industrial action as social workers.

Chapter 7 focuses upon partnership working. Over the past five years partnership working has become a key facet of working within personal social services. Changes to the way social workers work with adults and children are drawing previously disparate professional groups together as the current government seeks to 'modernise' the welfare state. This means that social workers need to be aware of the ethical implications of partnership working. This chapter then outlines the meaning of partnership and then develops some ethical principles to be considered for working in partnership. Little has been written on the ethical implications of working together and this chapter explores the challenges which social work professionals face in working in partnership with other professional groups such as the police, nurses and other health professionals.

Chapter 8 considers the ethical implications of social workers as employees of social work organisations. It analyses the advantages and disadvantages of social work organisations operating as bureaucracies and how some of the problems may be dealt with ethically. In particular it identifies the problems faced by social workers expected to be accountable to their employers' policies and procedures when these may act as barriers to meeting the needs of service users. It provides some alternative ways of working through the challenges when social work organisations operate in bureaucratic ways to limit the professional autonomy of social workers. It uses the concept of 'McDonaldisation' to investigate how social work may be increasingly operating towards business models of service delivery. Finally it returns us to the opening chapter by considering the idea of ethical practice from the example of whistle-blowing. Here the real-life example of a social worker is considered, who was involved in the North Wales Tribunal on child abuse, to assess the necessity for whistle-blowing. It concludes with a sober evaluation of the costs and benefits associated with whistle-blowing on an individual and social basis.

Learning features

The book is interactive. You are encouraged to work through each chapter as an active participant, taking responsibility for your learning, in order to increase your knowledge, understanding and ability to apply this learning to practice. You will be expected to reflect creatively on how immediate learning needs can be met in the area of social work values and ethics and how your professional learning can be developed to ensure an ethically based service for service users.

Case studies throughout the book will help you to examine the concepts and theories which underpin values and ethics in social work. We have devised activities that require you to reflect on experiences, situations and events and help you to review and summarise learning undertaken. In this way your knowledge will become deeply embedded as part of your development. When you come to practise learning in an agency the work and reflection undertaken here will help you to improve and hone your skills and knowledge.

This book will introduce knowledge and learning activities for you as a student social worker concerning the central processes relating to issues of daily practice in all areas of the discipline. Suggestions for further reading will be made at the end of each chapter.

Professional development and reflective practice

Great emphasis is placed on developing skills of reflection about, in and on practice. This has developed over many years in social work. It is important also that you reflect prior to practice, if indeed this is your goal. This book will assist you in developing a questioning approach that looks in a critical way at your thoughts, experiences and practice and seeks to heighten your skills in refining your practice as a result of these deliberations. Reflection is central to good social work practice, but only if action results from that reflection.

Reflecting about, in and on your practice is not only important during your education to become a social worker, it is considered key to continued professional development. As we move to a profession that acknowledges lifelong learning as a way of keeping up to date, of ensuring that research informs practice and of honing skills and values for practice, it is important to begin the process at the outset of your development. The importance of professional development is clearly shown by its inclusion in the National Occupational Standards and is reflected in the General Social Care Council (GSCC) Code of Practice for Employees.

Chapter 1
Preparing for social work

Social work values: the political and social context

Social work has undergone significant change over the past twenty years. The values of social work have been positively influenced by anti-discriminatory and anti-oppressive forms of practice. This requires social workers to account for difference in their practice and work towards social justice for those groups marginalised by the negative assessment of such difference. In addition, service user movements have taken an increasingly positive role in influencing the way in which social workers are required to put service user needs at the centre of service delivery. Less encouragingly, social work and social care has come under increasing media and government pressure (Harris, 2003a) to become more efficient and more effective in what it does. This is not necessarily a bad thing as, like any such statements, social workers are hardly going to argue against making their practice more efficient and more effective. The problem, as many commentators suggest (Parton and O'Byrne, 2000; Dominelli, 2002), is the way in which efficiency and effectiveness have been promoted through a singular vision which places social work within a wider process to 'modernise' public services. This concept of modernisation has been dominated by a managerial ethos that believes that social work would be improved through the introduction of procedures which ape the behaviour of private enterprise in the wider capitalist economy. Social work and social care services are increasingly required to operate as enterprises selling their products on the open market, with many aspects of the provision of services having been contracted out to the private sector. Thus public services have to compete to become more efficient, more flexible and treat service users as customers to become more like a private sector enterprise (Clarke, 2004).

As part of this process, social workers have become less able to use their skills in creative ways but are required to focus on standardised practice such as unified assessment procedures in the form of assessment frameworks. When social workers are not encouraged to follow narrow assessment protocols they are required to become managers of resources through the reforms introduced in the wake of the National Health Service and Community Care Act 1990. These developments have led many writers to suggest that the modernising project requires that social work becomes a rational technical activity. This means that social work is becoming an activity which is increasingly subject to managerial direction, working towards strictly determined practice policy and procedure which has as its goal the control of professional judgement and discretion. It defines social work as the rational application of such procedures in which questions of value become less important than what is achieved in terms of managerially determined service outcomes. In this view social work is not the quality of the service provided but quantity, i.e. the outcome, because outcomes can be measured. This distorts many aspects of social work, for example the quality of the relationships social workers forge with service users, because managerially they are less important as they are less easily measured.

This process is presented as a natural development to increase the efficiency and effectiveness of social work and therefore appears to be value-free and neutral. But this claim to neutrality has been used to wrest power from social workers to define and control the nature of their work. Managerial ideas and business-like solutions to essentially practical and moral problems faced by social workers marginalise professional and service user contributions to social work, and undermine the value base of social work. Harris (2003b) argues that this process is circular in that competition requires monitoring through contract specification that leads to the need for performance measurement to monitor the effectiveness of contracts which requires increased managerial scrutiny (see Figure 1.1).

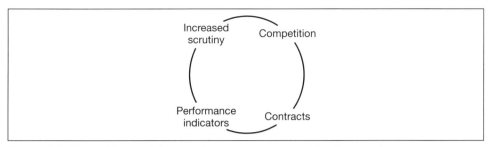

Figure 1.1 *Controlling social work: the management and business cycle*

- *Increased scrutiny*. Information technology systems allow detailed specification of social work activities and checks on their completion. Much of this control is expressed in computerised manuals, directions and guidelines that limit discretion.

- *Performance indicators*. Business-oriented measurable standards and pre-set standardised and repetitive systems with tightly defined criteria for eligibility for services.

- *Contracts*. The use of contracts ensures that control resides with the purchaser who has the power to make decisions and see them carried through. The provider has to implement the purchaser's decisions which are often determined in advance from a limited list which minimises contact time but calls for more throughput.

- *Competition*. The belief that competition among providers results in more economical, efficient and effective services (adapted from Harris, 2003b).

There is a danger that the process of social work can become a series of unrelated activities which prevent practice from being subject to ethical and theoretical scrutiny. As Parton and O'Byrne (2000, p31) state:

...even prescriptive assessment and monitoring schedules require interpretation and judgement to be made practical.

Social work is better described as a practical-moral activity. This means that social workers hold a privileged position within the public services in working with people who often experience profound problems and significant crises in their lives which require practical solutions but have important moral consequences. This requires social workers to exercise their judgement in informal settings and work in more informal ways. Much social work is carried out in people's homes and involves negotiation in which problems are jointly identified and then worked through by agreement with service users. Thus social workers are dealing with the practical activities of day-to-day living; for example how do service users parent their children so that they can thrive? Or how can an older person who may have a disability live a dignified life in old age where they can get the support needed to live independently? These day-to-day activities require social workers to make significant decisions that have a profound ethical consequence. So if, for example, parents are failing to parent their children, what actions ought the social worker take in order to work in the best interests of the child? Do they remove the child? Do they work with the parents? These problems challenge us to reflect upon our morality and our ethics as social workers.

ACTIVITY 1.1

Test yourself

Here are two statements showing how business thinking affects social work practice. Can you work out what is being discussed? (Answers below.)

A 'Mapping supply will involve an analysis of the market within which the service is operating. This analysis will include: an analysis of the existing stock, an analysis of the various elements of service, an analysis of services from other providers and an analysis of alternatives that can be spot-contracted.'

B 'Our interest is in best practice in terms of what works, why and how at the business level when customer-facing technologies are introduced. We have a services transformation practice and want to learn more about the art of the possible in order to help our clients solve their problems.'

Answers

A Senior manager writing about expanding the number of foster parents available to social workers to be used for placements of children and young people.

B Management consulting company explaining its interest in introducing telephone call centres into social services.

(Taken from Harris, 2003b)

Harris's prescient example of 'business speak' in social work must alert us to the damaging discourse which potentially distances social workers from engaging in ethical practice with service users. Such language can serve to infiltrate the consciousness of social workers and influence their way of thinking and ultimately their practice. To be immersed in a business culture distracts social workers from recognising the ethical content in their work largely because they are required to become mere deliverers of predetermined services. What predominates are resource issues and control over resources including social workers who are increasingly expected to acquire a better purchase upon an environment where resource management is the ultimate goal. Table 1.1 summarises the difference between the rational-technical as against the practical-moral approach to social work.

Table 1.1 *Rational or practical social work*

Rational-technical social work	Practical-moral social work
Management by direction	Management by consultation
Procedurally led services	Focus upon judgement and negotiation between worker and service user to meet need
Danger of early legal/procedural intervention	Legal/procedural intervention as last resort
Resource focused	Needs focused
Emphasis on outcomes	Emphasis on process of social work
Limit discretion of social work	Recognises negotiation, flexibility and uncertainty

Not surprisingly some workers can develop a siege mentality in which they are alienated from their organisations and become demoralised by the demands made upon them. Their work becomes the antithesis of the reasons which inspired them to enter the profession (Jones, 2001):

> It is not that business thinking and practices get in the way of 'real' social work. They have changed what social work is and what social workers do; they have implications for what social workers think, feel and are (Harris, 2003a, p213).

As you work with service users you will engage with ethical conflicts in deciding whether the increasingly rationed and procedurally-based focus of your work is in the best interests of service users. We shall see that our commitment to anti-oppressive social work which seeks as its aim to provide social justice for service users may then be compromised by the requirements placed upon social workers to work within a set repertoire of procedures and a limited resource base. This inevitably restricts the flexibility, availability and accessibility of services for service users. Waterson (1999), looking at this process in community care services, assesses whether the focus of community care social work is shifting from responding to needs to reducing or containing risks. She suggests that community care assessment is increasingly concerned with risk management. The focus upon risk means that resources increasingly follow high-risk cases which marginalises those service users who require more general support. Research by Martin et al. (2004) into adult care outlines some significant problems: the increased responsibility of social care professionals to comply with organisational priorities conflicts with their role of advocacy for their clients, a tension rendered all the more problematic by the perceived inadequacy of funding.

These shifts in the nature of social work present significant challenges to newly qualified social workers and as such require them to reflect deeply upon how they will engage in this new practice environment. Ultimately these imperatives derive from broader societal changes and therefore social workers need to think about how they should respond to these wider transformations. How then should social workers orient themselves to these wider societal imperatives and the values that underpin them? Clark (2000) outlines three approaches to the problem of how social workers can think about their relationship to the values of wider society. These approaches he characterises as:

- separatist

- constitutive

- intermediate.

Separatist

This approach suggests that occupying a professional role requires social workers to have a different set of values that separates them from the wider community. Professionals, by virtue of their expertise, have rights and responsibilities that are different and sometimes at odds with the wider society. For example, a social worker could be justified in not telling the truth (usually valued by most societies) to a service user if they felt it was in the service user's best interests or in the community's best interests. The justification for the professional comes from achieving a desirable end which the professional is expected to perform as part of a professional role. The use of deceit (only as a last resort) if it can be justified as an effective means to achieve such an end could be professionally justified in this way, but is clearly something which could be at odds with wider social values.

Constitutive

This position argues that professionals have no privileged value orientation and therefore have the same responsibilities as other members of society. Social workers should at all times uphold the values of the wider community in their work. Thus if the wider community considers deceit as morally wrong then social workers must abide by these common rules of morality in their dealings with service users. It suggests that the wider societal values will be adequate to enable social workers to work effectively with service users.

Intermediate

This argument is more complex, seeing professional ethics as an expression by society of its public morality. Although professionals might well have special responsibilities and privileges, these do not run separately from public morality but remain within it. This view suggests that the autonomy of professionals is important but they must be held to account when their actions cause public concern. Thus professional ethics will always be both part of the general public morality but also in tension with it. Social workers are therefore not immune from public accountability and responsibility, to which the many inquiries into the failures of social work hold testimony. However the unique role that social workers hold may mean that conventional morality is unable to provide justification for their actions in some cases. This in turn requires a different set of ethics which can navigate a way between professional responsibility and community accountability. This intermediate position is not an easy one to maintain but it does adequately describe the often ambiguous position that social workers find themselves in when assessing the validity of societal values in their practice.

---

*ACTIVITY **1.2***

Read the following extract by Norward (2002) of her experiences as a social worker in Apartheid South Africa.

Background
As a young black woman growing up in South Africa during the Apartheid era, the decision to become a social worker was an easy one. Not only was I limited in my career choices because of my educational background given the country's educational structure for blacks, but two of the most influential black female role models of my time who were very outspoken about the country's injustice system were social workers, namely Ellen Kuzwayo and Winnie Mandela. Thus to some women of my generation, social work was one of the vehicles to social change.

The political upheavals of the 1970s
The political volatility of the early 1970s espoused by the late Steve Biko redefined education for many of us who were attending black university campuses. The black consciousness movement was psychologically liberating and empowering. It also called on everyone to become an instrument of change and be involved in the struggle for black

---

liberation. For those of us who were pursuing social work as a profession, there was recognition that not everyone was capable of engaging in radical social work nor joining the underground movement. Hence, some opted for the most unpopular route of the time, working within the system to bring about change. The latter option turned out to be the most difficult one to implement.

The problem

One of the responsibilities of a social worker was to enforce the repatriation policy of all 'unproductive urban blacks' to their respective homelands. Repatriation was a major pro-vision of the policy of separate development which, under the Apartheid system, each of the black tribal groups who had received parcelled-out pieces of arid land from South Africa's central government, far removed from the flourishing industrial urban areas, were expected to engage in political, economic and social development, eventually leading to self-government, independent of South Africa. Ordinarily, repatriation suggests that one is being returned to one's country of origin or allegiance. Under the Apartheid system it symbolized a system of dumping. The term 'unproductive urban blacks' was used by the municipal white superintendents to describe urban black residents who were unemployed due to old age, disability or because of their illegal status in urban areas. Such individuals were deemed a burden to the city. Largely affected by this policy were migrant workers, the elderly and the disabled who could no longer contribute to the political economy of South Africa nor afford to pay the municipality for rented housing. Repatriation became the government's two-pronged approach to fostering inequalities, robbing blacks of their birthright and resettling them in barren unknown lands in the name of self-development and preserving the most developed parts of the country for whites. The latter were also rich in mineral wealth. Repatriation was also viewed as an answer to housing shortages in sprawling black urban areas, because by repatriating elderly residents, that freed up more houses. While it was easier for the mine industry to enforce this policy on migrant workers who could only reside in urban mine compounds and were able to obtain work permits under the government's Group Areas Act, enforcing such policy on urban citizens who were bona fide residents was much more difficult.

The resolution

Those at risk of repatriation were urban residents who faced eviction orders for failure to pay rent and for other infractions such as failing to show proof that they were legally per-mitted to reside in an urban area. Typically, such cases were referred by the municipal superintendent or senior clerk to the social worker for assistance with impeding recom-mendations for repatriation.

As social workers who had made a choice to work within the system, participating in this system, it could be argued, was contrary to the ethics of social work and the pledge of bringing about change from within.

In the absence of concrete resources, social work practice in South Africa called for high levels of creativity. Thus, where older people were affected by this policy, different strategies were utilized to keep them in their homes. Finding young married relatives, family friends or known trustworthy married couples who were on a waiting list for housing to agree to care for them, pay rent and in exchange have a place to stay was one approach. Collaborating with compassionate senior municipal clerks to sabotage the process was another approach. On rare occasions, social workers in consultation with senior municipal clerks, would go before the superintendent to plead for the expunging of the repatriation order.

(Adapted from Norward, 2002)

In what way did Josephine Norward reconcile her position working as a social worker in Apartheid South Africa?

In Clark's typology does this represent a separatist constitutive or an intermediate position in relation to societal values and social work values?

Comment

As Clark (2000) argues, accepting that social workers should at all times reflect the morality of the community leaves open the possibility that an immoral community may require social workers to act in immoral ways. For example, those medical practitioners and social workers in Nazi Germany who counselled the parents of children who were involuntarily sterilised or put to death through compulsory euthanasia (Proctor, 1988) must account for their actions in regard to their personal and professional ethics other than saying they were merely following the wishes of the community. For Norward the reality of working as a social worker was not an easy one and, as she says, it took her much time to assess her moral stance to the Apartheid regime. For her it would appear that she occupied an intermediate position in that she could not support the Apartheid regime yet she did not take a more radical position and uphold a total opposition. However, she could work within the system to limit some of its damage and also work effectively to uphold her own and her service users' dignity as human beings in not acquiescing to the Apartheid system.

Does Norward, by working within the system, uphold the values of Apartheid even in an indirect way?

Does she help to modify the worst excesses of the regime by trying to prevent those deemed as non-productive to remain in their own homes?

Can she through her practice also provide a symbol of resistance and subvert the system of Apartheid through the dignity and effectiveness of her actions?

By preventing some people from being 'repatriated' does this represent the best traditions of ethical practice required of her as a social worker?

Comment

When people are faced with having to make ethical choices in unjust and sometimes extremely threatening environments and decide not to comply with injustice then we can admire their courage and bravery as in the case above. On the one hand you may criticise Josephine Norward and argue that she should have nothing to do with the repatriation scheme. On the other hand you may think that working around the system enables some people to remain in their own homes who would otherwise have been forced back to a place with which they had no real connection or no hope of a reasonable life.

What would you have done?

As a social worker you will be faced with similar decisions to make but hopefully not in such extreme circumstances. Nonetheless, for the service users you will be working with issues of social justice are just as pressing within the context of UK society. As you work through this book you will discover that context is everything and involves:

- factors of time and place;

- the type and nature of the relationships involved;

- other people's reasonable expectations;

- the relevant history of the situation.

The factors above will all play their part in influencing the ethical principles that you apply. Thus ethical practice must be tempered by an understanding of their contingent nature. Principles can act as guides to decision making but cannot be more than that because each situation is different. The nature of the situation will therefore vary and in turn require you to weigh all relevant ethical principles within a specific context of social relationships at a particular time and place.

As a principle we would want to oppose the South African Apartheid regime as it was clearly a social system based on the suppression of the black majority by the white minority. However, if you are living within that system or any other political system then you have to make an ethical choice as to the relative benefits or losses that it confers upon service users. This means deciding whether to work within the system to ameliorate its worst excesses while still campaigning against it, or to practically oppose it in every way. This case you may think is rather an extreme one which may have little or no relevance for social work in this country. However, you will as a social worker be faced with similar problems which challenge your value base and pose serious ethical dilemmas for you. As a social worker how might you respond to the situation faced by asylum seekers in this country?

Mr and Mrs Hassan and their daughter Farina aged 12 have lived in the UK for the past four years while their application for asylum was investigated. They are Christians from Palestine. After much bureaucratic delay and investigation they have been told they must leave the country and are now categorised as failed asylum seekers. You have been working with the family for the past six months as Farina has Down's syndrome and you have been supporting the family to access appropriate support for her in her secondary school. Section 9 of the Immigration and Asylum (Treatment of Claimants, etc.) Act 2004 gives the Home Office powers to terminate all welfare support, except the accommodation of children in local authority care (under section 20 of the Children Act 1989), for failed asylum-seeking families who are deemed to be in a position to leave the UK. The Hassan family are very fearful of returning to Palestine and decide to try and stay in their flat where they have lived for three years. They ask you for help. Your team manager while sympathetic suggests that you will need to consider taking Farina into care as the family will soon be evicted from their flat and they will have no means of support.

ACTIVITY **1.4**

What similarities do you find between the situation in the case study and Josephine Norward described above?

Comment

As you can see, you are faced with a very similar dilemma to that of Josephine Norward. You can comply with your team manager's advice and reinforce the asylum legislation or find ways of supporting them and keeping the family together. If you support your manager's wishes then, as Humphries (2004) argues, you are drawn into supporting a racist policy and compromising your duty to act in the best interests of the child. Clearly, taking Farina into care merely because her parents have been forcibly pushed into dire poverty seems to work against some fundamental principles of social work. Dunkerley et al. (2005) in their study of asylum in Wales outline the negative effects of the asylum system upon service users:

> *...untreated mental health problems arising from experience of trauma in countries of origin, difficulties over access to education and health care, dissatisfaction with some accommodation and some children being placed with foster carers 'out of county'.* (p642)

On the other hand you can, as Dunkerley et al.'s (2005) research suggests, use your discretion to turn a blind eye. This could entail seeking to support the family outside of the system by using informal social networks or by involving voluntary campaigning groups such as Barnardo's to take up the cases of children of failed asylum seekers. Although in general the researchers are more pessimistic in that they found that most workers did not question their role with respect to asylum seekers, yet:

Our findings could be seen as more encouraging than the more pessimistic accounts of frontline staff in the asylum system. These workers are not accepting the system, but doing what they can to tinker around the edges of policy. On the face of it, the comprehensive National Asylum Support Service regulations allow little room for discretion on the part of practitioners, and yet, as indicated above, the large majority of failed asylum-seekers are not removed from the country. In part, this must arise from professionals 'turning a blind eye' or not actively pursuing such individuals according to the letter of the law. The research reported here provides at least some indication of such practices (Dunkerley et al., 2005 p649).

Thus as a social worker (see Figure 1.2) you are pushed and pulled between the competing responsibilities that social workers are required to attend to. Josephine Norward's example and the research on frontline staff in Wales suggest that social workers can make choices as to where their prime responsibility lies and can then make efforts on behalf of their service users to modify the worst excesses of such repressive systems in which they find themselves. But of course, this on its own is not enough. Social workers will need to engage in a political struggle both within the confines of their social work role and outside in terms of their rights as citizens to organise against the asylum system to provide an effective remedy for service users.

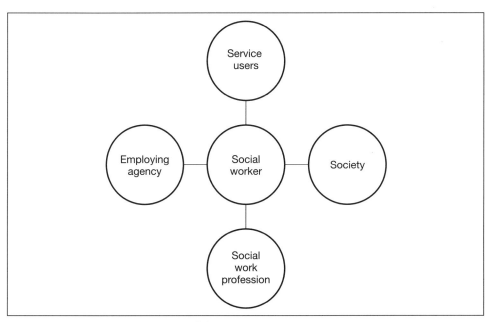

Figure 1.2 *Social workers' responsibilities*

ACTIVITY **1.5**

From looking at Figure 1.2, make a list of the respective duties that you think you owe to each of the areas outlined.

Comment

When social workers in their professional capacity engage with service users then they will need to have sound reasons for the actions they take. At the heart of their practice they must be able to take account of and morally justify their conduct. The aim of social work is therefore to be able to provide positive outcomes for service users at best, and at worst to provide the least harmful outcome. The positive sense of justification requires social workers to bring others to see that their actions are reasonable, that is that the balance of reasons would favour one course of action over any alternative. For social workers to justify their actions they need to persuade those to whom they owe their professional accountability to agree that their actions were indeed good ones. It is this sense of justification that is important for morality. Moral justification, then, means showing that there are more or better moral reasons weighing in favour of one course of action than against it.

Our rights and obligations as social workers come from the relationships outlined in Figure 1.2. These relationships can give us important moral reasons for certain kinds of actions. For example, relationships with service users means that we are obliged to treat them with respect and maximise their welfare. Our relationships with the wider society means we have a duty to maintain social justice to all groups in society and when necessary protect the wider community from harm. Our relationships to the social work profession means that we have a duty to be competent and effective in what we do in upholding the standards of the profession, usually laid down in guidance in the form of a code of ethics. It is important in this respect to think not just of the fact that a given relationship exists, but also about the nature and history of that relationship, and about the legitimate moral expectations that go along with it.

Trust and accountability

When social workers make mistakes either by omission through unconscious incompetence or commission through deliberate wrongdoing, trust in social workers breaks down. The media at its best inevitably play an important part in this process of accountability in which social workers' decisions are given publicity, but the media at its worst can also conduct witch hunts of social workers where every aspect of a person's life is open to the public gaze (Franklin, 1999).

One important step forward in protecting the standing of social workers has been to legally protect the title of social worker. The Care Standards Act 2000, which came into force on 1 April 2005, has been introduced to ensure that only those who are properly qualified, registered and accountable for their work describe themselves as social workers. It is a criminal offence for an unregistered person to use the title 'social worker' with intent to deceive. This is important because prior to this legislation anyone could call themselves a social worker; now it is illegal for anyone to do so. Service users have a right to expect that their 'social worker' is properly trained and accountable for their practice. The legislation also protects the professional status and reputation of the thousands of qualified and committed social workers in the UK against those who use the title illegally.

Section 61 of the Care Standards Act 2000 states that:

> *If a person who is not registered as a social worker in any relevant register with intent to deceive another a) takes or uses the title of social worker; b) takes or uses any title or description implying that he is so registered, or in any way holds himself out as so registered, he is guilty of an offence.*

A social worker stole £64,633 from a pensioner by fleecing her savings and keeping the cash after selling her house. (*The Sun*, Friday, 25 November 2005)

Unlike the example above, there are cases where social workers have upheld the highest standards of ethical social work practice much against the prevailing views of those in positions of authority over them. Alison Taylor, a residential care worker in a children's home in North Wales, became concerned in 1989 about the abusive and aggressive behaviour of her manager Nefyn Dodd who later had overall responsibility for all the residential child care services in Gwynedd, North Wales. Her allegations were not followed through and she was dismissed from her job. She continued to make her claims and told of other abuses across children's homes in North Wales. When a former child care worker Stephen Norris was convicted of the sexual abuse of boys at a community home in Wrexham, Bryn Esten, it was found that Dodd had also worked there. Taylor, with two local politicians and the newly appointed director of social services in Clwyd, unearthed previous allegations of child abuse in homes across North Wales which had not been investigated properly. After much pressure from Taylor and her colleagues, a tribunal (Waterhouse, 2000) was finally set up to look into the allegations leading to a final report in 2000 (Stanley and Manthorpe, 2004).

What are values?

Every person has a set of beliefs which influences their actions. Values relate to what we think others should do, or what we ought to do. They are personal to us, although we may realise that we share some basic values within our society or with others across societies. For example, a fundamental value shared by most people across cultures and societies would be to respect the lives of others. Other values may be more specific to certain cultures, for example maintaining a strict separation of the sexes in most public situations. In deciding those things in life that we value, we rely upon a sense of morality to inform us as to what is important, that is our own moral code determines what we value in life. However, this moral code does not come from thin air but forms through our own experiences of life as a process of personal development and socialisation. We are heavily influenced both by our past experiences and our current understanding of ourselves and the society in which we live.

ACTIVITY **1.6**

Make a list of those values which you feel are important for living what you consider to be a valued life.

Comment

As you can see, the importance of your value system is one which is very close to who you consider yourself to be, it is part of your identity. Your sense of values tells something to yourself and others as to the kind of person you think you are. If we are to define values then we are talking about those fundamental beliefs and principles which we consider constitute our morality and what Clark (2000) calls *the grand aspirations or big ideas of morality and politics such as freedom and justice, autonomy and community* (p28). Values refer to the way we want to live our lives. From a moral standpoint, they are fundamental principles which are the foundations upon which we judge others and act in the world. They have value in themselves, that is they have an intrinsic character which means they constitute an ultimate objective or end. They are not ideas which we use as a means to achieve some other goal, they are the goal. Consequently they are of such importance that they override any other preference, however practical and pragmatic or however useful. They are of such power that nothing should be allowed to overturn them.

ACTIVITY **1.7**

What would you feel if others questioned these values?

What personal feelings are involved if you have experienced such a situation?

Comment

As values form the core of your identity then it can be assumed that you would be compelled to engage with any person who challenged or questioned them. You may seek to understand and challenge, if appropriate, the other's point of view, but the importance for you of your own value base may require much effort for you to shift any of your values. In reading this book you will inevitably feel that your own values are challenged and it is clearly important that you look at alternative viewpoints, as this book is meant to encourage you to reflect on your own value base. In the course of this reflection you may think the power of the ideas presented warrant that you re-evaluate your values in the light of this new knowledge, just as the author did in researching this book and engaging in new and different ideas about social work values. In engaging in debate in this way, it is clear that strong feelings may be generated when our fundamental beliefs are challenged. This shows the essential importance of our values for who we are as people, our identity and how we act in the world.

Where then do our values come from?

Any basic sociological text book will identify the process by which individuals acquire the values of a particular society as a process of socialisation which is ongoing throughout our lives (Giddens, 2006). You can identify within this process the way in which different institutions in society seek to influence and pass on values to you. From birth your parents and carers are important in this regard. When you attend school then the influence of your peer group and friends is also important in developing your sense of value.

ACTIVITY **1.8**

What other influences upon your values can you identify?

Comment

The different influences may vary depending upon the particular culture which you inhabit. Thus for some people religious influence may be extremely important; others may identify their family as a formative influence. As we get older then the influence of family, for example, may not be so immediate and we may well develop and acquire other values from quite different influences. This process is always specific to a particular culture at a particular time. Political parties may be important here or trade unions, or the media or even the world of advertising may shape your values, particularly in societies where consumerism is becoming more pervasive. At the broader level then, our values are constantly being challenged. For example, new developments in technology mean we can keep people alive longer yet their quality of life may be minimal. Such changes in technology may thus require us to re-evaluate our values in the light of these challenges.

Radical thinkers

More specifically a number of radical thinkers have sought to explain how society and the powerful within society seek to influence us. Marxists use the term ideology to describe the way in which dominant ideas in society are managed by the most powerful groups who control economic and political power in a particular society (Ferguson et al., 2002). Thus they would point to the increasing value given to individualism and responsibility as powerful tools in controlling the way people think about themselves and the society they live in. For example, the conception of ourselves as individuals requires us to place less emphasis upon our capacity as social beings who also form groups, work collectively, cooperate together and live within wider communities. Indeed the notion of the individual is a specific construct of Western European societies. People from other cultures may have great difficulty in seeing themselves as distinct individuals separate from their family or wider community. Billington et al. (1998) argue that in Japan, for example:

> *The word 'I' cannot be used in a context free sense in Japanese and it is therefore difficult to form a sentence referring to oneself without placing oneself in the context to others.* (p48)

An influential Marxist writer in this regard is Antonio Gramsci who used the term hegemony by which dominant groups in capitalist society ... *maintain their dominance by securing the 'spontaneous consent' of subordinate groups, including the working class, through the negotiated construction of a political and ideological consensus which incorporates both dominant and dominated groups* (Strinati, 1995, p165).

The point to make here is that the acceptance of the dominant classes' cultural, political and moral values is developed through manipulating the consent of the majority of the population. This consent is not necessarily invisible but can be developed by using force alongside the more subtle forms of coercion through, for example, the media. What is important is that the truth of these dominant ideas appears as natural or as 'common sense'. This idea of common sense has to be continually developed, modified and renewed if it is to make perfect sense to people, but of course it can also be challenged and resisted (Williams, 1977). Thus in our society it is common sense then to see each other as individuals more or less separate from others.

More recent thinkers on this subject have used a related but different concept, that of discourse to describe the way in which persons are influenced in their thinking upon morality and values. The French social philosopher Michel Foucault (1977) uses the term 'discourse' for an authoritative way of describing things, in our case what constitutes social work values. A discourse acquires its authority by appearing neutral and is often seen in the way that professionals such as doctors or social workers draw on their professional knowledge to define what problems they should work on, and to define and control the people (service users) they deliver a service to. In this way a discourse has the power of an institutionalised way of thinking, a social boundary defining what can and cannot be said about a specific topic and about certain people. Discourses are seen to affect our views on all things and are pervasive; in other words, it is not possible to escape discourse. Discourses are propagated by specific institutions and divide up the world in specific ways. For example, we can talk of medical, legal and psychological discourses.

Closely connected with discourse is the idea of power and knowledge or 'Power/Knowledge', a term Foucault uses to highlight the fact that every description also regulates what it describes. It is not only that every description is somewhat 'biased', but also that the very terms used to describe something reflect power relations. Discourses promote specific kinds of power relations, usually favouring the 'neutral' person or professional using the discourse (the lawyer, psychiatrist, professor, doctor, etc.). One of the most powerful discourses in social work is that which is called the 'Psy discourse', this discourse takes the ideas of psychiatry and psychology as underpinning some of the key assumptions about the nature of service users' problems and the ways in which social workers should treat them (Healey, 2005). Thus when we explore social work values we are also engaged in forms of power by deciding what constitutes a social work value and therefore what can be described and talked about as ethical social work.

For example, two different discourses can be used about the people who were involved in the 7 July 2005 bombings in London. Those who adopt what can be described as an Islamic fundamentalist discourse may see the perpetrators as martyrs, those on the receiving end of such actions may define them as terrorists. In other words, the chosen discourse delivers the vocabulary, expressions and perhaps also the style needed to communicate. The way that the debate is then developed is confined to the way in which the perpetrators are defined by the discourse which underpins and constrains what can be said about them and how their actions are evaluated.

The purpose of social work values

The purpose of social work values is to provide a common set of principles, which social workers can use and develop as a means of working in an ethical way with service users. Working from a professional value base has a number of benefits. For example:

- they can be guides to professional behaviour;
- they can maintain a professional identity;
- they can protect service users from malpractice.

The importance of having a value base for social work is that it is intended to guide the action of social workers and protect the interests of service users. Thus it is more appropriate to talk of social work ethics. Ethics guide action and are therefore reflections of value statements given flesh by being put into action. It is of little use for social workers to have a professional value base which does not inform and influence their practice as social workers. We can therefore understand social work ethics as values put into action (Banks, 2006).

Why act in an ethical manner?

> ### First social worker conduct hearing scheduled
> *29/03/2006*
>
> *A public hearing into the conduct of a Registered Social Worker will be held next week, from 5–7 April, in Newcastle by the social care workforce regulator of the General Social Care Council (GSCC).*
>
> *The case will be heard against a social worker from Darlington who is alleged to have committed misconduct and breached the GCSS's code of practice for social care workers by advertising herself as an escort.*

The following section asks you to consider why social workers should act ethically. What influences our decision to act in a way which is compatible with our sense of morality?

ACTIVITY *1.9*

Read the narrative below and answer the questions which follow.

Eric Slater walks into the house after introducing himself as a social worker from the local social services office. He has been asked to visit Mrs Johnson, a 45-year-old recently widowed, by her local GP, who has become increasingly concerned about her mental health. 'Social services, is it? Have you come to help me or what?' she asks. Mrs Johnson lives in a very big house. Must be worth at least a million, thought Eric, she must have a few quid stashed away. Mrs Johnson has been wandering lately and was found by one of her neighbours in the local park crying. Then two days ago, before Eric visited, the police found her in the bus station trying to get a bus back home but she couldn't remember where home was.

Eric sits down in the front room and Mrs Johnson asks him if he would like a nice cup of tea or something stronger from the half-filled whisky bottle by the side of the TV. They get chatting about nothing very interesting. In fact Eric is feeling quite bored. When is she going to shut up, ponders Eric. Then Mrs Johnson shows Eric her jewellery and shows him a suitcase, stuffed with ten pound notes under the staircase, stored there in case of accidents! Mrs Johnson tells Eric that he reminds her of her deceased husband. She asks him whether he would like the money under the staircase and perhaps take some of her fine diamond brooches, and begins to call Eric by her husband's first name.

Eric starts to think and almost says, 'No, shouldn't you put that money safely in a bank?' But something stops him and he begins to calculate. Perhaps he should take the money and jewellery as by the next day Mrs Johnson wouldn't remember him or her belongings. Eric suppresses a grin but then opens up, smiling expansively at Mrs Johnson and becomes Mrs Johnson's husband. 'Thanks my love, I'll just take this stuff to the bank.' Picking up the suitcase after some more chit-chat and sliding the brooches into his coat pocket, he leaves Mrs Johnson whom he knows will be none the wiser by the next day.

1 Does Eric offend your sense of morality in anyway?

2 Has Eric done anything wrong?

Comment

I hope that Eric is offending your sense of morality. Generally, morality refers to a system of rules that guides your behaviour in social situations. It concerns something which you consider to be of value to you and therefore requires upholding against actions which may harm the principle you support. Morality sets guidelines or rules by which you can assess your and others' actions, to judge whether they are good or virtuous. But, as noted above, morality does not exist in a vacuum. It is not something which we as individuals magically acquire, but something which develops when people interact with each other. This suggests that morality is a shared set of values justifying a chosen course of action. Many cultures share values that appear to be constant and attract wide agreement, for example truth-telling and restrictions on lying. In addition, all cultures appear to have rules against doing unnecessary harm to other people (although variations occur as to what 'unnecessary harm' means).

If Mrs Johnson would be upset at Eric refusing to take the money and jewels then surely he should accept them to protect her feelings? After all, as she now seems to see him as her former husband, if he told her who he actually was, would she not become distressed? For example, if faced with lying to protect someone's feelings, which value should take priority? It is on questions like this that we are most likely to differ, even if in Eric's case he has made off with money and valuables. So if there are some values which we cannot safely agree on, why don't we agree to live and let live and agree to differ? The issue we outlined above is that morality is social and therefore we need to justify our actions to each other (if not to the police at least in Eric's case if he ever got caught!). Although this may sound flippant in the situation outlined this has implications for professional social workers who have to justify their actions to a range of interested parties to whom they owe responsibility.

The importance of shared values cannot be underestimated as in many situations daily life would be intolerable if we did not share with others a common set of values. However, when these shared values break down or are not shared by some sections of the community then there can be dangerous consequences. Many cases of racial attack and murder highlight the potential for undermining our daily existence. Consider if you are a white person having to contemplate the possibility of abuse or attack from those who see the colour of your skin as a moral threat to their existence. Racially motivated attacks are still a growing problem, as charges brought under the Crime and Disorder Act 1998 and Anti-Terrorism-Crime and Security Act 2001 show in Table 1.2.

Table 1.2

Charges prosecuted	3190	3597	4029	4719	6208
Year	2000–2001	2001–2002	2002–2003	2003–2004	2004–2005

Source: CPS 2005

The importance of having a basic value system which is shared by citizens within a society is crucial in enabling all members of a community to live their chosen lives. If we return to Mrs Johnson this does not mean that every person will respond in a non-harmful way.

People can act in a number of ways when faced with Mrs Johnson based upon how they reason or rationalise the situation. One example of this kind of rationalisation is called prudential reason, more easily understood as self-interest. Prudential reason concerns our interests, what we want, what we desire and therefore what we can have (Rowland, 2003). If we desire money and jewels, Mrs Johnson has these in abundance, she is offering them and nobody will be the wiser, then why not?

Or we can believe we are acting from a sense of duty and what we consider to be the right thing to do. This may not be in line with our own self-interest or give us an advantage in any way but purely because we think it is morally right. So why shouldn't Eric take the money and run?

Essentially there are many reasons why people may choose to behave in a moral way. They may be inspired by a faith in God. For example, good Muslims should behave in a way that glorifies Allah and included in this command is to show charity and compassion to the poor. This is institutionalised in the practice of Zakat, the giving of a proportion of one's income to charitable works. Socialists may believe they have a moral duty to create the best social conditions, usually understood in terms of greater equality and social justice for all people in society. Figure 1.3 provides some of the reasons why you may choose to act morally.

ACTIVITY **1.10**

Which of the reasons in Figure 1.3 best fits your own rationale for acting in a moral way?

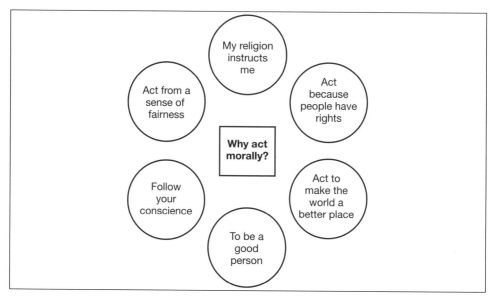

Figure 1.3 *Why act morally?*

Comment

When we act in a moral way we are saying something about what we value in life and how we ought to behave in society. To act out of a sense of justice means that we value fairness so that people receive their due entitlements. We may extend this to a notion of social justice in which we seek social fairness in which the resources, goods and benefits of a society are distributed fairly to all groups in that society.

In this book we are exploring the values and ethics of social work and we are doing this by asking you to explore your values and what they mean for you. However, the values you live by are not necessarily matters of individual preference or opinion. If all ethical matters were matters of opinion or preference we would be unable to evaluate the ethical practices of others. Ethical preferences which are based upon misinformation or a lack of perception would, I suggest, be evaluated as less worthy than those principles based upon the necessary information being available and informed by a shrewd perception which has stood the scrutiny of others (Bochel et al., 2005).

We can also recognise that values may not be expressed solely by individuals but may also be adopted by wider groups in society. People from different cultures often have a distinct set of values which informs their way of life. Likewise, professional groups such as nurses or social workers seek to regulate their members' behaviour as defined by codes of practice which set the standards by which professionals should act.

Traditional social work values

For social workers, traditional values were widely adopted prior to the development of anti-oppressive practice. The radical social work movement of the 1960s and 1970s drew upon an analysis of class conflict within capitalist societies to criticise social work as largely reproducing class inequality. These ideas were later developed and expanded upon by feminist and anti-racist approaches and then further enhanced by service users and survivors' movements to include issues of disability, mental health, age and sexuality.

Traditional values typically focused upon the social worker/service user relationship and therefore developed a value system which could develop ethically appropriate principles of action based in the most part upon the individuality of the service user. Thus if service users experienced inequality, the solution was understood as developing the same access and the same treatment to all, irrespective of any other characteristics such as differences based upon gender or race. Three authors stand out as being particularly influential in relation to traditional values, namely Timms (1983), Biestek (1974) and Butrym (1976). These authors argued that their ethical principles were universal and capable of application within any social work context. Figure 1.4 illustrates the respective lists of ethical principles which these authors developed.

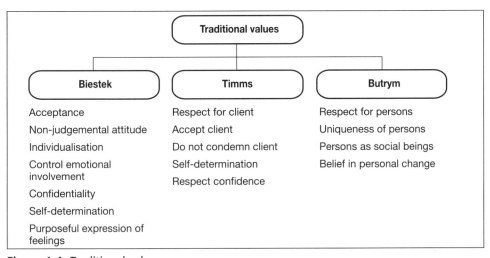

Figure 1.4 *Traditional values*

ACTIVITY 1.11

From the respective lists in Figure 1.4 can you identify where at least two of the writers share a common value principle?

Comment

The value principles which seem to be shared by at least two of the writers at any one time are:

- acceptance;
- respect for the client;
- self-determination;
- non-judgementalism/do not condemn client.

There is much that these authors share in their assessment of which values are important for social work. This has led Horne (1999) to argue that the core of social work values in these traditional approaches focuses upon respect for persons. As he comments, this value is the mainspring from which all other values are derived. It is not the purpose of this book to investigate in depth the meanings of these values and you are advised to consult Horne's book to explore these further. The purpose here is to contrast traditional approaches with the concerns of this book, which will focus upon anti-oppressive approaches to social work values. Chapter 2 begins to explore these values in greater depth.

C H A P T E R   S U M M A R Y

This chapter has introduced the importance of understanding the political and social context in which social work values are applied. Increasingly managerial and business-like solutions in social work are being introduced as the government seeks to develop what it considers to be efficient and effective social work and social care services. This chapter has sought to restate the importance of values for social work and, in particular, the practical and moral engagement with service users for which ethically-based social work strives. Allied with this has been the centrality of understanding how social work values should engage with the wider society in which they are situated. This necessity means that social workers are sometimes caught between representing service users on the one hand, while on the other being required to uphold wider societal values. Social workers' ethical concerns to support service users who may be seen to transgress societal values or who may, just by expressing their difference, be seen as a threat to the moral order is at the heart of the challenge. This inevitably places social workers in ethical conflicts and dilemmas as to how best to negotiate this relationship and promote the interests of service users.

FURTHER READING

Harris, J (2003a) *The social work business*. London: Routledge.
A thought-provoking book on the way in which social work is increasingly influenced by the culture of managerialism and private enterprise.

Horne, M (1999) *Values in social work*, 2nd edition. Aldershot: Ashgate.
A thorough and well written outline of the key values in social work.

Chapter 2
Anti-oppressive practice

This chapter will begin to help you to meet the following National Occupational Standards:

Key Role 6 Demonstrate professional competence in social work practice.

- Work within the principles and values underpinning social work practice.
- Identify and assess issues, dilemmas and conflicts that might affect your practice.
- Devise strategies to deal with ethical issues, dilemmas and conflicts.
- Reflect on outcomes.

This chapter will also help you follow the GSCC's Code of Practice for Social Care Workers:

1 As a social worker, you must protect the rights and promote the interests of service users and carers.

This includes:

- promoting equal opportunities for service users and carers;
- respecting diversity and different cultures and values.

It will also introduce you to the following academic standards as set out in the social work subject benchmark statement:

3.1.1 Social work services and service users

- The social processes ... that lead to marginalisation, isolation and exclusion and their impact on the demand for social work services.
- Explanations of the links between definitional processes contributing to social differences (for example, social class, gender and ethnic differences) to the problems of inequality and differential need faced by service users.
- The nature of social work services in a diverse society (with particular reference to concepts such as prejudice, inter-personal, institutional and structural discrimination, empowerment and anti-discriminatory practices).

3.1.3 Values and ethics

- The complex relationships between justice, care and control in social welfare and the practical and ethical implications of these, including roles as statutory agents and in upholding the law in respect of discrimination.

Anti-oppressive practice: orientation and values

On the one hand, AOP represents a general value orientation towards countering oppression experienced by service users on such grounds as race, gender, class, disability, etc. (See Figure 2.1). On the other, it also contains specific practice values; these are the values of empowerment, partnership and minimal intervention.

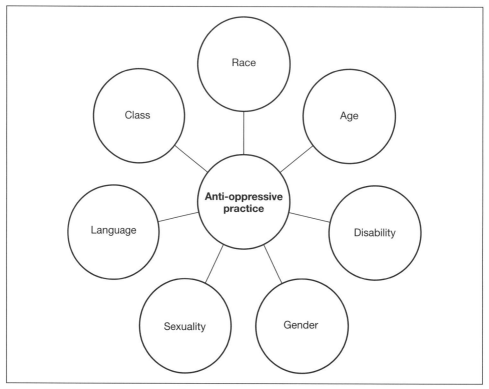

Figure 2.1 *AOP as value orientation*

AOP is therefore the means to achieve social justice for service users. It is not adequate to merely analyse a service user's situation and acknowledge their social location. It requires us to achieve real change with service users by enabling respect and fairer treatment from society.

In order to develop our understanding further we must clarify what we mean by AOP. Dalrymple and Burke (1995) make a distinction between AOP and anti-discriminatory practice (ADP).

Anti-discriminatory practice

An approach to social work practice which seeks to reduce, undermine or eliminate discrimination and oppression, specifically in terms of challenging sexism, racism, ageism, and disablism... and other forms of discrimination encountered in social work. Social workers occupy positions of power and influence, and so there is considerable scope for discrimination and oppression, whether this is intentional of by default. Anti-discriminatory practice is an attempt to eradicate discrimination from our own practice and challenge it in the practice of others and institutional strictures in which we operate. (Thompson, 2001)

For Dalrymple and Burke AOP is a much broader term which seeks to challenge the power differences between groups, and understands such power differences as embedded in society to such an extent that they have a pervasive impact both in public and private life. They suggest that ADP is limited in this extent in that it deals with more visible forms of oppression that can be amenable to social reform through, for example, making it illegal to discriminate on such grounds as race or gender.

Anti-oppressive practice requires:

- personal self-knowledge;
- knowledge and an understanding of the majority social systems;
- knowledge and understanding of different groups and cultures;
- knowledge of how to challenge and confront issues on a personal and structural level;
- awareness of the need to be 'research minded' (Everitt et al., 1992);
- commitment to action and change.

(Dalrymple and Burke, 1995, p18)

For Thompson the difference is in the process, so that *discrimination is the process (or set of processes) that leads to oppression* (pxii). He recognises the need for a much broader approach that goes beyond reforming the legal system to account for discrimination, and sees differences between AOP and ADP in practice as minimal, becoming semantic problems rather than ones which may require different theoretical explanation. Whichever term you use it is important to understand that there are differences in how the concept can be used and therefore students need to understand if they are adopting a reformist or a radical model (see figure 2.2). A reformist model seeks to make relatively small incremental steps to achieve change within the structure of society. For example, a reformist approach to child care might seek to improve the law relating to how children are treated in the family which would target the behaviour of parents to prevent physical or sexual abuse. A radical model would focus on the unequal powers that adults have over children in the wider social structure, seeking to empower children by stressing their potential for collective action to counter abusive situations inside the family. It may even challenge the concept of the family as the only or most appropriate way of bringing up children, believing that children should be cherished by the wider community as well as their parents.

	Reformist	Radical
Changes	Legal powers	Social inequality
Targets	Individuals/organisations	Social structure

Figure 2.2 *Competing models of AOP*

AOP understands that inequality is a persistent feature of modern capitalist societies. Inequality is experienced in a number of different ways that relate to the manner in which society is divided or differentiated (Giddens, 2006). This process of social differentiation creates inequality when hierarchies of power and influence, including the control over key resources, are attached to different positions. This results in some groups achieving a position of dominance and superiority over others. When social divisions such as these arise, they persist over time and become entrenched within a given society. When this occurs we can see the way in which social divisions form the social structure of a society.

ACTIVITY 2.1

Look at the list below:

Social division	Category
Gender	Female
Race	Black
Class	Working

Q. *If you were a working-class black woman would you consider yourself as having much power in society at large?*

Q. *Now identify the opposite for each category in the list above so that the list would look like:*

Social division	Category
Gender	Male
Race	White
Class	Middle

If you were a white middle-class male would you consider yourself to have more or less power than a black working-class woman?

Comment

The relative power of groups reflects the control that they have over some of the key resources in society. The experience of advantage or disadvantage structures the way that individuals and groups come into contact with welfare services and their own life chances. Perhaps the starkest example of this can be seen in the different mortality and morbidity rates experienced by socio-economic circumstances and residential area.

This is just a snapshot of the way in which inequality determines the range of experiences and life chances of different social groups in society. However, in terms of social workers' ethical practice a general commitment to countering such inequalities is essential. Social workers invariably work with service users who form the most disadvantaged and oppressed groups in society. Any effective social work practice must involve an assessment of such debilitating circumstances as a starting point to any social work intervention.

RESEARCH SUMMARY

White et al., (2005) looked at the effect that place of residence and individual socio-economic circumstances during 1971–91 had on the subsequent mortality (in 1995–2001) of a sample of men aged 26 or over in 1971. Some key findings include the following:

- *Neighbourhood deprivation in 1991 made the strongest contribution to predicting mortality. For example, the odds of dying in 1995–2001 were nearly a third higher among those who had lived in the most deprived neighbourhoods compared with those in the most affluent;*

- *Social class in 1971 continued to have a strong influence on mortality risk in 1995–2001. For example, the odds of dying in 1995–2001 were 54 per cent higher among those in partly skilled and unskilled occupations compared with those in professional occupations.*

Valuing difference

From a values perspective, understanding the process by which social groups experience disadvantage and how they cope with the challenges of such discrimination is essential for AOP. This requires a positive orientation towards those groups in society and the individuals within them who may have alternative ways of viewing the world and who therefore may have a quite different understanding of what constitutes a 'good life'.

Valuing 'difference' is therefore a complex process that requires social workers to be open to understanding these different conceptions of the 'good life'. Unless individuals follow this path, their reaction to 'difference' is not to value it, but to either dominate it or exterminate it.

An example of this process of domination and extermination can be highlighted by the film *Rabbit-proof Fence* (Noyce 2002). During the first half of the twentieth century Australia took children of mixed aboriginal/white origins from their homes, trained them in boarding schools and sent them to work in white communities. The majority of the children never saw their parents again. The purpose was to break up mixed families, civilise the children and absorb them into white society. *Rabbit-proof Fence* is the true story of three young girls who ran away from boarding school at the Moore River Settlement. Living off the land and on hand-outs, they eluded trackers and the police for months. Two of the girls made it home while one was recaptured.

A.O. Neville, then 'Chief Protector of Aborigines' in 1930s Western Australia, ordered the roundup (i.e. kidnapping) of all 'half-caste' (known now as dual heritage) girls (girls of half Aboriginal and half white descent) from their Aboriginal families for mandatory education into the ways of white society, leading to eventual low-level employment as domestic servants. Neville was simply enforcing the 'Aborigines Act', a law designed with the intention of 'salvaging' 'half-caste' girls from Aboriginal life and integrating them into the white Australian world.

From the brief description of the film above what comparisons could you draw between the actions of the Australian government at that time and other similar examples you might know about from history?

Comment

Comparisons can be drawn between the Australian government's plan to eliminate 'half-caste' Aborigines through the dilution of their so-called Aboriginal genes and the Nazi policies (during the same time period) of eliminating minority populations (Jews, gypsies, etc.) through extermination. Other comparisons can be made between the Australian policies and recent attempted genocides in Rwanda, ethnic cleansing in the Balkans and, in the UK, the policy developed at the turn of the twentieth century of separating people with learning disabilities from the community by placing them in 'special hospitals' as the authorities feared that allowing people with learning disabilities to reproduce would degrade the genetic pool of intelligence in society.

Valuing 'difference' goes against common-sense socialisation which portrays difference as 'inferior' or deems it in pathological terms as 'deficient' as in the way Aboriginal culture was suppressed. Many disabled people who campaign for the civil rights of disabled people would make such a claim when they argue that many social workers have practised in a way that sees disabled people as dependent, where disabled people are assessed against the norms of the non-disabled world. Barbara Lisicki, an activist for disabled people and a member of the Disability Action Network (DAN) and who is disabled herself, comments:

> *It is absolutely crap for disabled people to attempt to fit into the 'normal world' and to live a 'normal life'. We are not accepted as normal, but then nor are black people, single parents, gay people – there are so many exceptions to normality.*
>
> *Normality is a myth. There is no substance to it. We are told to be part of this normality. If we want to change something we are told we have a 'chip on our shoulder'. If we say: 'I don't want to make a fuss', we are putting up with all sorts of compromises and personal difficulties.*
>
> *DAN is really in your face. It is not about making compromises. Sometimes we are accused of radicalism. Tell me a better way. Nothing else has worked. We force people to have an opinion. We force them to discuss the issues. You will never get rid of impairment.*
>
> *Even if you screen every genetic condition out of existence people will still have accidents. Impairment is a part of life. It always will be. The important thing is to remove the fear that surrounds it.*
>
> *Like the black and gay movements we are saying: We are proud. We are what we are. You can't change us. We have been ridiculed, separated and abused. We know that difference is hard to deal with. Black people were viewed as devils and chained in slavery not that long ago. We need to look at who has power and how they are using it? How are they abusing it?* (Farnworth, 1997)

ACTIVITY **2.3**

In what ways does Barbara Lisicki use the idea of 'normality' to challenge the treatment of disabled people?

Comment

Lisicki argues that disabled people are different yet experience similar prejudice to other marginalised groups in society. She is concerned to challenge the notion that to be different is to be inferior. The casting of people as different from oneself into a subordinate status is central to the process of 'othering' them, the 'them and us' approach which places 'them' as the subordinate minority and 'us' as the superior and therefore normal majority. The 'othering' of individuals or groups withdraws 'them' from the circle of humanity and facilitates the denial of 'their' human, social and political rights. This othering can be overtly oppressive in denying access to services and citizenship or can be less visible where some groups, particularly disabled people, are seen as the objects of pity. This view leads to the added misconception that oppressed people are passive victims who are unable to act for themselves, something that DAN has challenged very effectively.

Understanding differences

Moving beyond common-sense attitudes about 'difference' requires the social worker to literally inhabit the world of the 'other'; this exercise of empathy requires a deep understanding of the other person's world and their values. It also requires the social worker to reflect upon their own values and their own understanding of their identity, what privileges they have had, what struggles they have experienced. In identifying differences, social workers can reflect on their position of power in society and identify ways that power can be shared with others. In addition, by reflecting upon the struggles they have experienced when they have been in a powerless position, they can see the similarities that they sometimes share with service users. In understanding similar experiences we are creating service users as part of 'us'. In reflecting upon and identifying our differences we are aware of the potential for creating service users as part of 'them' and therefore are in a position to share our power with respect and competence to minimise the practice of 'othering' (Billington et al., 1998). This process of othering requires a broader social understanding of the ways in which discrimination and oppression can be exacerbated by a lack of access to adequate welfare resources. Thus different oppressed groups may all be competing for restricted welfare resources, setting one group against another. Dench et al., (2006) show how the lack of affordable public housing (new local authority builds have virtually ceased since the 1980s) in Tower Hamlets has had the consequence of developing hostility among some of the white working-class population against the incoming Bangladeshi population. Thus we have a relatively impoverished group of white working-class people turning against an even more impoverished incoming group. Discrimination is exacerbated against the incoming population and anger directed at them rather than against the inadequate housing policies developed as a result of the Conservative government's 'right to buy' policies of the 1980s and continued under the present Labour government. This requires social workers to be sensitive to the ways in which a struggle over inadequate resources can lead to fear and resentment among some groups being directed against others. The importance of being sensitive to these issues and being able to respond to those fears and resentments requires a confidence in understanding the reasons for racist hostility. It requires appropriate assertiveness to challenge those fears alongside an appreciation of difference to tackle the social inequalities that arise for all groups to achieve social justice.

Summary

Anti-oppressive practice requires social workers to focus their understanding on three levels:

- intellectually – to grasp its central principles and methods of working;

- emotionally – to feel secure about and confident in working in anti-oppressive ways, and to be able to recognise and learn from the mistakes they make when reality falls short of their ambition to work in this way;

- practically – to be able to implement the principles they have learnt and feel that they are competent in their practice.

Cultures, values and relativism

Having argued for the need to value difference and not judge others from a position of normative superiority, does this mean social workers and social care workers should never pass a judgement on others or challenge the different practices, including cultural practices, of others? In referring to cultural practices we are recognising the centrality of culture to the way in which different groups live their lives, understand the world they live in and conduct themselves. Culture refers to:

- a particular society at a particular time and place;

- the knowledge and values shared by a society;

- the attitudes and behaviour that are characteristic of a particular social group or organisation.

In short we mean: *the accumulated habits, attitudes, and beliefs of a group of people that define for them their general behaviour and way of life; the total set of learned activities of a people.*

The importance of being sensitive to different cultures is a crucial element of AOP, for effective social work needs to counter monocultural practice. White culture in the UK is often reflected in the content of social work services. This means not just those practically oriented services such as domiciliary care or family support, but also the whole process of social work from assessment through to the evaluation of practice. If social workers assess service users using a 'culturally blind' approach this will result in poor or inappropriate services being offered or no services being offered at all for those who do not fit into a white cultural norm. For example, hospice services have historically been delivered by the voluntary sector. Research into the needs of people from ethnic minorities show that there is a perception among some that hospices, with their Christian roots, cater only for white

Christian communities (Gatrad and Sheikh 2002). This leads these authors to conclude that there are no effective national provisions in place for the training of professionals in tran- scultural social work and medicine as it affects hospice work, few professionals will therefore have had any real opportunity to learn about, for example, death rites in differ- ent cultures (Gatrad and Sheik 2003). A recent review of the provision afforded people from ethnic minorities echoes similar concerns in the personal social services.

RESEARCH SUMMARY

Chahal (2004) reviewed the research studies undertaken on behalf of the Joseph Rowntree Foundation since 2000 in relation to ethnic minorities. The conclusion was as follows:

- *Minority ethnic communities continue to experience mainstream services as operating on the basis of stereotypes and assumptions.*

- *They also believed they were subject to prejudice and discrimination in the delivery of services*

- *Services were seen as 'monocultural' and therefore inappropriate to meet their own needs in terms of language, religion and culture.*

- *Staff could be seen as unrepresentative and organisations lacked guidelines relating to working with minority ethnic users.*

- *There was inadequate information about service provision.*

- *There were high levels of unmet social, care and identity needs.*

- *Formal parenting support was not culturally sensitive. Inappropriate assumptions were made by service providers about the extent and nature of informal family support.*

- *Ethnic monitoring, despite being required by law, often did not take place in both statutory and voluntary agencies.*

ACTIVITY 2.4

Why would a middle-aged Muslim daughter insist on maintaining a day and night hospital vigil at the bedside of her dying mother?

Why would Hindu parents wish their terminally ill child to die as close to the floor as possible?

Comment

Unless you have a first-hand knowledge of such issues then I would assume that you have little understanding at this stage. If we are unable to engage with the beliefs of different communities and their cultural practices then we will by omission be endorsing oppressive practice. As a value position social workers should be aware of the culturally different possibilities for validating death and dying. This is achieved by being open to difference and by being committed to enabling people to have a dignified death that meets with their cultural rituals and practices. It is not possible to have an immediate knowledge of the many different cultural practices of different groups living in the UK. However, the practical and ethical expectation in relation to AOP is that you will have the commitment to research and acquire such knowledge and then integrate this into practice.

Cultural and ethical relativism

In addressing difference as unique and therefore not comparable with our own view of the 'good life' are we implying therefore that each group's chosen practices are immune from any assessment as to their validity? If we are, this approach is known as cultural and ethical relativism. Cultural relativism is a form of moral relativism asserting that all ethical truth is relative to a specific culture. According to cultural relativism, we can never pass judgement on different cultures' social practices; it can only ever be true that a certain kind of behaviour is right or wrong relative to a specified culture.

In demonstrating the value of a culturally relativist approach to AOP it can be argued that it allows social workers to hold onto their own culturally distinct values without having to be judgemental about other people's culture. This principle has a long and honourable history in the ethics of social work, i.e. non-judgementalism. We have already noted in relation to the film *Rabbit-proof fence* the dangers of imposing cultural values upon others.

Cultural absolutism was one of the defining ways in which the colonisation of Africa, Asia and other parts of the globe by the European powers (in particular Great Britain) in the nineteenth century was reinforced. Imperialism as a form of cultural domination tended to destroy the indigenous culture and replace it with that of the colonisers. Indeed that process has also been identified within social work practice itself in imposing Western conceptions of social standards upon other cultures. Social workers applying a social work practice framework underpinned by Western European cultural norms have tended to apply these culturally embedded practice norms to persons from culturally different backgrounds. The limitations imposed, for example, by assessing immediate nuclear and even extended family networks as the norm marginalises other family structures, for example from Africa, where a diverse and wider family structure which takes cousins into account, limits the appreciation of the importance of African family networks:

> Thus the ethnocentric worldview constructs a 'universalism' of social work practice and imposes a value system and construct which may compromise the psychological wellbeing of black children (Graham, 2002 p72).

Cultural relativism allows us to evade this difficulty; our moral code applies only to our own society, so there is no pressure on us to hold others to our moral standards at all.

The importance of cultural toleration and respect cannot be underestimated if we are to understand the ways in which children and adults from different cultures are often made to feel that their culture is inferior. Phinney (1990) puts forward the idea of 'identification by proxy' as a means by which, in his example, black children learn to negotiate and manage their relationships with what they consider to be a hostile white world. Black children are raised in a society that does not generally recognise them as having value and as a consequence they experience racial discrimination. They are then left to assess who may treat them with respect and fairness. This experience will affect the degree to which a black child is able to disclose information about themselves honestly or to make an identification with the white worker. The child will put forward a proxy or pretend self to the worker for self-protective reasons.

ACTIVITY **2.5**

You are a white social worker visiting Ahmed, an 8-year-old Muslim boy whose parents came from Pakistan. He is with you in a summer playgroup which you have helped to set up with your colleagues from a local voluntary group. You are chatting in the group and Ahmed is the only Muslim child. You ask the children what they like to eat for breakfast. Most of the children reply that they have cereal and toast, but when your colleague asks Ahmed he replies a bit nervously bacon and eggs.

- *In what ways might Ahmed be exhibiting identification by proxy?*

- *How might you encourage a different response from Ahmed?*

Comment

Clearly Ahmed, coming from a practising Muslim family, is unlikely to have eaten bacon and eggs for breakfast given that pork is seen as unclean and therefore in religious terms would be spiritually damaging for Ahmed. Given that Ahmed is the only Muslim in the group he may wish not to identify himself as different from the rest of the group and may feel frightened, embarrassed or ashamed that somehow he might eat something quite different for breakfast. Thus he responds in a more or less stereotypical way by giving what he thinks is an answer which will at best give him status in the group and at worst be seen as being culturally typical. As his social worker, you would need to allow Ahmed to be able to express himself and be proud of his own culture and traditions. One way would be for you to get the children to think about different cultures and what they might eat for breakfast and allow Ahmed to explain the different food he might eat.

Does taking a morally and ethically relativist position pose problems for social workers? Should relative cultural values always take precedence over all other values? It can be argued that cultural relativism allows us to avoid some thorny ethical problems by not judging the moral status of other cultures. But what should social workers' ethical response be to judging the moral status of another culture? Under what conditions would it be necessary to do so? For example, some cultures have openly approved of slavery and others have felt ambivalent at best to infanticide, particularly where the child is a lesser valued female.

In respect of our own cultural practice, does it also excuse us from judging our own culture? For example, the treatment of older people is often seen as highly discriminatory to such an extent that ageism will soon be subject to equal opportunities legislation. Maybe our practice of placing older people in residential homes with little contact from family and friends may require us to view our own culture more critically. If we refrain from ethically evaluating other cultures then why should we evaluate and criticise our own? If we do not reflect upon our own cultural practices then we may also reinforce harm to members of our own culture as in the case of older people. We have already highlighted in Chapter 1 that there could be a basis upon which to evaluate our actions from an ethical standpoint which invokes a standard that is not culturally relative.

Parekh (2000) argues that there are four principles which are generally employed to evaluate different cultural practices.

- *Human rights principle*. An appeal to universal human rights (see Chapter 1) has been one approach by which to make evaluations of other cultural practices.

- *Core values*. Every society has acquired over time a character or identity embodied in its core values. These core values form the basis of its way of life and therefore it is both right and proper to suppress practices which offend core values.

- *No harm principle*. Given that moral values are cemented into the foundations of society offending cultural practices should only be disallowed if they cause harm to others.

- *Dialogue principle*. Since there are no universally-valid moral principles, the concept of core values by which to judge others is problematic. Since harm can be equally defined as being differently evaluated then what is required is to engage in an open dialogue. This requires an open minded and serious conversation which seeks as its outcome a consensus.

Parekh favours the last approach, as he argues that core values in any society should not be sacrosanct but should be negotiable. Dialogue would entail a trade-off between groups where this kind of interaction would help us decide on a generally acceptable response to cultural disputes. He calls this intercultural dialogue. This is a useful idea for social workers in responding to cultural difference and therefore can enable social workers to engage in a cultural dialogue with service users they work with. However, there may be occasions where dialogue is unsuccessful. Social workers may then have to assess the relevance of a cultural practice from the point of view of the no harm principle. This may be the case where statutory responsibilities placed on social workers may not allow for an open-ended dialogue, for example where a person may be put in danger through a particular cultural practice.

The 'no harm' principle may also be tied in with a human rights perspective where basic human rights, if they are violated, constitute harm. However, human rights legislation does not seek to impose specific moral standards but rather seeks to encapsulate general or universal principles which can be applied cross culturally. Thus the problem is not easily resolved. For example, when the Human Rights Act 2000 refers to the right to family life, it provides no guidance as to what family life constitutes since there are different forms of family life across different cultures. It leaves us to explore the specific case and then make a judgement. To explore these issues further consider the Activity below.

ACTIVITY 2.6

You are working with a Somali family. The father Mr Abdullahi 'Issa Mohamud has been concerned about his daughter Mariam not coming home at night and being disrespectful to him and his wife. He is concerned she is mixing with a local group of Somali youngsters who have been involved in street violence. Sometimes in his frustration with Mariam he has locked her in her room and kept her a virtual prisoner, particularly over the weekends when he fears Mariam may go out and mix with the street gang. There are six children of which the eldest is Mariam who is 14 years old.

Mariam confides in you that she is about to go on holiday, returning to her parents' village for two weeks. She suspects that she will be required to undergo female circumcision as is the custom in her culture; she suspects this because her father is saying that when she returns she will be a woman and will no longer need to go out with her friends.

She asks for your advice as she is not sure whether she wants to undergo this ritual.

Some information

Female circumcision is a practice common in equatorial Africa that is unfamiliar to many Westerners. Included under the term 'female circumcision' are several different procedures in which varying amounts of genital tissue are removed. This ranges from the removal of the clitoral hood, leaving the rest of the genitalia intact (known as 'sunna' circumcision), to removal of the clitoris and anterior labia minora, to removal of the clitoris, the entire labia minora, part of the labia majora and suturing of the labia majora leaving a posterior opening for the passage of urine and menstrual flow. This latter procedure is known as infibulation, and is the most common form of female circumcision in Somalia. In Somalia, the procedure is usually performed by female family members but is also available in some hospitals. It is usually performed between birth and five years of age.

In the last twenty years much attention has been focused on the medical and psychosocial complications of female circumcision. However, most Somali women view circumcision as normal, expected and desirable. It has become the centre of a debate about potentially harmful traditional cultural practices, and as such has become a complex and emotionally-charged subject (taken from **www.ethnomed.org/ethnomed/cultures/ somali/somali_cp.html***).*

Immediate complications

This depends upon the kind of circumcision carried out with the sunna method being relatively less physically harmful and akin to a male circumcision. Complications can include severe pain, shock, haemorrhage, tetanus or sepsis, urine retention, ulceration of the genital region and injury to adjacent tissue, wound infection, urinary infection, fever and septicaemia. Haemorrhage and infection can be of such magnitude as to cause death.

Long-term consequences

*These include anaemia, the formation of cysts and abscesses, keloid scar formation, damage to the urethra resulting in urinary incontinence, dyspareunia (painful sexual intercourse) and sexual dysfunction, and hypersensitivity of the genital area. Infibulation can cause severe scar formation, difficulty in urinating, menstrual disorders, recurrent bladder and urinary tract infection, fistulae, prolonged and obstructed labour (sometimes resulting in fetal death and vesico-vaginal fistulae and/or vesico-rectal fistulae) and infertility (as a consequence of earlier infections). Cutting of the scar tissue is sometimes necessary to facilitate sexual intercourse and/or childbirth. Almost complete vaginal obstruction may occur, resulting in accumulation of menstrual flow in the vagina and uterus. During childbirth the risk of haemorrhage and infection is greatly increased. (***www.unfpa.org/about/ ondex.htm***)*

In the light of the information presented above how would you approach advising Mariam?

Comment

This case study is problematic and very difficult as it presents you with a clear dilemma in relation to Somalian cultural practices. If you advise Mariam to comply with the wishes of her family then what are the consequences for her?

- *Arguments in favour*. On the positive side she will be seen as undergoing a vital rite of passage in Somali culture which will enhance her status as a woman. If she values the idea of marriage to another Somali then, as the information suggests, she will find it easier to marry as she will not be seen as 'unclean'. She will be honouring her father's wishes which may improve the treatment she receives from him.

- *Against this view*. Mariam, if she is to undergo this ritual will certainly be physically and maybe psychologically damaged, whether she agrees to the practice or not. As a social worker does this constitute a child protection problem in which you have a duty to protect Mariam?

In deciding which course of action may be the best, it is important to take into account choice:

- Does Mariam have a real choice here, what options are available to her? Although options are present does this constitute a real choice if she is being forced into having the procedure?

- Does your decision require you to give control of the situation back to Mariam?

- What criteria should you employ in deciding to overrule the wishes of Mariam's father and the cultural practices which are included in this, if Mariam does not wish to proceed (see Figure 2.3)?

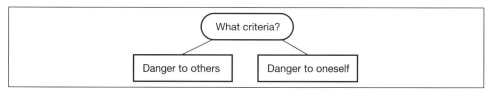

Figure 2.3 *Criteria for intervention*

In this case Mariam's situation does not directly involve danger to others. In relation to the second criteria then we can see that this action may very well involve some considerable harm. If Mariam does not want to go ahead with this procedure then we may have a duty to act. However, what if Mariam decides in the end that she will go ahead with the procedure? Do we have a right then to intervene against her wishes, given that she is still a minor? We have to take into account the level of understanding of a 14-year-old. All things being equal we would have to conclude that she is capable of making her own decisions and that she is aware of – or we would ensure she is aware of – the likely physical harms that could develop. Even with that proviso in mind do we still have a duty to go against her wishes? After all, legally she is still a child and this procedure constitutes harm. Given the knowledge we have of this procedure in Somalia, this practice is usually done when a girl is first born and most certainly done before the child is five years old, so the possible trauma and damage that could be caused to a young person is likely to be considerable. What does the Children Act 1989 have to say about the duties of a social worker in this situation?

Section 31 requires that social workers should take action if the child experiences 'significant harm' and this must be of a severity that the child experiences or is likely to experience an impediment to their health, physical or emotional development.

In this instance the procedure is a very dangerous one for a 14-year-old girl and this is verified by the information provided above. If we decide to act then what action should we take? If we remove Mariam from the family home what would be the likely consequences for her? Inevitably she would be separated from her brothers and sisters and her parents. How could we ensure that she could maintain her own cultural lifestyle? This may be very difficult if her father, as would be likely, disowns her. She may be seen as a highly unworthy person by the majority of people in her own community. What cultural supports could be put in place for her?

Any decision that we make in this case is therefore fraught with ethical dilemmas. In making a decision to intervene against particular cultural practices we must be very clear as to the purpose of this intervention and the likely consequences for Mariam. We would need to ensure that Mariam was able to access as much cultural support as is possible in allowing her to make her decision, which in this case is to go against her father's wishes. It is important to realise that cultural practices are not set in stone and that the process of acculturation, the description of how cultures change over time, is a significant concept when considering the importance of specific cultural practices. Many women's groups across the UK, in Africa and indeed in Somalia, continue to campaign against this procedure. Indeed, such groups no longer term this procedure 'female circumcision' but 'female genital mutilation'. Thus in considering any foregoing or specific cultural practices we need to understand that cultures change and are open to influences which render the whole nature of culture a living social phenomenon. To assume that specific cultures contain within them any particular views, in this case in favour of female circumcision, would be to deny the very defining characteristics of all cultures which are living, evolving and sometimes changing quite rapidly. As Clarke (2004) argues in relation to UK culture, we cannot reduce this culture to any essential notion of 'Britishness'. National cultures, are differentiated, as we have already analysed in relation to social divisions, and undergo continual contestation which renders any culture more dynamic and open to change. We may well be falling into the trap of seeing our own culture as necessarily dynamic and open to change while not recognising similar processes in other cultures.

FGM is not uncommon, it is estimated that 74,000 women in the UK have undergone the procedure, and about 7,000 girls under 16 are at risk. This estimate is based upon the number of women and girls living in the UK who originate from countries where FGM is traditionally practiced.

FGM has been illegal in the UK since the Prohibition of Female Circumcision Act 1985, this legislation has been strengthened by the Female Genital Mutilation Act 2003 which prohibits FGM and in addition makes it illegal to take girls abroad for FGM. Guidance issued to local authorities is useful in this regard:

> *Where a family has been identified as at risk, it may not be appropriate to take steps to remove the girl from an otherwise loving family environment.*

Experience has shown that often the parents themselves are under pressure to agree to FGM for their daughters from older relatives. It might be helpful, therefore, to talk to the family outside the home environment to encourage them to acknowledge the impact FGM would have on their daughter/s. It might also be necessary to ask the police to get a prohibited steps order, making it clear to the family that they will be breaking the law if they arrange for any of their daughters to have the procedure.

In areas where there are large practising communities, social services departments should consider incorporating more detailed guidance on responding to concerns about FGM to their existing child protection procedures, in partnership with other local agencies and community groups. (Department of Education and Science 2004)

Service users: empowerment, partnership and minimal intervention

Since the early 1980s developments in social policy legislation have made service user participation a key requiremen. For example, the National Health Service and Community Care Act 1990 made consultation with service users a legislative duty for local authorities. Since 1997 and the election of a Labour government there has been an increased momentum requiring active service user (and carer) participation in service development, for example in government directives on Best Value for local authorities and the legislation associated with the public service 'modernisation' agenda (DoH, 1998). Unfortunately practice has fallen short of the legislative requirements and requires an increased effort to enable further involvement from service users. The role that social workers take in this is therefore an important one given their privileged position in working closely with service users.

Having looked in considerable depth at the issues of AOP and culturally-sensitive social work it is now important to look at the specific values that we identified above that relate to AOP. These are:

- empowerment;
- partnership;
- minimal intervention.

As we argued above, these values make sense only as part of an anti-oppressive approach if we contextualise them within a general AOP perspective which commits the worker to the value of social justice (see Figure 2.4).

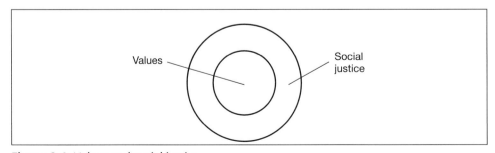

Figure 2.4 *Values and social justice*

Empowerment

Empowerment requires the development of personal, interpersonal and political power to allow individuals or collectives to enhance their life situation. It requires the full participation of people in the formulation, implementation and evaluation of decisions determining the functioning and well-being of themselves and their wider social environment.

Addressing the ethics of empowerment in your work requires you to consider the power that you can exercise in relation to service users. It requires you to consider ways in which that power can be shared with and optimally transferred to the service user. Thus the social and personal barriers which prevent service users from achieving control in their lives is paramount as control implies power to decide on what constitutes a 'good life'.

Empowerment is a contested concept, some writers emphasise the importance of individual empowerment while others focus upon collective and social aspects (Adams 2003). While individual empowerment is important and necessary it is the contention here that it is not sufficient. Parker et al. (1999) argue that social workers must be wary of an uncritical approach to the concept. They suggest that empowerment is often *done to you by others, or done by you to others* (p151). What they mean by this is that professionals have colonised the practice of empowerment so that service users are therefore in passive receipt of empowering practice by professionals which, they suggest, is the opposite of the project of empowerment. As a first step in developing empowering practice, the social worker is required to enter into the world of the service user. This is akin to an empathetic approach but goes beyond this by requiring the social worker to see the commonalities of one service user's experience with others. In this approach the service user's interpretation of events and problems in their lives must take centre stage. At this stage it requires social workers to view this narrative as legitimate. It requires understanding on the part of the social worker and an acceptance for its validity for the service user. It is not something which requires changing by the social worker as if it may lack a true reflection of a situation or a lack of consciousness on the part of the service user. To take the view that the service user's consciousness of their situation needs to be changed at this stage is the complete opposite of empowerment.

> *A person who, for example, has derived most meaning and satisfaction in their life from caring for others is likely to experience being looked after in a nursing home very differently from someone who has been used to having others meet their needs in many ways throughout their life. Someone whose occupational role has been a major part of their identity may interpret the experience of going to a day centre differently from someone whose identity was more closely defined by the quality of their relationships with others. These are factors which will have a profound influence not only on a person's care needs generally, but also on how they can be most meaningfully involved and consulted* (Allan, 2001).

In considering the dynamics of empowerment two aspects are important:

- control – so that people define their own situation and their needs within this;
- self-actualisation – enabling service users to then take power for themselves through developing their confidence and self-esteem, their skills and knowledge.

Partnership

Partnership refers to the way social workers should work with service users. This means in effect working with service users in a systematic way but with the service users' consent.

If we look at the basic model of systematic practice, we can highlight how partnership working is integrated in each stage of the process.

- *Assessment* – investigate and analyse the needs of the service user with them, checking out the validity of the information gathered at each stage, drawing out the strengths which the service user has as well as those needs which require further development.

- *Plan* – agree a course of action with the service user but do not impose your own strategy.

- *Intervene* – draw on the service user's strengths, agree on what they can do and what you will do, and review intervention with the service user on a regular basis. Agree on how much time will be devoted to the task.

- *Evaluate* – discuss what achievements have been made with the service user, and agree on what has been achieved and what might need to be addressed in the future.

Partnership as a principle is equally valid with involuntary service users. For example, in regard to statutory child care, these principles should continue to be adhered to so that service users have the maximum amount of choice and control over their situation as possible. These principles of partnership working have been validated by families involved in statutory child care who felt that even though they were subject to intervention in which they had no choice they were far more positive about this experience where social workers had worked in partnership (Aldgate and Statham, 2001).

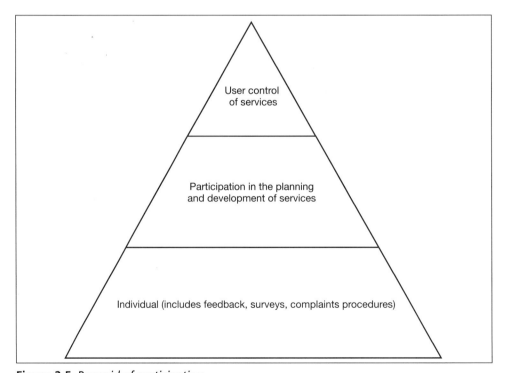

Figure 2.5 *Pyramid of participation*

We could look at partnership as a pyramid with the apex being user control and management of services, descending towards participation in planning of services, down to the base of individual consultation via surveys of service user's views to gain feedback on the effectiveness of services. (see Figure 2.5).

Democratic and consumerist approaches to empowerment

Distinctions have been identified between consumerist/market approaches and citizenship/democratic approaches to empowerment (Crouch, 2003). The extent to which service users are able to exercise their voice depends upon their ability to influence agency-led initiatives to achieve this. Voice becomes more potent where user-led initiatives have been able to control the pace and extent of partnership.

Partnership	Approach	Degree of service user control
Agency-led	Exit	Low
Service-user-led	Voice	High

Consumerist – exit

This suggests that service users have power as consumers of the service to either purchase the service directly or have it purchased on their behalf by care managers. This implies that service users will be given a choice over the kinds of service that they want. This is based on a market model in which a person who is unhappy with a particular service can withdraw their purchase of one service and transfer it to another. In terms of consultation, service users as consumers contribute to consumer surveys to voice their satisfaction or otherwise with the service which is in theory adjusted to meet consumer demand.

Democratic – voice

This suggests that service users should have a voice in the organisation and delivery of services. This means developing processes of consultation and participation in which service users are consulted as to the kinds of service they want and how they ought to be delivered. The more voice, i.e. the more service users have power of decision in planning and organising services, then the more control. This involves membership on planning and management committees as partners with personal social services, or to have control of the planning and organisation of services with service users in the majority.

At various times social workers and service users may find themselves at different points of this continuum, depending upon how tolerant service users are of being excluded from this process, and how proactive social workers are at actively involving service users in the process.

Partnership is often synonymous with participation, and in the literature is often indistinguishable from it. The extent of participation and partnership by service users in determining the kinds of service that they need depends upon the level of power and the process of empowerment to achieve control over the delivery of services.

Underpinning the concept of partnership is a value that all citizens should be involved in making decisions which affect their lives. The value of partnership has been emphasised in both community care and children's services, and as such has been promoted by the state even within statutory situations such as child protection or mental health work. For example, research into the placement of children away from their parents showed in the 1980s that the outcome for children was much better when parents were involved in the placement process (Aldgate and Statham, 2001).

Minimal intervention

Minimal intervention as a specific value of AOP refers to the need for social workers to be aware of the formal power they have in relation to the lack of formal power of service users. Power used by social workers can be positive as well as negative. The use of social workers' power to advocate and intervene at levels of organisations which have proved inaccessible for service users is one such example. The intervention of social workers to protect service users from the illegitimate actions of others is another. To avoid the disempowering of service users by recourse to early intervention Payne (2000) highlights a three-stage approach (see Figure 2.6).

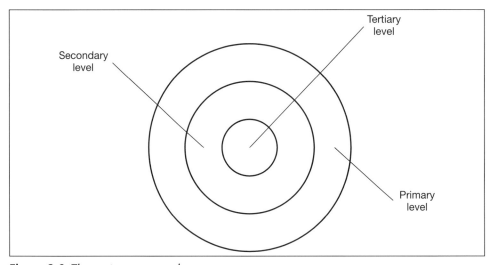

Figure 2.6 *Three-stage approach*

- *The primary level* – to prevent problems arising. Services might be adapted to be appropriate and helpful to clients, community resources mobilised to help, and the public and people involved given information and education to enable more control of the process.

- *The secondary level* – to catch problems and try to deal with them early, before they become serious. This reduces the amount of interference in clients' lives.

- *The tertiary level* – to reduce the consequences for people when something has gone wrong or action has been forced on the agency.

A good example of how minimal intervention has been compromised is in the area of child support and protection. In the context of the many public inquiries into failures within the child protection system, it is not surprising that social workers take the less risky option and put families through the child protection process rather than providing family support. Yet this has the inevitable consequence of stigmatising and oppressing many children and their families (Waterhouse, 2000). This process was particularly evident in research by Gibbons et al. (1995) who found that only 15 per cent of families who were originally referred were finally placed on the child protection register, while Farmer and Owen (1995) outlined the traumatising effects this process had on children and parents alike. This focus upon incidents of abuse rather than supportive work has been highlighted by Devaney (2004) whose research suggests that the monitoring of the refocusing of children's services through the measurements of performance is designed to monitor the operation of the system rather than the actual impact of services and interventions on the lives of children and their families. Little (2004) concurs with this and his literature review of the research on the child protection system identified that children often undergo too many assessments by numerous agencies, resulting in wasted time, lost information and feelings of alienation on the part of the families.

C H A P T E R   S U M M A R Y

This chapter has explored AOP and ADP. It has suggested that, to be effective, AOP must examine and counter oppression across the social structure. Efforts to reform the oppressive actions of individuals and organisations, while necessary, are not sufficient to counter oppression, which requires a multilevel approach which seeks to change the unequal social relations that constitute the structure of society. Appreciation of difference does not mean being indifferent to injustice in our own or others' cultural practices. As social workers, we must tread very carefully in assessing the likely impact of any intervention which challenges embedded cultural practices upon the service users concerned.

FURTHER READING

Thompson, N (2001) *Anti-discriminatory practice*. Basingstoke: Palgrave.
This book is still the classic text on anti-discriminatory practice and is a well-written and highly accessible book.

Dalrymple, J and Burke, B (1995) *Anti-oppressive practice*. Buckingham: Open University Press.
This book looks at the issue of anti-oppressive practice and engages in an interesting critique of Thompson's approach.

Parekh, B (2000) *Rethinking multiculturalism: Cultural diversity and political theory*. London: Macmillan.
A challenging read and one which argues for cultural dialogue around issues of multiculturalism. Chapter 10 is valuable in discussing cultural relativism

Chapter 3
Principles and consequences

A C H I E V I N G   A   S O C I A L   W O R K   D E G R E E

This chapter will begin to help you meet the following National Occupational Standards:
Key Role 6 Demonstrate professional competence in social work practice.
- Work within the principles and values underpinning social work practice.
- Identify and assess issues, dilemmas and conflicts that might affect your practice.
- Devise strategies to deal with ethical issues, dilemmas and conflicts.

This chapter will also help you follow the GSCC's Code of Practice for Social Care Workers:
1 As a social worker, you must protect the rights and promote the interests of service users and carers.
This includes:
- treating each person as an individual;
- respecting and, where appropriate, promoting the individual views and wishes of both service users and carers;
- supporting service users' rights to control their lives and make informed choices about the services they receive;
- respecting and maintaining the dignity and privacy of service users.

It will also introduce you to the following academic standards as set out in the social work subject benchmark statement:
3.1.3 Values and ethics
- The nature, historical evolution and application of social work values.
- Aspects of philosophical ethics relevant to the understanding and resolution of value dilemmas and conflicts in both interpersonal and professional contexts.

CASE STUDY 3.1

Joyce Phillips, aged 69, cares for her mother Megan Davies, who is 90 years old. She lives just a few streets away from her mother's house and has spent increasing amounts of time with her mother, particularly since her mother was widowed some two years ago. Megan is becoming increasingly forgetful. Joyce's husband, aged 70, suffered a stroke two years ago and relies heavily on Joyce both physically, as he can no longer wash and dress himself, and emotionally, as he sees little of his friends who find it difficult to visit him.

Joyce gets very tired having to juggle between caring for her husband and her mother. She has never asked for any help from social services. When a social worker did visit her at home she said that she didn't require help. After all, social workers only help people who can't help themselves, and anyway she felt it was her duty to look after her husband and her mother. She added: If everybody just dumped their loved ones onto social services then the whole reason for being in a family would just die*.*

Whether we agree or disagree with this statement Joyce has a clear reason why she wishes to continue to care for her husband and mother. What Joyce is expressing here is not only her own justification for her continued care of her family, but also a deep-seated moral stance about the responsibilities, as she sees it, of family members to one another and what that means in practice.

Introduction

In Chapter 1 we looked at different justifications for why people act ethically. Some people had a strong religious belief which they felt inspired them to act; others came from a secular belief system which involved an ethic of social justice, a sense of what was fair. Similarly Joyce (in the case study above) is expressing her reasons for continuing to care, invoking a principle where she sees care as a duty requiring her to look after her husband and mother.

In this chapter we will examine two underpinning philosophical perspectives that have informed the practice of social workers, i.e. principled and consequentialist perspectives. Having established our understanding of these approaches, we will examine some recent alternatives which have challenged these previously-dominant ideas in social work values. These are virtue theory and a feminist ethic of care.

Social workers, despite the increasing managerial controls on their professional discretion, still have significant autonomy in their dealings with service users and have been characterised as 'street-level bureaucrats' (Evans and Harris, 2004). This refers to the way social workers are able, through use of their professional discretion, to sometimes subvert accepted policy as laid down by their employers when working alone with service users. In effect they create policy through the decisions they make when working directly with service users, when managerial supervision is at its weakest. Professional autonomy remains important for social work practice as social workers have to apply and interpret policy in relation to individual cases. In this chapter we explore the philosophical and ethical approaches upon which social workers can assist service users in making those moral practical decisions.

We can either base our approach upon clear principles to inform our action, for example always tell the truth, or we can decide to weigh up the likely consequences of our actions to see who will benefit the most (see Figure 3.1).

We can consider approaches which call upon our understanding of what an ethical social worker would do in such a situation or we can take into account feminist approaches which require that the social worker considers an ethic of care.

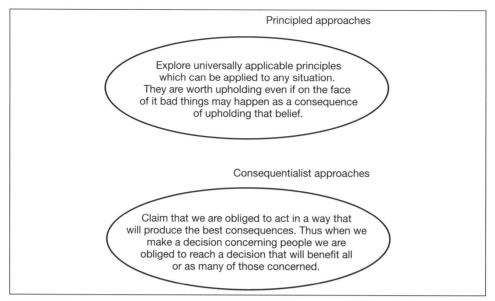

Figure 3.1 *Principled and consequentialist approaches*

Given the relatively simple definitions in Figure 3.1, how can we apply these principles to Joyce's situation in Case Study 3.1 above?

ACTIVITY **3.1**

Make some brief notes on what position you think Joyce is taking in Case study 3.1.

- *Does she justify her actions based on a particular principle which she believes is important?*

or:

- *Does she justify her decision to care for her mother and husband in terms of its consequences, i.e. that it will have the greatest benefit to the majority of the people involved?*

Comment

From the brief description of the two approaches so far, I would hope that you identified that Joyce was employing a principled approach to the care of her husband and mother. Joyce has justified her actions through a principle of responsibility to the other members of her family. Remember that the principled approach is only concerned with the rightness of this principle and that any other reasons should not be considered in justifying the decision. So even if Joyce is finding the reality of caring very difficult to manage and maintain, these difficulties are of lesser importance than upholding the principle of family responsibility.

By contrast we could analyse this situation in consequentialist terms. Joyce could reduce the amount of time caring for her mother by accessing home care for her mother; in turn this could lead to Joyce feeling less tired and giving more time to her husband which could improve her relationship with him. In those terms the consequences would benefit two out of the three people involved in this situation so justifying the reduction in the time spent with Joyce's mother.

Kant's principled approach – also known as deontology

Emmanuel Kant (1724–1804) was a German philosopher. His moral theory grew out of the Enlightenment which was the revolutionary intellectual movement that influenced all areas of social life (mostly in Western Europe) by the late eighteenth century, reaching its peak with the French Revolution of 1789. It inspired philosophers and scientists to think in radically different ways. The core of Enlightenment thinking asserted that human beings are the centre of all things, and claimed that human reason should replace traditional ways of thinking and the social institutions supported by it. The goal of many of the Enlightenment thinkers was to use reason as the basis to overturn the superstition of the past. In particular this meant removing God as the source for explaining the world, and replacing this with the power of science. Rational scientific thinking would provide the basis for understanding the natural and social world and lead to human progress. Progress out of the dark ages of tradition could be achieved through the application of scientific knowledge. In Britain, the Enlightenment *was primarily the expression of new mental and moral values, new cannons of taste, styles of sociability and views of human nature* (Porter, 2000, p14).

For Kant the problem was to develop a moral theory which was informed by rationality. Rationality enables people to understand what their duties are and how their duties enlighten what they do in the world. The issue for Kant was to develop universal principles or guidelines that parallel the way in which religion informs people of their duty, replacing the spiritual tenets of religion with a rational consideration of what one ought to do.

For an action to be moral we must act in accordance with rational principles, which must be true for everyone. In order for us to determine if a principle and the act flowing from it is moral, it must be able to be applied universally, i.e. has the scope to be applied to all situations in which we might need it. A good example of this is the act of lying. If through our reasoning of the universal principle we show that lying can be applied successfully, then we can act on it as a principle worth upholding:

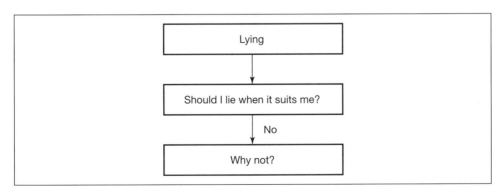

Because if everyone lied (universal principle) then nobody would know what was truthfulness and what was falsity. Universality is the benchmark for testing through the application of reason. A principle is moral only if it can be universalised. If lying was universalised then the confusion of not knowing which was truth and which was falsity would break down social life and lead to chaos. In this way then it is an immoral act. Thus we should only act on those principles that can be universalised. So for Kant one of his key principles was always to tell the truth:

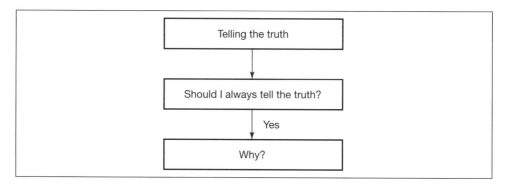

ACTIVITY 3.2

Apply the universalist test to the proposition that it is always moral to tell the truth.

CASE STUDY 3.2

Two years pass and Megan Davies is now in residential care after Joyce has been persuaded that this is the best place for her mother. Megan has now acquired senile dementia; she continually asks when her husband is coming to see her. The care staff once told Mrs Davies that her husband had died which upset her to such an extent that she was crying continually for a number of hours afterwards. This has been repeated on a number of occasions. Mrs Davies's fellow residents also become very distressed at the way that she becomes grief stricken and they have asked that something must be done. The care staff also feel increasingly uncomfortable telling Mrs Davies the truth and find they have to spend a lot of time with her, which means they are often unable to complete their duties for the rest of the residents. The owner of the home, concerned for her staff and other residents, as well as wishing to do the 'right thing' by Mrs Davies, asks your opinion as to the best course of action to take. She feels it is far better to lie to Mrs Davies, to avoid the repeated distress Mrs Davies experiences when she is told her husband has died.

ACTIVITY 3.3

What advice would you give if you accepted Kant's categorical imperative regarding truth telling in relation to Megan Davies?

Can you envisage any problems with the advice you have given?

Comment

When we have established such a principle (through the universalist test) it becomes for Kant a 'categorical imperative' (a command which must be followed). Act only on that maxim through which you can at the same time will that it should become a universal law.

If we accept that always telling the truth is a categorical imperative, then every time Mrs Davies asks us whether her husband is coming to see her we must as duty instructs tell her he has died. There is a problem: explaining that her husband has died many times during the day, given Mrs Davies's poor short-term memory, will cause her great distress. In effect she continually relives the anguish when hearing her husband has died. It may also be very stressful and time-consuming for the members of staff to spend time with Mrs Davies and deal with her unhappiness. It may also be stressful for other residents if they witness Mrs Davies's distress.

Kant believes that people's humanity is defined by the ability to think rationally about one's position in the world. Thus we can use our reason to determine what the 'right thing to do' is. Morality is the product of our reasoning as humans and this enables us to organise our conduct and live a moral life. The moral life is one that has been arrived at through the reasoning mind formulating rules of behaviour, which tell us what we ought to do, not what our human desires want us to do. The reason why we should act in this way is because by acting rationally we are living up to our status as human beings.

Moral considerations therefore have precedence over all other considerations such as personal pleasure; moral considerations are therefore commands that require us to act in a certain way. To do what is right is then our duty and duty comes before all else. For Mrs Davies our duty is to tell her the truth. Focusing upon one's duty has led people to perform both heroic and horrific acts in equal measure. It provides strong motivations that can often blind people to the consequences of their action.

In the book *Hitler's Willing Executioners* (Goldhagen, 1996) the author draws on witness testimony of the Nazi murder squads in Eastern Europe during the Second World War. These men were volunteers who justified the brutality of their acts with the comfort that although what they did was horrifying, it was justified through their duty to the Fuehrer and the Fatherland. The writer Jung Chang in her autobiography of her family *Wild Swans* (1991) writes movingly of the way her father, an important civil servant, would always put his duty to the Chinese Communist Party before his family, preferring not to unfairly favour his family above others.

Before exploring Kant's principled approach further, it is worth considering at this stage some of the assumptions Kant makes here and relate them to social work. The first assumption to consider is as follows:

- that to be human is to be a rational being.

ACTIVITY **3.4**

Make a list of service users who are likely to be unable to act in a rational way.

Comment

Social workers often work with people living in situations who may have difficulty in thinking and acting in a rational way. A woman seeking refuge from a violent partner clearly living under periods of extreme stress, may require much support to overcome her fear for herself and her children if she has any. Do people with severe learning disabilities whose ability to think rationally may be impaired mean they are less human? How should a social worker respond ethically to such people if they adopt a Kantian position?

- The second assumption to consider is as follows: emotion is illegitimate.

ACTIVITY **3.5**

Think about the reasons you decided to train as a professional social worker and make a list of the most important. How far do they relate to issues of duty in the sense that Kant talks about?

Comment

Perhaps one of the reasons you chose to become a social worker was that you were motivated by a desire to help others in a constructive way. You may have been moved by a sense of injustice that many people live dangerous and difficult lives with little material and emotional support to help them. These are strong motivations to want to make a difference in the world. To focus upon the rather austere sense of duty and rationality leaves little room for those feelings of compassion that inform our sense of duty and responsibility to change the world in which we live. Without the motivation of our desires and feeling for our fellow human beings, we would not be able to put ourselves in a position to act morally.

For Kant there is a constant struggle taking place between our higher rational selves and what we consider to be our duty, and our lower desires and instincts and how we satisfy them. Fans of *The Simpsons* TV programme will be aware of the battle between Homer, who exhibits a continuing desire to satisfy his basic instincts, particularly in the realm of food and drink, and his wife Marge, who attempts to elevate his thinking and remind him of his duties, often unsuccessfully. Kant argues that rational beings, therefore, are higher because they rise above the so-called baser instincts; as such they are worthy of respect. They are worthy of respect because rational beings set their own goals in life, which also requires us as rational beings not to impose our own goals upon them. We must not treat others as a means to acquire our own goals but as ends in themselves capable of forming their own goals just as we do.

Rationality is the means by which human beings become free from self-interest and the pursuit of animal pleasure. This must have seemed very liberating at the time of Kant's writing because this not only frees us from our instincts but also from the strictures of the church and the state. Kant calls this freedom 'autonomy', a concept which means that I decide on the principles that inform the way I live my life free from the external influences of others. This is a highly individualistic approach which has met with much criticism because it fails to look at the consequences for all those involved in a particular situation. Individuals are important but we must also take into account that individuals live in societies with others and therefore moral decisions do not exist in a vacuum but have inevitable consequences for others.

Utilitarian consequentialism

The best known moral theory which develops consequentialism is Utilitarianism. This philosophy was developed by Jeremy Bentham (1748–1832), one of the most original and extraordinary thinkers of his day. Bentham believed in, among other things, suffrage (votes) for women. He was also a prison reformer and advocated a legal system based on his theory.

Utilitarianism looks at the consequences of actions balancing the relative advantages and disadvantages of a particular course of action from the standpoint of creating the greatest good for the greatest number of people. Utilitarians hold that it is not the capacity for rational thought which enables human beings to decide on the right course of action, it is a person's basic drives of seeking pleasure and avoiding pain. This is known as 'the principle of utility'. For Utilitarians the assessment of how much happiness can be drawn from a particular action as against how much pain, is central; if more happiness is gained for more people then that is the right course of action. Each person's happiness in this understanding is the same as anyone else's; in other words, let each person's happiness count as one. This principle was developed further by Bentham's disciple, J. S. Mill, who argued that actions should be judged on the greatest good for the greatest number, which leads us to two principles informing Utilitarianism:

- a principle of justice – let everyone count as one and no one's happiness count as more than that;

- a principle of utility – to ensure the greatest good for the greatest number.

For social work there is a constant tension between these two principles.

CASE STUDY 3.3

A family resource centre has been given an increase in its funding (£50,000) for the next year. After much consultation with the local community two proposals have emerged:

- *Proposal 1. To renovate the children's play area (which has been closed on health and safety grounds) so that all the children in the community can play safely at the centre .*

- *Proposal 2. To renovate part of the play area for all the children but use the rest of the money for an outreach worker to work with the local Somali community to encourage greater use of the centre for all children in the area.*

If you were the manager what course of action would you take and give your reasons for your decision?

Comment

Is the point of social work to create the greatest amount of happiness in the situations we are faced with, or are other criteria more important, for example creating as much equality as possible, ensuring social justice and fairness for service users? In the case above it would seem that Proposal 1 does open up the resource to all the children in the community (the justice principle). However, Proposal 2 questions how effective this is if some groups in the community do not feel their families can use the centre (the utility principle).

ACTIVITY 3.7

Let us now apply the Utilitarian principle to Mrs Davies's situation as outlined previously. In considering this situation two of the questions a Utilitarian is likely to consider are:

- *What would be the consequences of lying to Mrs Davies?*

- *What might be the options to achieve the least harmful or most advantageous outcome overall for all involved with Mrs Davies?*

Comment

Traditionally, Utilitarianism has considered that any decision should account for the balance of pleasure over pain. In looking at the actions of the care staff, we assess in what ways those actions contribute to a balance of pleasure over pain experienced by Mrs Davies and all those involved with her in the home. This can be defined as act utilitarianism. We are evaluating the action or actions of the individual or group of individuals and quantifying the balance of pleasure (benefits) over pain (costs).

Alternatively, we might suggest to the owner that she develop some guidelines/procedures which could increase the balance of pleasure over pain. In this respect, guidelines about the treatment of service users with senile dementia could be developed and then assessed as to how they minimise harm to all concerned. This is known as rule utilitarianism. We are assessing a principle, based here upon guidelines, to see what the relative benefits and costs are when it is enacted.

However, there is a number of problems with the utilitarian approach. Measuring the balance of pleasure over pain tells us nothing about whose pleasure or pain we are accounting for. If we are measuring the total amount of pleasure promoted, whose pleasure do we take into account, for example Mrs Davies, the care staff, the matron, the other residents, Mrs Davies's relatives? To measure the total happiness produced from one course of action, then, we need to measure all those whose happiness is affected by lying to Mrs Davies. This is a purely mathematical procedure but is happiness easily quantified? How do we measure the relative happiness of, say, Mrs Davies who expects her husband to be coming soon against the care staff that no longer have to deal with the distress of counselling Mrs Davies when she experiences the grief of losing her husband again?

This led some Utilitarians, as we identified above, to propose that every person's happiness counts for one, i.e. that it has the same value. This was developed by Mill to suggest the greatest good for the greatest number. However, if this is the case then we can assume that the power of the majority in any situation may well win over the needs of minorities. Would we want to live in such a society?

Let us use an example from social work in Wales, although the problem could apply to any situation where there is a linguistic minority.

Your local social services department has instituted a policy to provide information to local service users about the services they have on offer. The area covers both a rural and an urban population. Those living in the urban area form the majority and predominantly use English as their first language; those in the rural area, who form the minority, use Welsh as their first language. Your social services office decides to put most of its resources into providing leaflets and adverts in the local press within the urban areas, as this will affect the majority of likely service users, and they argue that people in the rural areas speak English anyway. This could be justified quite clearly if you took a Utilitarian approach but it would be unfair on first-language Welsh speakers. In this case the needs of all service users must be accounted for so that all receive the information in the language of their choice, which is likely to improve overall take-up of all services.

As in the previous case study we are again faced with two competing imperatives:

- On the one hand we have a principle which urges us to produce as much good as possible (utility) from this perspective so we distribute the leaflets to as many people as possible.

- On the other hand the second imperative requires us to distribute this good as fairly as possible (justice) and ensure that the leaflets are also distributed to those whose first language is Welsh.

Often these imperatives of utility and justice clash as we saw in the case of the family resource centre above and therefore taking a majority approach to the distribution of information in this case would fail the test of justice and fair treatment.

The importance of the principled and consequentialist approaches

Principled approaches provide a set of guidelines which can act as a framework within which social workers can assess when actions should be undertaken. It provides a benchmark in advance of the situations they are likely to face. Social workers who were asked to visit and counsel the parents of learning disabled children subjected to euthanasia in Nazi Germany may well have felt their role was entirely justified in reducing what were considered to be a malevolent influence that was degrading the quality of the Aryan master race. They may have felt intimidated and feared that they would suffer punishment if they didn't comply. Or they may have taken a principled approach and refused to undertake such work. This is important, as we have seen with the example of the Welsh language where principles of justice which extend the rights of a minority have historically been denied first-language Welsh speakers because they are not in the majority and they can speak English anyway. Social workers who work with individual service users must be able to justify their actions to them, but also be able to represent and advocate on behalf of service users when their managers, who may try and ration and prioritise services, could compromise their needs. Social workers who can argue effectively from a sound principled position will therefore be able to advocate for service users much more effectively than those who try and second guess what might be in the interests of the majority.

Consequentialist approaches also have their strengths when policy-makers and managers have to make decisions about the appropriate allocation of resources. The case studies outlined above show that decisions have to consider issues of the greatest good for the greatest number when dealing with the allocation of resources across a number of competing groups. This is not to say that this approach is the only or final one but it can provide the means to understand the problem, and weigh the competing interests of one group against another when scarce resources mean that some groups may lose out.

Both approaches apply formulas to situations. Irrespective of context you are required either to do your duty whatever the situation might hold, or calculate the consequences of action. Both formulas tend to ignore the overall context in which these decisions are made. Yet social workers have to exercise their judgement in specific contexts, and although principled and consequentialist approaches may provide useful frameworks to inform a possible course of action, it will not fully inform the social worker. Each situation is unique and requires social workers to understand the specific practice situation. For example, requiring a social worker to never lie to a service user may be highly problematic if the service user in question is a violent estranged husband seeking the whereabouts of his partner and children.

Likewise, to always require social workers to uphold the principle of confidentiality when the child you are working with discloses that her father has physically abused her may again require further action and the breaking of that confidentiality.

For these reasons critics of these approaches have looked to the nature of social work and suggested that the exercise of judgement requires social workers to have particular qualities of character which cannot be read off from the maxims of Kantian or Utilitarian theory. Social work often operates in an uncertain and unpredictable environment which cannot be tamed by the application of broad ethical maxims. McBeath and Webb (2002) make such a point when they argue:

> *Kantian and Utilitarian ethics to a degree rely, respectively, upon the mechanical application of rights-claims and adherence to duties, or upon the comparison of anticipated outcomes* (p1018).

Given the contingent aspect of social work, in exercising their judgement social workers had better do this in the most effective and informed way possible. This often draws upon the special qualities of social workers as human beings who are required to call upon their reserves of character in order to work in ethical ways. One of the key approaches which stresses the importance of character is virtue theory.

Virtue theory

Virtue theory proposes that ethical practice must be cultivated by 'good' social workers; it focuses development upon the character of the individual social worker. For example, social workers who are unable to suppress their feelings of homophobia in their private lives are likely to carry this prejudice into their professional lives. Virtue theory requires individuals to develop themselves as good people as well as good social workers. If social workers are often required to make judgements about service users then they should make sound judgements. The development of sound judgement requires the exercise of qualities such as courage and wisdom; these cannot be taught through the application of rules advocated by deontologists and consequentialists. As Clark (2006) argues, for example, it is important to show respect to service users, but ethical lists do not tell the social worker how to do this within particular practice-situations and contexts. This requires the social worker to interpret the meaning of respect within that particular culture and society. These ideas come from the ancient Greeks, in particular the philosopher Aristotle (384–322BC). Aristotle was concerned with developing the moral qualities of individuals so that they could embody a good life within themselves. Following the good life required the acquisition of character and the qualities which flowed from that such as kindness, courage, etc. The concept he identified in this regard was that of flourishing (*eudemonia*). For Aristotle, living the 'good life' meant individuals were required to follow the 'golden mean', a rule of thumb by which the individual avoids excess. This is not to say that the virtuous social worker should avoid being angry but that anger should be evidenced in appropriate ways and at appropriate times. Cohen (2003) provides some useful examples that can be applied to social work, such as the Goldilocks test (from the children's story) where Goldilocks tests which bowl of porridge to eat and chooses the one that is 'not too cold and not too hot' (see Figure 3.2).

Sphere of applicability	Too much	Too little	Just right
fear	rash	cowardly	courageous
anger	irritable	lacking spirit	patient
social skills	flatterer	cantankerous	friendly
social conduct	shy	shameless	modest

Figure 3.2 *Aspects of virtue*

When developing character, social workers should seek to develop those qualities on the right of Figure 3.2.

Problems with virtue ethics

Houston (2003) has critiqued the development of virtue-based social work. He suggests there are difficulties in establishing virtue. For example, in order to develop virtue we need to define what it actually means. For Houston, this is problematic because if we consider a virtuous person to have such character traits as bravery, courage, justice and truth, where do these come from? As Houston argues: *to establish virtue we must refer to the virtuous person but in order to identify him or her, we must have some idea of what virtue is in the first place* (p820).

Social workers seeking virtue are bound to move around in circles. Virtue is what the virtuous person exhibits and the virtuous person exhibits virtue in an endless circular argument. A second criticism concerns suggestions made by virtue theorists that what must be developed is the moral intuition of individuals so that they can decide on what is virtuous. This ignores the dangers of a solitary individual determining what is good without any reference to others. As Houston suggests *all manner of cognitive bias and unconscious self-manipulation can be present, hardly a firm basis for the development of a virtuous social worker* (p821).

These are important criticisms, which the social worker wishing to adopt virtue theory would do well to acknowledge. However, virtue theory does point the way to the importance of sound moral judgement in social work. As Banks and Williams (2005) show, many student social workers when faced with an ethical challenge often feel intimidated because of their status as students, as matched against the powerful professionals whom they identify need to be questioned. As Banks suggests, these dilemmas and conflicts relate to professional confidence, competence and commitment. In echoing virtue theory she suggests that merely to develop an understanding of different ethical principles and arguments is necessary but not sufficient to equip student social workers to practise ethically. It is essential to develop:

> qualities in students that enable them to recognise ethical issues and dilemmas (moral sensitivity) and to act on their decisions (courage and strength of will (p749).

Clark (2006) supports this view suggesting that social workers require a sense of vocation involving an ethical commitment in which their identity and their character are inextricably mixed.

ACTIVITY 3.8

To help you think about the virtues of social workers put yourself in the position of an interviewer selecting students for the degree in social work.

Is it possible for a social work student to hold prejudicial views about people from ethnic minorities in private while working in a non-discriminatory way in public as a social worker?

What qualities would you look for in a prospective student social worker?

What qualities would you judge to be inappropriate for a social worker?

Comment

As you may be able to see from the first question, it would be unprofessional to allow a student social worker onto a social work course who evidenced such prejudice while professing to uphold anti-oppressive principles in their public role as a social worker. We would expect that the character and motivations of the student would be congruent with those aims of professional social work including anti-oppressive practice. We could not expect such prejudicial beliefs to be held back when faced with many service users from minority ethnic backgrounds.

Drawing on Clark (2006) it is possible to outline those appropriate and qualities (see Table 3.1).

Table 3.1 *Qualities of social workers*

Appropriate qualities	Inappropriate qualities
Commitment to learn new skills	Technically incompetent or inept
Commitment to social justice	Discriminatory and neglectful
Enabling	Over-controlling
Morally inclusive	Poor moral character
Competent in social situations	Poor social communication/engagement

Adapted from Clark (2006).

This is not an endless list but it points to the necessity for social workers to develop qualities of character that can be overlooked by deontological and consequentialist approaches.

A feminist ethic of care

In addressing virtue ethics we have emphasised the importance given to the moral qualities of the social worker. Virtue ethics then eschews more abstract ethical perspectives and asks social workers and social care workers to look towards themselves and their capacities for empathy, courage and compassion. As Hugman (2005) argues, there is a growing interest in placing emotions at the heart of ethics. The helping relationship is one in which the emotional content is often silent in the discussion of ethics. When we considered Biestek's list approach to ethics we recognised the importance of controlled emotional involvement by the helper. However, this may underestimate the difficulties of achieving such control by social workers in emotionally charged and disturbing situations, for example, when a child may have to be removed from its parents or carers, or when an older person has to relinquish their independence and move into long-term residential care. Professional ethics then must attend to the importance of emotion and in particular those feelings of compassion within the helping relationship because as Hugman (2005) argues,

> *to attend to compassion involves the recognition of the person or situation, in a way that demands a moral response (p66).*

Froggett (2002) supports this argument, suggesting that as rational technical responses in social work become prevalent, so the ability to feel and show concern by social workers through their professional role has been marginalised. In recognition of how abstract principles of ethical practice are unable to attend satisfactorily to these qualitative issues, arguments for an ethics of care attempt to provide a framework that can account for and include these 'softer' aspects of ethical practice.

Banks (2004) calls the development of an 'ethic of care' by feminist writers as being part of a broader range of *relationship-based ethics* (p89). This means that a moral significance is given to the characteristics of people's relationships. The approach is one which situates ethical decision-making in the quality of the relationships people maintain with one another, in particular where people are in vulnerable or dependent relationships that require a specific orientation, such as compassion or care within the relationship. This is similar to virtue ethics in that the ethically sensitive practitioner is required to show a quality or attitude towards the ethical problem that confronts them.

Gilligan (1982) proposes what she calls an 'ethic of care'. This work was a response to the work of Kohlberg (1984) who suggested that there were definite stages to moral development. Kohlberg's approach explored the idea that moral judgement is acquired developmentally in tandem with the development of other cognitive and intellectual skills. Kohlberg distinguished six stages of moral development, each stage developing out of the one before (see Figure 3.3). These stages move from the basic level of learned obedience and avoidance of punishment, to a middle phase concerned with maintaining and developing social relationships, which he called a conventional morality, through to the most advanced which is characterised by identifying complex moral issues and developing and applying universal principles.

Level	Stage	Social orientation
Pre-conventional	1	Obedience and punishment
	2	Individualism, instrumentalism, and exchange
Conventional	3	'Good boy/girl'
	4	Law and order
Post-conventional	5	Social contract
	6	Principled conscience

Figure 3.3 *Kohlberg's classification*

Level 1 reflects the level of thinking which is dependent on looking to what is socially acceptable – people act in a way which is socially sanctioned by an authority figure. This is reinforced through accepting that punishment may rightly follow any transgression of the rules and therefore deviant behaviours are to be avoided.

Level 2 has moral thinking developing in response to approval-seeking by others and orients itself in society to doing one's duty through obligations imposed by society, by following existing moral and legal codes.

Level 3 is where moral thinking is relatively rare in Kohlberg's estimation. This thinking is grounded by the valuing of fraternity and an authentic concern for the welfare of others. This leads into the highest stage for Kohlberg based on the valuing of independent moral principle, reflected in the developed conscience and respect for universal principles of justice, for example, which may challenge notions of conventional law and morality.

Moral development requires individuals to move through each stage in turn. In order to move to the next stage, individuals first have to appreciate the moral principles informing the previous stage.

Kohlberg's research, although claiming universal applicability, had been conducted upon men only. When Gilligan conducted her research on young women she found that the 'lower' morality concerned with maintaining relationships predominated in her sample. For Gilligan this reflected not a lower state of moral development in women but a different one. Gilligan called this the 'different voice', an ethic of care based upon maintaining social relationships, rather than an ethic of justice determined to develop the right action from abstract principles of justice. For Gilligan women's, moral voice has been silenced by the male concern for developing abstract principles to inform moral development. The dominance of male philosophers and ethical theorists reinforces this process by insisting on the universal applicability of such terms as rationality and objectivity in the development of ethical theory.

ACTIVITY 3.9

Ask your male and female friends to solve the problem below.

Joseph is playing with his sisters Frances and Zoe. Joseph wants to play 'firefighters' and suggest they all build a fire engine out of the kitchen chairs. Frances and Zoe want to play 'casualty'. None of the children want to play the others' game. How could you overcome this impasse?

Comment

Gilligan's research showed that male and female respondents might solve this problem differently. While most men take the option called 'turn-taking' – we play firefighters and then we play Casualty – based on a justice model of equal turn-taking, most women by contrast would seek to resolve the problem by including or merging both games into one, something like 'let's play firefighters who need to go to Casualty' (see Figure 3.4). This emphasises the essential connected nature of the game, meaning both viewpoints are reconciled through maintaining relationships within the group so that all are included.

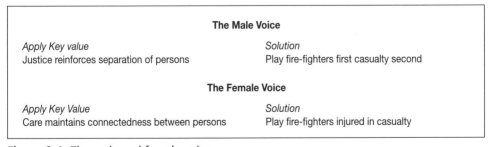

Figure 3.4 *The male and female voice*

According to Gilligan, most of our moral concepts have developed from a male perspective and are characterised as abstract principles. They have ignored the particular situations within which people make moral choices. For example, the major approach to moral philosophy over the past several hundred years has been what might be called an 'ethic of justice', which is deeply rooted in a desire for individual autonomy and independence. The concern for an ethic of justice is to balance the competing interests among individuals. Gilligan points out the troubling consequences of an ethic of justice that does not take into account an 'ethic of care'.

Such formal concepts as duty and justice often result in an objectification of human beings or, at least, a distancing of the parties involved in and affected by moral decision-making. Caring, on the other hand, requires a closer relationship between parties and recognition of the other as a subjective being. Gilligan suggests that the quality of caring is best understood as coming from the feminine, though not exclusively so. Caring considers the needs of both the self and others – it is not just concerned with self-survival. In considering the needs of both self and others, moral decisions should make allowances for differences in the needs of others. Tronto (1993) develops this further suggesting that the idea of care is a basic and valued premise of human existence. It is founded on the fact that we depend upon others and that we have the capacity to care for others. Care is a process and a practice that has four phases to it:

- caring about – recognising the need for care;
- taking care of – assuming a responsibility to care;
- care giving;
- care receiving.

From this, she derives four ethical elements of care:

- attentiveness;
- responsibility;
- competence;
- responsiveness.

This conception is based on an 'obligation to care', From this perspective we view ourselves as part of a network of connected individuals whose different needs create a duty in us to respond. By responding, we must attend to the details of the need which is expressed, and to the outcome of our response on others potentially affected by our actions.

This does not mean that every need requires a response. We must also weigh:

- the seriousness of the need;
- the likely benefit derived from our response;
- our ability to respond to this particular need;
- the competing needs of others in our network.

Almost all ethical decisions require us to weigh competing interests. What an 'ethic of care' requires is to relate the need on an emotional level, a consideration lacking in deontology and consequentialism.

ACTIVITY 3.10

1 Look at Figure 3.5 and link the individuals into a network by joining lines between them. For those which you consider are more significant, draw a double line between the respective participants in the network.

2 Look at Figure 3.5 and identify possible conflicts between the partners which have the potential for disrupting the relationships from the point of view of Mrs Davies.

3 Now decide how you can ensure that all the participants in Figure 3.5 can retain those valued relationships so that the network can be sustained.

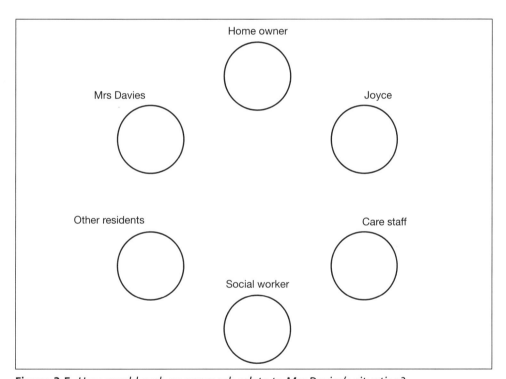

Figure 3.5 *How would such an approach relate to Mrs Davies's situation?*

Comment

From Figure 3.5, you can see that the social worker is part of the complex of relationships which have developed around Mrs Davies. To this end, you must take account of your practice within the social network created and the quality of the relationships forged by all the participants. Instead of acting from outside and judging what your duty might be, or what the most beneficial consequences are, you are ethically required to take account of the lived experience and emotions of all those within this network of relationships. For Mrs Davies the ethic of care requires us to respond to her immediate need, i.e. her despair at continually repeating her feelings of loss for her deceased husband and to her development as a moral person of worth within the residential home. Within the network of relationships then, the immediate others are also implicated in this and each of those people's needs must also be weighed in this way. Therefore what becomes the right course of action will nurture the existing social relationships within Mrs Davies's network. To tell Mrs Davies the truth may ultimately destroy her relationship with her daughters as her daughter becomes increasingly wary of talking to her mother if she is being continually asked about her deceased father and then witnessing her mother's grief. This ethical thought process can then be integrated with others in the social network of Mrs Davies. Although you as the social worker may arrive at the same decision, as if you were operating, for example, from a consequentialist approach, the importance is derived in the care and attention given in the process of decision-making. The quality of the individual's relationships are attended to and given due attention. In this regard the process of arriving at the decision is as important as the decision itself.

Problems of an ethic of care

Criticisms of care ethics have come from writers from the disability movement. These criticisms derive from their concern that care has been used oppressively with disabled people whose demand for greater independence may be compromised by an uncritical adoption of such an approach. Shakespeare (2000) has argued that two alternative theoretical models for reforming care are available. The first derives from the disabled people's movement and sets out a model of independent living. The second is the feminist ethic of care. Both criticise the way care has been promoted, but they diverge in their vision for an alternative. Disabled writers underpin their critique by emphasising the civil rights of disabled people, suggesting that independence can be achieved via personal assistance schemes. Feminist approaches, as identified above, question the whole notion of care and wish to recast it with the recognition that care is not special but forms the normal part of everyday life in which we are all involved and reliant upon.

While the recasting and recognition of care is important, disabled and feminist writers would criticise the tendency to idealise the caring role and the implication that caring may be a natural attribute of women. Users of care services often feel a lack of control over who provides care and how that care is provided. In addition they may feel their voice is minimised and ignored and their very bodies neglected and abused by carers. A disability rights perspective argues for justice in care so that disabled people have the autonomy and independence that some feminists (see Silvers et al., 1998) argue is a patriarchal barrier undermining an ethic of care.

CASE STUDY **3.4**

Let us assume Mrs Davies does not acquire senile dementia but becomes more physically dependent upon her daughter following a series of falls. Mrs Davies, although preferring her daughter to care for her, realises that she cannot ask her daughter to do more for her as she can see how exhausted her daughter gets. Following an assessment of her needs by her social worker, Mrs Davies is given a significant package of care. Mrs Davies did not like to complain but she felt that the social worker was a little brusque in her attitude and seemed to be rushed. A support worker will visit three times a day to help Mrs Davies get up in the morning, visit midday to get shopping and visit at 8 o'clock in the evening to help Mrs Davies into bed. Mrs Davies, although grateful for the care, is unhappy that many of her social needs are not taken into account. She has asked that some of the care hours could be used to enable her to visit her daughter or go to the cinema which she enjoys, but these do not fit into the carers' rota given they have to organise their time efficiently to meet their commitments to the other people they have to visit.

ACTIVITY **3.11**

In what way does the organisation of Mrs Davies's care deny her independence?

In what way does the nature of the care provided limit Mrs Davies's care?

Comment

Mrs Davies's independence is compromised by the way that her care is organised. She is unable to maintain her social contacts and her presence in the wider community as the care provided for her is narrowed to her basic care needs. Her independence is compromised further by the way that her assessment was done to her rather than with her.

In respect to care, this provision limits Mrs Davies's options, particularly when the carers are getting her to bed at 8 o'clock.

Feminist writers such as Sevenhuijsen (1998) and Lister (2003) have sought to develop an ethic of care alongside an ethic of justice. They recognise that there is a darker side to care in which frustration, conflict and abuse can be present, unless this is tempered by a concern for justice in care. However, there is still considerable tension in these approaches. Disabled people continue to fight for the right of independence and observe that just as women's dependency is socially constructed so it is for disabled people. The priority for disabled people is to be able to make choices to exert control over their own lives rather than question independence. As Shakespeare (2000) argues:

> *Rather than challenging the goal of independence, disabled people want to be empowered to become independent. The crucial move is not just to recognise that everyone has needs, but to break the link between physical and social dependency* (p80).

The goal of independence as a first step for disabled people is crucial but this should not prevent the ethical social worker from questioning independence. A feminist ethic of care does point towards reconciliation between care and justice and an ethic in which all persons should have the right to care for and be cared for by others. For some disabled people the severity of their impairment may be such that developing the kind of independence argued for above is difficult to achieve but must always be aspired to. This requires an ethic of justice in attending to the validity of those people's needs and ensuring their fair treatment, while at the same time recognising the mutual interests and interdependency that we all share. How care and justice is linked can be evidenced by the claims of some disabled people to be supported to have children. In this regard they have the right to be able to bear and look after children if they so choose. In the achievement of such a right we are attending to the necessary development of disabled people as interdependent as care givers and care receivers. Research by Tarleton et al. (2006) shows how problematic this issue is, finding that 50 per cent of the parents with learning disabilities researched have had their children removed into care.

C H A P T E R   S U M M A R Y

This chapter has explored the range of philosophical approaches to ethics and related these approaches to social work. It has shown the importance of deontological and consequentialist approaches in social work and has emphasised their significance. We have suggested that any philosophical approach has to be applied in a specific context which requires the social worker to assess the validity of each approach for that particular service user. By contrast we have then considered virtue ethics and suggested that character has importance for social workers in reflecting and living out those principles considered important for ethical social work practice. Finally we have considered a feminist ethic of care and shown how this has been an undervalued approach in social work. The advantages and disadvantages of an ethic of care have been investigated using the critique developed by Shakespeare (2000).

FURTHER READING

Banks, S (2006) *Ethics and values in social work*. 3rd edition. Basingstoke: Palgrave.
Banks's book provides good coverage of all the main philosophical approaches identified in this chapter.

Porter, E (1999) *Feminist perspectives on ethics*. London: Longman.
Porter provides a highly accessible introduction to feminist ethics.

Chapter 4
Being accountable

This chapter will begin to help you to meet the following National Occupational Standards:

Key Role 5 Manage and be accountable, with supervision and support, for your own social work practice within your organisation.

- Manage and prioritise your workload within organisational policies.
- Carry out duties using accountable professional judgement and priorities and knowledge-based social work practice.
- Monitor and evaluate the effectiveness of your programme of work in meeting the organisational requirements and the needs of individuals, families, carers, groups and communities.
- Use professional and managerial supervision and support to improve your practice.

This chapter will also help you follow the GSCC's Code of Practice for Social Care Workers:

6 As a social care worker, you must be accountable for the quality of your work and take responsibility for maintaining and improving your knowledge and skills.

This includes:

- meeting relevant standards of practice and working in a lawful, safe and effective way;
- informing your employer or the appropriate authority about any personal difficulties that might affect your ability to do your job competently and safely;
- seeking assistance from your employer or the appropriate authority if you do not feel able or adequately prepared to carry out any aspect of your work or you are not sure about how to proceed in a work matter;
- working openly and cooperatively with colleagues and treating them with respect;
- recognising that you remain responsible for the work that you have delegated to other workers;
- undertaking relevant training to maintain and improve your knowledge and skills and contributing to the learning and development of other service users and carers.

It will also introduce you to the following academic standards as set out in the social work subject benchmark statement:

2.5 The expectation that social workers will be able to act effectively in such complex circumstances requires that honours degree programmes in social work should be designed to help students learn to become accountable, reflective and self-critical. This involves learning to:

- think critically about the complex social, economic, political and cultural contexts in which social work practice is located;
- work in a transparent and responsible way, balancing autonomy with complex, multiple and sometimes contradictory accountabilities (for example, to different service users, employing agencies, professional bodies and the wider society);
- exercise authority within complex frameworks of accountability and ethical and legal boundaries; and
- acquire and apply the habits of critical reflection, self-evaluation and consultation, and make appropriate use of research in the evaluation of practice outcomes.

What do service users value?

RESEARCH SUMMARY

Virtually all our respondents wanted some advice and someone to listen, and when they did get this they were enormously appreciative. It also appeared to work. One couple, for example, where the father had only managed to elicit advice and support over the telephone about their teenage daughter, said it had made all the difference. The young woman (aged 13) herself stated that things were now better because they had all sat down as a family to talk about difficulties. Another mother with two late teenage children felt alone and needed some help and advice: she appreciated the short burst of help and, although critical overall about the provision, liked the fact that the social worker was very clear about her role (Leigh and Miller, 2004).

Research undertaken on service users from the 1970s onward shows a remarkable consistency in what service users value from social workers (Mayer and Timms 1970; Rees 1978; Winefield and Barlow, 1995). Social workers are valued:

- for their ability to listen;

- for engaging empathically with service users;

- for being clear about what they can and cannot do;

- for providing basic and effective help.

For example, a literature review of research undertaken by the Joseph Rowntree Foundation's Older People's Steering Group (2004) found that:

The forms of support or services which older people valued concerned negotiating the ordinary things in life – relationships, learning in later life, transport, housing, contact – 'being comfortable', having 'that bit of help' (Older People's Steering Group, 2004, p1).

However, what service users value from professional social work and what sometimes is provided does not always tally. Social workers can sometimes inhabit a provider ideology which limits service user's options. Beresford and Croft (2001, p300) criticise such an ideology which they argue leads to:

- restrictions on the rights of people who use them;

- institutionalisation;

- an emphasis on social control;

- widespread abuse and neglect;

- shortcomings in standards;

- failure to ensure equal access and opportunities.

Such an approach subverts the needs of service users to the requirements of social work-ers and the organisations which employ them. This leads to an entrenchment of organisational and professional values which marginalises the rights of service users to a responsive service. Professionalism in this view has for too long limited what was available to service users through what was considered professionally expedient. Professionalism in this sense is closely associated with the concept of 'welfarism' (Froggett, 2002). This reflected a commitment to the provision of universal welfare services, defined, adminis-tered and delivered by professionals which ignored service users' definitions of need, leading to a 'one size fits all' approach. Delivering welfare services resembled the mass production of consumer goods infamously associated with car manufacturer Henry Ford who is rumoured to have said, *Any customer can have a car painted any colour that he wants, so long as it is black*.

Welfarism institutionalises a hierarchical relationship of social worker and client with power residing with the social worker using their professional expertise to decide upon client need. This expertise encapsulated a strong professional identity clinging tenaciously to expert power arraigned against social work clients and other professions to limit chal-lenges to their professional status (Asquith et al., 2005).

This view of professional social work is now more or less discredited. Service users have become more vocal in their demands to have their needs recognised, stimulating a debate as to what constitutes professional social work. In Scotland, for example, Asquith et al. (2005) have begun this debate by focusing on the professional identity of social workers. They observe that pressures upon this identity have come from the move away from direct work with service users and the requirement to fulfil a more limited organisational func-tion within local authority social work departments. This has been reinforced by the requirement to work across agencies, for example with health and education profession-als. They suggest that social work organisations may no longer be necessary in their present form. Similar processes have begun in England where the requirement for greater partnership, working in adult care with health and child care with education, is leading to new organisational structures such as Children's Trusts.

> *Do we now need a different kind of social work service from that devised in the sixties? Is social work best provided by local authority social work departments – or would service users be better served by a strong professional social work element within education, health and other agencies?*

> *From the leadership perspective the distinctive identity of the social worker may well be threatened by increasing integration with other services. This does not necessarily indicate that professional social work will cease to exist. But it will be all the more important for social work to clarify and consolidate its professional identity in the world* (Adapted from Asquith et al. 2005).

ACTIVITY *4.1*

Make a list of those attributes which you would expect a professional social worker to have.

Here is my list (not exhaustive) – how far is yours different?

- *Knowledge of social problems – understanding of poverty, discrimination and its effects on different groups.*

- *Knowledge of individual problems – child development, mental health.*

- *Possession of appropriate skills, e.g. communication skills.*

- *Motivation to help people in constructive ways.*

- *Sound value base that informs their practice.*

Comment

Apart from these attributes that we would expect of a professional social worker there is something more about a profession which takes us beyond the competency of the work that professionals do. Friedson (2001) constructs an ideal list of attributes which encompasses both competence and wider social and political attributes of professions. These are:

- specialised knowledge;

- power to organise and control own work;

- sole legal power to offer a service;

- only fellow professionals can supervise and scrutinise work;

- dedicated to service of the public.

As Friedson (2001) argues, these attributes are only ideals and as such the reality contains positive and negative characteristics. As identified in Chapter 1 the behaviour of some social work professionals does not live up to the ideal. Professionals may collude together to protect their status and income from the encroachment of others. Social workers, like other professions, are increasingly subject to pressure from service users and the state (see Figur 4.1). On the one hand the state has introduced both tighter control through the use of service targets and a greater use of the private sector in the provision of services. On the other hand service users are demanding a greater voice in the planning, organisation and delivery of services.

Social work as compared with other professions is less independent of state control and is therefore more vulnerable when faced with pressure from the state. These differences can be attributed to wider social and political factors which the work of Larson (1977) and Abbott (1988) identify well.

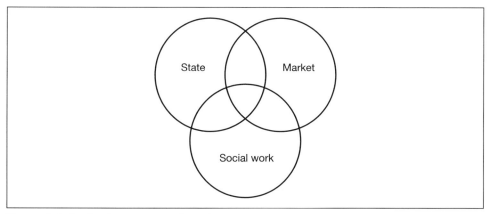

Figure 4.1 *Professions, state and market.*

Larson:

> *Looks at the historical process by which a limited group of occupations strategically increased their social status as against other occupational groups to gain a monopoly in the marketplace. Thus professions gain economic advantage for themselves by restricting the supply of practitioners and striving for a favoured place in society in terms of the respect and influence afforded to them. Thus a profession gains status or loses it by its ability to control the market for its skill and the extent to which it is then respected by wider society.*

Abbott:

> Looks at the way occupations gain and maintain the control over specific occupational activities. This is viewed through the division of labour in which different occupational groups compete over control of different occupational activities and how they maintain their own social and official boundaries. Thus the ability of a profession to maintain its status relies on maintaining this strict division of labour. He points out that 'professions' (i.e. what members of such professional groups and others normally call professions) develop when jurisdictions become vacant; groups of expert workers convert their work and knowledge into a currency. They present their work as expertise different from other expert work. In turn they can claim an expert status beside other expert groups (occupations, professions).

Social work therefore is in a different position from some of the professions analysed by the two writers above as they focus mostly upon more traditional professions, for example doctors, lawyers, etc. Social work's history is different and is not comparable to those traditional professions. In essence, social work as part of the 'caring professions' is mandated by society to perform certain activities which it is hoped will lead to the general well-being of individuals and the society within which they live (Hugman, 2005). But this social mandate is under increasing pressure as noted above by pressures from the state and service users. Service user groups have mounted formidable criticism of social workers, for example the disability movement has successfully criticised the welfarism of social services in reinforcing ideas of dependency on service users. The state, largely as a response to some well publicised cases which impute neglect on behalf of social workers, has increasingly introduced legislation to require more partnership working with other professionals (DfES, 2004). When social workers have tried to develop their own critical practice through anti-oppressive approaches they have been opposed by those groups who wish to control and punish those whom social work seeks to empower. Throughout the 1980s and 1990s the tabloid press ran a number of stories which purported to expose the 'political correctness' emanating from so-called left-wing councils and social work departments (Franklin, 1991). In 1987 an unheard of rise in the diagnosis of child abuse involving some 121 children who were compulsorily separated from their families led to a major inquiry into the methods used to diagnose children suspected of being abused and the subsequent handling of procedures to remove children from their homes. The subsequent report (Butler Sloss, 1988) criticised the way suspected child abuse was diagnosed and the lack of inter-agency cooperation.

Such pressure had a significant effect with the appointment of a lawyer, Jeffrey Greenwood, as chair of Central Council for Education and Training in Social Work (CCETSW) in 1993. He declared his commitment to equal opportunities, but also pledged to rid social work training of 'politically correct nonsense'. This led to a revision of training policy where explicit orientation to such politically charged references to race and anti-racism were dropped (Mclaughlin, 2005). The focus upon social work and its presumed mistakes at this time highlights the relative weakness of the social work profession to resist efforts to limit its professional discretion, but also reveals the nature of accountability in social work.

Accountability

To be a professional social worker is to be accountable. Accountability means that as social workers we are prepared to be open to the scrutiny of others for our actions, be prepared to accept praise and blame in equal measure and be prepared to explain our actions. Social workers' accountability is not necessarily transparent. Is social workers' primary accountability to service users, to the wider community who provide the resources for social work or to their employers? To be accountable involves:

- explaining one's actions;

- justifying one's actions;

- admitting one's actions may have been at fault;

- countering unjustified criticism.

On a personal level, accountability requires social workers to be open to criticism which can be threatening to one's self-esteem, whether criticism is justified or not. But to be a professional requires the worker not to personalise this criticism and understand it as an aspect of the professional role to develop ethical practice. Being accountable not only involves the passive sense, it requires an active engagement in which the social worker may seek to counter unjustified criticism. Practically, being accountable involves social workers keeping case records, attending case conferences, writing case reviews, attending court, giving evidence and writing court reports. All of these actions place the social worker under public scrutiny, and calls practitioners to account.

CASE STUDY 4.1

Brian's social worker, Caroline, has written a pre-sentence report for the Youth Court. Because of the pressure to complete the report on time, Caroline did not check the grammar before sending it to the court. Although she made some recommendations on Brian's behalf, this was unsupported by research or other evidence. The magistrates remark on the poor grammar used which made parts of the report hard to follow. Unfortunately, to compound the situation further, Caroline attended the court in a pair of jeans which she did not have time to change out of as she had been working with a group of young offenders on a playgroup scheme.

On the face of it these may seem fairly minor infractions and ones which Caroline would not repeat if she could choose, or could she?

Comment

In addressing the practical issues of accountability we need to consider the following:

- *How far did Caroline prepare?* Did she read the appropriate research and allow enough time to write a thorough report? Often social workers are pressured by their managers to take more work than they can cope with. It is essential that Caroline learns to be more assertive with her manager if this happens. By Caroline managing her time and not over-burdening her caseload she will be able to be more thorough in her report writing. Likewise Caroline must plan for the day in court. She will then have time to prepare herself for any questions asked or consider what might be the appropriate dress for the occasion.

- *How far did Caroline practise?* Did she go through any information she may want to present in advance? If there are legal issues involved, she should ensure her familiarity with them and reflect how the court might respond. Researching the practice issues and making sure she is prepared enables her professional persona to flourish in any public forum. When she is on public show not only the content of her communication is scrutinised but so is her general demeanour. How she presents and handles herself in public reflects upon her professionalism and is a part of her professional accountability. Ultimately her practice is designed to provide the service user with the maximum representation through the effective employment of her professional knowledge and her personal engagement in court.

If Caroline presents negatively by being inappropriately dressed, lacking knowledge of the case and being poorly informed, she is signalling her unprofessional approach. If she presents as too casual in her demeanour, can she be trusted, particularly if she appears hesitant and unable to give a clear account of the case? This will therefore reflect on the person, i.e. both Caroline and the service user, and risks any case she might be involved with.

The law and accountability

Social workers are empowered with duties and powers deriving from the authority given to them by law and statute. But what right do social workers have to intervene through the law? What authority do social workers have and where does it come from? Clark (2000) outlines three basic justifications for professional social workers to exercise their legal powers:

- Professional power is exercised through the law and therefore what constitutes appropriate conduct must relate to how the law defines the rights of citizens and the duties of social workers to intervene.

- Law should be made through the consent of citizens and it should both promote the general good and not compromise human rights in doing so.

- Professional power should be informed by professional expertise to promote the general good and protect human rights.

This legitimacy to act becomes complex when confronting the messiness of social work practice and the way in which the law is codified. This requires social workers to interpret what the relevant statutes actually intend. The law by itself is not value-free or objective. It embodies values of its own which reflect the power of dominant groups in society to frame and influence what the law should embody. Social workers need to view the legislative process with some scepticism and constantly scrutinise its operation.

One example can be gleaned from the NHS and Community Care Act 1990: sections 46 and 47 impose a duty on local authorities to provide information to service users about services and a duty to assess need. The problem from a values point of view is that there is no duty to provide the services that the assessment has identified. Yet on the other hand the law does not say the local authority can do nothing as a result of the assessment, so there may be areas for social workers to negotiate and intervene on the service user's behalf to achieve an element of what the assessment identifies in terms of service delivery. In respect of community care legislation, the Act enables local authorities considerable flexibility in deciding which needs are addressed.

Local authorities also have the power to withdraw services. This followed the Gloucester judgement which decided that services could be withdrawn subject to a reassessment of need if a local authority was faced with resource problems requiring resources to be rationed to prevent overspending (*R* v *Gloucestershire County Council, ex parte Barry* [1997] 2 WLR 459). For social workers then, it is imperative that they understand both the potential to use the law in respect of protecting people from harm, and also its limitations. Our example of community care law shows the way in which limitations affect the rights of service users when their social support is reduced.

Disabled people take care issues to court

In 1995 six disabled people launched a test case in the High Court over the right to community care services. Five pensioners, one of them a Mr Barry, challenged decisions by Gloucestershire County Council to reduce or cut home help and respite care services because of lack of money.

ACTIVITY *4.2*

Let us assume that you are the social worker who originally assessed Mr Barry's needs and you are working with him. You have realised that he, along with many others in the local authority, has had his domiciliary support reduced.

How should you respond when he asks you:

1 To explain the actions of the local authority that you work for.

2 To explain where your accountability lies.

Comment

This case identifies the difficulties social workers face when explaining policy which they disagree with. On the one hand you are accountable as an employee to the local authority which employs you, but you are also accountable to Mr Barry. To use a colloquial expression you are caught between 'a rock and a hard place'. On reflection, it is appropriate for you to inform Mr Barry that you do not personally agree with the decision. You could also take the case further by suggesting that Mr Barry uses the legal route to appeal against this decision and you could offer to link him with one of the many local and national pressure/service users groups who might take his case further. You could take the issue back to your managers and lobby on Mr Barry's behalf; you might also join with other social workers who have experienced similar problems and put together a case to feed back to your managers. You might take the issue through the local branch of your union (*Unison*) to apply pressure through the local joint committees upon which employers and union representatives sit.

As a social worker you are not just an employee, but a professional who has a range of responsibilities which do not begin and end with your responsibility to your employer, although this clearly constitutes one of your responsibilities. As social workers are increasingly involved in rationing resources and prioritising cases, they are caught in a dichotomous accountability in which a concern for individual service users and the service they receive is constantly challenged by the need to ration and control resources. To be accountable, social workers need to balance the corporate responsibility they hold and their duty of service to service users.

The tensions highlighted above draw attention to the ambiguous nature of accountability. Social workers' professional associations have recognised this, as the definition of social work below identifies:

2. Definition of Social Work

Social workers will:

(a) Strive to carry out the stated aims of their employing organisation, provided that they are consistent with this Code of Ethics;

(b) Aim for the best possible standards of service provision and be accountable for their practice;

(c) Use the organisation's resources honestly and only for their intended purpose;

(d) Appropriately challenge, and work to improve, policies, procedures, practices and service provisions which:

- Are not in the best interests of service users;

- Are inequitable or unfairly discriminatory; or

- Are oppressive, disempowering, or culturally inappropriate;

(e) Endeavour, if policies or procedures of employing bodies contravene professional standards, to effect change through consultation, using appropriate organisational channels;

(f) Take all reasonable steps to ensure that employers are aware of the Code of Ethics for Social Work, and advocate conditions and policies which reflect its ethical position;

(g) Uphold the ethical principles and responsibilities of this Code, even though employers' policies or instructions may not be compatible with its provisions, observing the values and principles of this Code when attempting to resolve conflicts between ethical principles and organisational policies and practices.

BASW Code of Practice (2001)

ACTIVITY 4.3

If we return to the case of Mr Barry, we have already outlined in the comment possible courses of action. From the definition of social work in Figure 4.2 from the British Association of Social Workers (BASW), what elements could be used by you to justify challenging your employer's actions?

Comment

Clearly paragraph (d) supports an ethical stance to challenge your employer. In particular, the bullet points outlined make it clear your duty is to challenge if you feel an employer's policies run counter to the interests of service users, especially if they operate unfairly or are oppressive and disempowering. Your employer may argue that by cutting domiciliary services across the board they do not discriminate against any one service user. However, you may want to argue that in respect of Mr Barry the cut in service may have the consequences of being particularly oppressive and discriminatory if it means he is unable to support himself in the community like others in a similar position.

By advocating for Mr Barry you are operating in a responsive fashion within the constraints of your position as a social worker, paid by the state to enact a particular role. This means as a paid employee you are subsequently accountable to your employer and if you are unable to manage this tension between service users and your employing organisation then you need to consider if the role of social worker is one that you feel capable of carrying out (see Table 4.1).

Table 4.1 *Nature of conflicts with service user*

Enact social change	Enact social control
Advise	Direct
Enable	Control
Advocate	Manage

Accountability and the law

One of the main reasons for becoming a social worker comes from the desire to help those at risk of exploitation and social exclusion. As a social worker, it is easy to see the law as a hindrance to what you might think of as real social work. The law, as noted above, is imperfect but at any one time it represents what is considered to be the will of the citizens in a democratic process whereby law is legislated through Parliament. The law gives social workers much room for exercising their judgement and discretion but cannot work unless that discretion is used wisely. The law, with all its problems, provides a framework which:

- establishes social work agencies and sets out procedures for helping;

- sets standards for when it is appropriate, and when it is necessary, for action to be taken;

- provides a framework for holding social workers to account.

  The law often needs improving, but, for the social worker and others, it cannot be ignored. It is law, and not ideals, which sets out, sometimes with clarity but sometimes with confusion, what social workers are required to do, who they are accountable to, who they have responsibilities towards, and to some extent the overarching principles which govern public services. This is not to say that law is separate from ethics; best practice is both legally and ethically informed, but the imperative for the social worker in deciding how to respond to complex ethical dilemmas is to ensure that their chosen course of action is lawful (Brayne and Carr, 2005, p1).

In being accountable it is clear that when service users' interests conflict with the state's interests, an ethical conflict is presented to the social worker. In certain cases this conflict is less problematic. To override a service user's wishes may result in the protection from harm of that person or protecting others from the harmful effects of those service users' actions. Using force or acting against service users' wishes if they are damaging others may be difficult to enact but has as its justification the prevention of harm. As Clark (2000), argues, social workers are ultimately accountable to the state and their actions must be seen in the light of the purposes which the state has in regulating the behaviour of its citizens. As he observes, the function of social work in society is to *regulate and control* (p106).

Ethics and accountability

In recognising the importance of accountability it is necessary to investigate the role that a code of ethics has in providing guidelines by which social work professionals can be called to account. Ethics refers to the professional obligations which act as rules of conduct by which social workers should practice. A written code of ethics enables social workers to judge their practice against an ethical standard. Just as importantly, a code of ethics enables service users to understand what they should expect from a social worker in terms of their conduct. By definition then, social workers' actions can be judged as ethical or otherwise by reference to a code of practice. As student social workers, you will be required to adhere to the General Social Care Council's Code of Practice (**www.gssc.org.uk/**) which acts as an ethical framework. But there are other codes which you may adhere to. The British Association of Social Workers (BASW) also operates a code of practice and as such, if you become a member of the association, you will be required to uphold its code. However, this code is chosen voluntarily. With the GSCC Code of Practice you have no choice and you are duty bound to uphold it.

The code of practice for social care workers was launched in September 2002. The code is intended to provide a guide for all those who work in social care, setting out the standards of practice and conduct workers should meet. The code is a crucial element in regulating the behaviour of social workers and social care workers. Section 62 of the Care Standards Act 2000 requires that the GSCC keep the code under review so that they meet with the contemporary requirements of social workers and service users. The importance of the code is clear when social workers are considered in breach: they can be removed from the social care register and cannot practice.

Enforcing the codes of practice

The codes mean that, for the first time, the social care sector will have similar regulation to doctors and nurses. Registered social care workers who breach the codes could be removed from the Social Care Register.

- Over time, it is expected that employers will introduce code compliance as a contractual requirement for all their staff. If an employer feels an issue brings a worker's registration into question, a registered social care worker can be referred to the GSCC, which will investigate and consider whether their case should be heard at a conduct hearing.

- The Commission for Social Care Inspection (CSCI) takes the Code of Practice for Social Care Employers into account when enforcing care standards.

(www.gscc.org.uk/)

As research by Banks and Williams (2005) has shown, codes of ethics and codes of practice comprise a range of pronouncements containing rules, principles and general statements, for example rules of professional practice which workers must comply with. They may also include ethical rules, such as maintaining confidentiality. The list below highlights this further.

- **General statements**
  - These may include statements which outline the general mission of a profession as in social work which may include the enhancement of human well-being.
  - Such statements outline the attributes of a professional social worker, such as professional social workers should be honest and trustworthy.

- **General principles**
  - These describe the general ethical attributes of practice which social workers should adhere to, such as respect for the autonomy of service users or the promotion of their general well-being.
  - These are the principles of professional practice which describe the means by which social workers can meet the needs of service users, such as collaboration with colleagues, maintenance of accurate case notes.

- **Specific rules**
  - These are rules of professional practice such as not accepting gifts from service users.
  - These are ethical rules such as protecting the confidentiality of service users.

ACTIVITY **4.4**

*To understand the importance of the code of practice look at the GSCC code of practice for social care workers on the website (****www.gscc.org.uk/****). Using the general list adapted from Banks above make a list of those statements which contain:*

- *general statements about the nature and purpose of social work;*

- *general principles which social workers should adhere to;*

- *specific rules which social workers must adhere to.*

Comment

You should have been able to identify quite a number of answers to fit the specific categories above. To test your answers I have provided a brief and therefore not exhaustive list below.

- **General statements about the nature and purpose of social work:**
  - As a social care worker, you must uphold public trust and confidence in social care services.

- **General principles which social workers should adhere to:**

  - Respecting and maintaining the dignity and privacy of service users.

- **Specific rules which social workers must adhere to:**

  - Adhering to policies and procedures about accepting gifts and money from service users and carers.

  - Promoting equal opportunities for service users and carers.

  - Respecting diversity and different cultures and values.

Note I have deliberately not identified from which of the six areas these statements have come. If you have not recognised any of these elements go back and check where my selection has come from to reinforce your learning.

It is important to recognise that the code of practice, because of its prescriptive nature, tends to focus upon more specific rules and principles rather than making more gener-alised statements about the nature, and purpose of social work. It is interesting to note that references to the ethical aspects of the recognition of difference as part of an anti-oppressive practice does not figure as a specific principle, but becomes part of points I and 5, identified in the GSCC codes of practice as referred to in Activity 4.4.

For reference go back to these parts of the code and identify those aspects of AOP which are referred to here.

This is instructive of the way in which AOP has been given less prominence by the code. Despite this, its importance is fundamental to ethical practice, as we argued in Chapter 3.

Accountability and practical reason

Professional social workers, by claiming the right to work with service users by dint of their specific knowledge and expertise, must therefore take responsibility for their actions. They have a position of trust in which their knowledge is legitimised by the state and in many respects recognised as of value by service users. Over the past thirty years at least, there has been a succession of reports and inquiries which have investigated the various failures of the social work profession in their unsuccessful attempts to care for or protect service users (Stanley and Manthorpe, 2004). However, as Clark (2005) argues, it is almost impos-sible to highlight in many of the inquiries who is responsible, as there are many agencies and many different people involved. Nevertheless, from an ethical point of view, social workers must take responsibility for the actions they have control over and must be able to account for their actions if they are to behave in a truly professional manner.

In terms of ethical practice, social workers must draw on their training in which they learn about different ethical responses to practice situations, yet as we observed in Chapter 1, they must also interpret this knowledge in the light of the context in which the practice problem is situated. This requires the ethical problem to be reconciled within that particu-lar practice context. This reconciliation can be called 'practical reason' and has to be filtered through the way each individual social worker's personal character and ability enables them to respond to a practice problem.

The development of this position is based upon the work of Schön (1987) who argues that professional workers learn from the people they serve in their practice. Professional workers then reflect back on practice, using theory both in action with service users and also when later evaluating practice. For Schön, real professionals learn to live with uncertainty, hold the ambiguous moment and are confident to act even when they are not sure what the right answer is. Effective professionals use 'tacit knowledge'. That is, the repertoire of theories and actions which have worked well in the past and can be used to measure and assess the right action in the moment of current practice. The professional social worker therefore acts more at an intuitive level, acting politically and creatively to find solutions as the situation calls. As an ethical practice, reflection is focused upon what service users need rather than what is available from a preset menu of services or standardised managerial responses.

The ethical content of reflection can be outlined by its use in avoiding oppressive practice. To work in an anti-oppressive way requires social workers to be in a mode of constant critical reflection. This means stepping outside of one's practice and measuring it against the methods and ethical principles of anti-oppressive social work. Critical reflection means questioning the existing set of social relations as the norm, for example between social worker and service user. It is a critical process, what Schön calls 'a reflective conversation with the situation' (see Mullaly, 2002). Critical self-reflection can be broken down into how we reflect upon:

- knowledge about ourselves;
- how our identities are influenced by dominant ideologies and discourses;
- knowledge of our social location;
- our own power to dominate which may reinforce discriminatory practice;
- our lack of power when we are subordinated to others;
- the sources of our beliefs, values and ethics which may be derived from the dominant ideology and which may itself impose constraints upon our freedom to act.

As Mullaly (2002) argues:

> *Critical self reflection is a form of 'internal criticism', a never-ending questioning of our social, economic, political, and cultural beliefs, assumptions and attitudes* (p207).

Fook (2002), drawing on an analysis of discourse, provides another way to develop critical self-reflection. She argues that discourse shapes the meaning we give to practice through how we describe and label social work intervention, which in turn shapes our experience as social workers. Challenging a dominant discourse requires a four-stage process (see Figure 4.2).

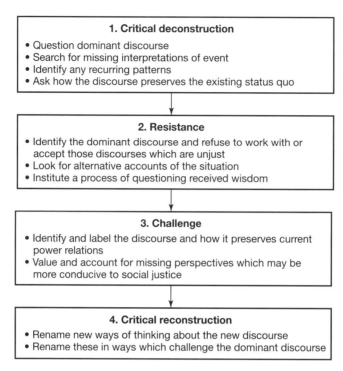

Figure 4.2 *Critical reconstructive process*

(Adapted from Fook, 2002)

CASE STUDY 4.2

In your case allocation meeting the team is discussing a new referral upon a well-known family they have been referred a number of times over the past four years. This family receives Income Support and has done so for the past four years following an accident at work which meant that the husband, who was the only member of the family in work, could no longer remain employed. This has led to many financial problems resulting in much stress in the family. At about the same time as the husband was forced to give up work, both parents experienced problems with their own relationship and their relationships with their children which led to a number of investigations by the social work team into allegations of neglect of the children. One member of the team becomes highly critical of the family saying they are a classic dependent family whose parents haven't a clue how to parent their kids. *Another says,* Yes, they want us to do everything for them, always asking for money. If I didn't know better I'd call them a bunch of scroungers.

ACTIVITY 4.5

Using Fook's approach of critical deconstruction how would you challenge your colleagues' standpoint in the above scenario?

Comment

One strategy may be to pose to the rest of the team how comments that have been made help us to understand the family situation. It may require you to remind the team of the family's history. You could identify words like 'dependent' and 'scrounger' and suggest alternative ways of looking at the family. You could highlight the difficulties any family would experience in living on long-term Income Support. In particular, words like 'dependent' and 'scrounger' legitimize the low and inadequate levels of benefit paid to families with children and place the blame for their poverty on their so called 'dependency' rather than the inadequacies of means-tested Income Support. You may then ask your fellow team members whether they could exist on the amounts that this family has. You might want to use some evidence which you could get from a number of campaigning groups such as the Child Poverty Action Group. Becker (1997) showed that the vast majority of users of the personal social services (PSS) are in receipt of state social security benefits and that their problems are often compounded by social workers' lack of understanding of the realities of living in poverty. More recently a project undertaken by the University of London Royal Holloway (Gupta 2004) identified the effects of what they call the discourse of 'povertyism' used by some social workers.

Some examples of 'povertyism' were:

- A lack of knowledge, understanding and appreciation about the impact of poverty on children and families – a poverty-blind approach. Poverty is seen as the 'norm'.

- Prejudices and pre-conceived ideas – you are irresponsible (need vouchers not cash); likely to neglect your children (no food in cupboard means you are not feeding your children); if you were in care you must be a bad parent.

- Poverty as a risk factor – being blamed for being in poverty and having difficulties – 'It must your fault because other people cope on benefits'.

- 'Povertyism' is a system can make people feel they don't matter, their perspectives and needs are not recognised, e.g. having to wait three weeks when in a crisis; not listening to what families feel would help and support them.

- 'Povertyism' means that workers don't consider the implications of their actions on people's self-esteem – treated without respect, being made to feel grateful for services, 'beggars can't be choosers'.

(**www.swap.ac.uk/about/miniproject7.asp**)

As a result of this you might suggest that your team members think about this family's problem from the above perspective, and try to challenge the discourse of 'povertyism'. Your colleagues might think of different ways to describe this family, such as a 'family living in poverty'. Reframing this family's problem in this way opens up the possibility of working with them in a less oppressive manner.

This process of critical self-reflection is an important part of developing accountability to oneself as a professional social worker, but also to service users. Service users have the right to expect that social workers continually reflect upon their practice to ensure that they are knowledgeable of the service user's social location and competent to engage with it in a non-oppressive way.

C H A P T E R S U M M A R Y

This chapter has explored the issue of accountability for social workers and has focused upon the importance of a code of ethics for social workers. It has made a distinction between a code of ethics and the code of practice for social care workers and suggested that both are important, the first because a code of ethics provides a set of general statements and principles about the nature and purpose of social work by which social workers can develop sound principles of practice, the second because the code of practice provides more direct guidelines which social workers can follow and their behaviour be assessed and therefore called to account.

There is a number of issues with codes of practice for social workers that need to be addressed and are important to outline as these criticisms can provide the basis for social workers to use their codes in a critical and reflexive way.

One of the key criticisms which has been levelled at codes of practice is the way in which ethics can be reduced to one of individual relationships between service users and social worker. Friedson (2001) argues that the practice ethics based on this one-to-one relationship may not be the most essential part of professional ethics. He argues that the economic, political, social and ideological circumstances create many of the moral problems of professional work. He calls these elements 'institutional ethics' a concern for those defining characteristics of professional practice requiring an ethical critique and a more collective approach to resolve the ethical dilemmas caused by such factors. Dominelli (2002) develops this further for social work practice, arguing that ethical principles, particularly those more traditional values based upon Biestek's approach, ignore the social context by focusing upon the helping relationship. As a result ethics have become a matter of individual professional applicability rather than embedded within wider social contexts. As we have seen above, ethical codes have a number of different features that may provide general guidelines for the profession to follow. They may be more specific in outlining rules of conduct or they may deal with general practice principles. In the code of practice for social care workers we have seen that all three elements are present, and this would be true of BASW's (2001) code of ethics if we subjected that to the same scrutiny. Thus different codes of ethics and practice have different purposes; they are trying to achieve different things either to act as general or more specific guides to practice.

It is important to note the way that ethical codes have changed considerably over time in response to changing circumstances. Thus the code of practice reflects a significant input from service users in terms of ensuring the rights of service users. It may be that as the code is developed further the room for discretion by professionals would appear to be limited (Banks, 2004). However, no code can be entirely prescriptive, and while professional social workers are given the power to operate and use their professional judgement, there will always be interpretation of even the strictest of codes. By having a separate code of ethics, the special nature of social work is reinforced in which the ethical prescriptions included in codes of ethics will be separate and distinct from ethics of everyday life, as we have noted in Chapter 2. Ethical codes will therefore remain imperfect; they will need continual reappraisal in the light of changing circumstances. The importance of codes of ethics therefore remains, both in terms of providing some basic guidelines which protect service users and of providing some identifiable principles which social workers can reflect upon to enable them to be effective.

FURTHER READING

Banks, S (2004) *Ethics, accountability and the social professions*. London: Palgrave.
Banks provides a challenging but excellent discussion of the key issues surrounding accountability for social workers and other helping professions.

Chapter 5
Managing risk

A C H I E V I N G A S O C I A L W O R K D E G R E E

This chapter will begin to help you to meet the following National Occupational Standards:
Key Role 4 Managing risk to individuals, families, carers, groups, communities, self and colleagues

This chapter will also help you to follow the GSCC's Code of Practice for Social Care Workers:
4 As a social care worker, you must respect the rights of service users while seeking to ensure that their behaviour does not harm themselves or other people.
This includes:
- Recognising that service users have the right to take risks and helping them to identify and manage potential and actual risks to themselves and others;
- Following risk assessment policies and procedures to assess whether the behaviour of service users presents a risk of harm to themselves or others;
- Taking necessary steps to minimise the risks of service users from doing actual or potential harm to themselves or other people;
- Ensuring that relevant colleagues and agencies are informed about the outcomes and implications of risk assessments.

It will also introduce you to the following academic standards as set out in the social work subject benchmark statement:
3.1.4 Social work theory
- Models and methods of assessment, the nature of professional judgement and the processes of risk assessment.

Risk and social work

Risk refers to the likelihood of an event happening which in contemporary circumstances is seen as undesirable. Risk is often defined as a hazard which must be accounted for, evaluated and then avoided. However, risk in this sense is one-sided and does not fully describe those aspects which confront a person in a 'risky' situation. Risk constitutes not only a hazard but can also be seen as offering an opportunity. As Douglas (1992) has argued, this meant in the past that risk was associated with gain as much as loss. In more traditional societies the notion of risk has been concerned with the vagaries of nature –

natural risks beyond the control of human beings. With the rise of scientific and rational thought in the Enlightenment, the promise was that risk in the natural world could be tamed. Science could control the uncertainties of the natural world for the benefit of all. The development of social science extended the possibilities of control to social risks associated with poverty, unemployment and so on through the rational application of planned intervention in society to maintain incomes and limit the impact of unpredictable capitalist economies. Risk in the social world became calculable and therefore controlled by the development of statistical calculation and the idea of a normal distribution of occurrences around the 'bell curve', which provided an element of certainty about how human actions could be predicted against this 'normal' distribution (Hacking, 1990).

The development of the welfare state after the Second World War in the UK was based upon the idea of social insurance in which the social risks of, for example, ill health and unemployment could be mitigated by universal systems of welfare provision, based on the pooling of risk. In contemporary times, risk has become understood by some sociologists (Beck, 1992; Giddens, 1994) as no longer tameable in the way that the architects of the welfare state hoped. For Beck, the success of a welfare state in limiting social risks to its population has been bought at the expense of an untrammelled materialism which produces technological sophistication but also 'man (sic) made' risks that have changed the social perception of risk. As Penna and O'Brien (1998) argue, the pooling of risk opened up opportunities for marginalised populations to have a limited share in the welfare cake of modern society and wider consumer satisfactions. But what happens if ... *the cake is intrinsically poisonous, its production is the cause of individual and collective sickness* (p174).

Beck argues that we now live in a 'Risk Society' which has been created by the very means with which societies attempted to tame the risks of old. Thus the degradation of the food chain by the technological manipulation of agriculture leads to the poisoning of the environment and the risk of serious damage to animal and human life through such occurrences as BSE or the genetic modification of food. Paradoxically those societies which it is claimed have solved the problem of scarcity and absolute poverty are the very societies most responsible for and most susceptible to these new risks. The concern from an ethical standpoint has increased in the light of these perceived threats to the environment so that, for example, the BASW Code of Ethics (2002) now includes the protection of the environment as one of their principles, the principle of social justice (BASW, 2002).

It is with these wider concerns about the nature of risk in modern societies that the current concern with risk within social work can be understood. For Kemshall (2002) this process has led the welfare state from attempting to use the collective resources of society and the state to protect its citizens, to one that is now concerned with the limiting of social risks by increasing individual capacity to protect against such risk. Policy directed towards marginalised populations such as single parents or the long-term unemployed are not couched in how a universal welfare state can meet the needs of such groups. The argument is one in which a risk-averse society can limit the perceived threat of such groups to the social fabric. The individuals caught up in this web of risk avoidance are no longer identified as the accidental products of a rapidly changing industrial society but more individually responsible for changing their own marginalised position in society.

As we will see, the concern with taming risk within the lives of social workers and the service users they work with, may work in the same paradoxical way that, it is argued, general society has developed. The same procedures and guidelines instituted to tame risk may be the very processes by which risks are produced, for social workers and service users alike. This may sound fairly abstract but it is important to move away from seeing such arguments as distant from real life, because they now inhabit much of the terrain in which social workers operate. In order to understand the importance of risk in social work we must define what we mean by risk and why risk needs to be understood in its more traditional sense of a choice between potential hazard and potential opportunity. Let us use an example from Chinese mythology.

A group of eight Chinese merchants have to transport their merchandise across the fast flowing Yangtse River. They each own a boat which is full of the goods they wish to take to market. In the past at this time of year the river can be very treacherous – last year one merchant lost his entire stock when his boat sank as he tried to traverse the river. It is important that they try and sell their merchandise now, as at this time of year the majority of the farmers from the surrounding countryside descend on the market at this particular time.

ACTIVITY 5.1

How might the merchants minimise the risk of one of their number losing their entire stock?

What constitutes the hazard here?

What constitutes the opportunity?

Comment

For the merchants to minimise the risk, they decide to fill each boat with a part of their merchandise so that all their stock is distributed equally across the eight boats. Thus if one boat sinks in the fast-flowing waters then all will lose just an eighth of their stock. Obviously the hazard presented is that if they do not try and spread their risk then one of the merchants faces the distinct possibility of financial ruin by losing all their stock to the river. But the nature of this risk could be ignored by them all agreeing to take a chance and hope that they all get to the other side, or they might gamble and hope that it won't be their boat that goes down, something more prudent merchants would find an unacceptable risk to take. The opportunity presented here is that if they do nothing and decide not to risk their merchandise they may have to wait a considerable time before they can sell their stock in the market. To manage the risk as they have done means that in the worst case scenario they will only lose a part of their stock and in the best they all reach the other side intact. Nevertheless, they will have taken the opportunity to sell their stock while the market is at its best.

Risk management

This scenario of course mirrors much risk management in social work – the child protection panel conference in which a group of professionals decides on the appropriate course of action in a child care case is such a form of risk sharing. Here every member of the panel will bear responsibility for making the decision and every member has an input into providing and sharing information on the case to arrive at a considered decision. This in theory minimises the risk of one individual making a decision in isolation without having the necessary knowledge or support to reach an appropriate outcome. Below is an example of information given to parents by Gateshead Social Services Department on what happens once a decision is reached within child protection.

What sort of decisions can the conference make?

The only decision the conference can make is whether your child's name should be placed on the Gateshead Child Protection Register. This will happen only if the conference feels there is, or is a likelihood of, significant harm to the child and that a child protection plan is necessary.

If the decision is to place your child on the register, a Social Worker will be nominated for your child and the other people who will be involved in working with you and your family will be identified. This is known as the 'core group'.

The conference will also make recommendations which will form the child protection plan. These could include:

- whether other kinds of services are needed;

- whether there needs to be further assessment;

- whether it is necessary to take legal action.

You will be sent a copy of the decisions and recommendations within a day or so of the conference, followed by a copy of the minutes of the meeting a few days later.

If there is anything you are unhappy about you should raise it at the conference or arrange to talk it over with the Social Worker or the chairperson afterwards when they will try and sort things out. If you are still unhappy, however, they will explain what further action you can take. (**www.Gateshead.gov.uk/socserv/conferences**)

So far we have explored the idea of risk management and given an example of the child protection conference to outline the importance of risk in social work. You might be thinking at this stage what connection risk has with social work values? When social workers talk of risk they are employing values. When social workers decide that a particular situation is risky, this rests on beliefs about what is good and what is bad in a situation (Brearley, 1982). Let us take an example of working with people with learning disabilities:

Mrs John is a single parent with a young daughter Yvonne who is 18 years old. Yvonne has been asked to go out with her friends from college dancing in a local nightclub. Yvonne has Downs Syndrome and her friends all have different learning disabilities. Mrs John is unhappy that the college has encouraged her daughter and her friends to go out dancing as she is concerned that Yvonne may put herself at risk. As she says, this will be the first time Yvonne has gone out on her own with her friends.

ACTIVITY 5.2

What values might be in conflict here?

Comment

The social work value in conflict here is that of autonomy, or the client's right to self-determination in Biestek's terms. The autonomy of Yvonne to choose what activities she wishes to do conflicts with her mother's concern that her daughter may be putting herself in danger. Problems of risk are particularly poignant here in terms of people with learning disabilities' rights as citizens to make and act on their own decisions. In the past, of course, people like Yvonne have been seen as socially incompetent and in need of protecting from the risks and dangers of life. We should not forget about the safety needs of any young person going into an adult environment for the first time, but we account for Yvonne's right to go out with her friends and her right not to be put in a situation she may not be able to handle. How might Mrs John's position be modified if Yvonne and her friends had over a period of months been enabled through different forms of social skills and situation training to go out into adult situations? As social workers and care workers, if we value principles of inclusion in society and the autonomy of disabled people to make their own life decisions, then we need to enable people to make positive decisions on their own behalf and have the social skills and support to be able to put them into practice.

Although we have not gone into the detail of risk analysis here, it is clear that values are an inextricable part of such risk analysis, as they form the principles upon which a risk analysis takes place, enabling us to choose what is valuable in determining an acceptable or unacceptable risk.

The increasing focus upon risk in social work and indeed wider society has been linked with a tendency to avoid all risk (Kemshall, 2002). In a society increasingly worried about threat, governments become less concerned with maintaining levels of material welfare and more concerned with containing risk through the control and compliance of populations. Individuals are encouraged to make their own life plans through an enhancement of choice in those areas governments withdraw from (i.e. welfare services) but outside of this social conduct is increasingly regulated (Webb, 2006).

> *Increasingly expert interventions are less concerned with fathoming the great riddles of unconscious life than with a modest sense of problem solving in the face of risk. Experts are particularly concerned with life planning and risk regulation during what*

Giddens calls 'fateful moments'. Fateful moments, such as bouts of depression, marriage breakdown and loneliness, are all by-products of a reflexive culture with its emphasis on self-governance and responsibility. If individuals are unable to undertake the responsibility for their own self-governance then experts are required to do it for them. Indeed it's during fateful moments and crises that experts like social workers are involved (Webb, 2006, p38).

Many social work commentators argue that a preoccupation with risk lies at the heart of child protection practice (Parton, 1998). It has become a key motif around which the work of the personal social services is organised. With social workers preoccupied by risk, they increasingly make decisions which are defensible, rather than decisions which they consider to be ethically appropriate. This has led to an unacceptable number of families being involved in child protection procedures experiencing considerable distress and trauma only to be filtered out of the registration process when they are deemed not to warrant further action (see DoH, 1995). Lymbery (2005) suggests that a similar inflation of risk in assessing older people leads to the overprotection of individuals who are deemed unable to make their own judgements about what kind of life they should lead. This becomes more acute when an older person is assessed as being unable to live independently, for example with the onset of Alzheimer's disease. Society's failure to adapt itself to the needs of older people leaves older people more open to the dangers of risk. For example, the numbers of older people not claiming their basic pension entitlement leaves an estimated 800,000 older people living in poverty below the minimum considered desirable by the government. In addition, as social work departments become increasingly focused upon risk, then service users who represent the most risky become the prime recipients for social work intervention and resources, rather than those whose needs may be potentially greater. This in turn leads to a greater focus upon risky service users as the main beneficiaries of resources, particularly when resources become tighter.

RESEARCH SUMMARY

Table 5.1 shows the percentage spent upon services for people with different degrees of support needs, comparing 2004/5 with 2005/6.

Table 5.1 *Percentage spend on services*

	2004/5	2005/6
Low	6.2%	4.1%
Moderate	36.4%	28.3%
Substantial	52.9%	58.9%
Critical	4.5%	8.7%

Seven out of ten people now only receive support if their needs are substantial/critical. 80 per cent of councils plan to tighten eligibility criteria for learning disability, physical and sensory disabilities and mental health services, with 77 per cent doing the same for older people (Local Government Association, 2006).

In a climate of risk aversion what constitutes risk is dominated by the concerns of professionals and their fears rather than an assessment of what may constitute a risk for the service user. Ethically, the implication is that the needs of the social worker and his/her employing organisation may therefore outweigh the needs of the service user. Risk increasingly within social work tolerates little uncertainty or ambiguity. Practice must follow that which is certain and which can be accommodated within the set menu of policies, procedures and guidelines, giving the illusion of safety. This expectation of the modern-day social work organisation is inherently unreasonable, life is a risky business and the removal of all risk, even from those seen as dependent, is a life devoid of any real content. Lownsborough and O'Leary (2005) argue that risk is now conceived in a narrow and limited way. They oppose this, suggesting a focus upon a well-being orientation which they differentiate from a risk orientation (see Table 5.2).

Table 5.2 *Differentation of orientation*

Risk orientation	Well-being orientation
• Risk equals danger	• Community governance
• Risk is individualised	• Focus on structure
• Threat, fear and distrust	• Leadership and trust
• Intrusive risk reduction	• Community focus
• Punishment focus	• Strength focus
• Defensiveness	• Supportive
• Vigilance	• Family sensitive
• Distrust	• Trustful

Source: Lownsborough and O'Leary (2005).

By emphasising well-being we are posing different questions about the possibilities inherent within any social work situation. It asks us as social workers to act in an ethically positive and anti-oppressive way. It requires social workers to think of minimum intervention in the sense of avoiding unnecessary use of statutory procedures. Additionally, it requires social workers to look at supportive and life-enhancing aspects of a service user's situation. This asks social workers to focus upon the strengths of communities to manage and support those experiencing problems and by orienting practice around a more trusting orientation as an initial response. Its focus is positive, assessing the strengths of service users and the situations they find themselves in.

Risk: conflicts and dilemmas

When we investigate the nature of risk it is impossible to remove uncertainty in decision-making. As we noted above, social workers, their managers and policy-makers can attempt to minimise such situations; for example, the Children Act 2004 in England and Wales includes the development of Local Safeguarding Children Boards (LSCBs). LSCBs replace Area Child Protection Committees (ACPCs), which currently commission serious case reviews. Likewise, in the area of adult abuse, the Protection of Vulnerable Adults (POVA) guidelines have been introduced to protect vulnerable adults. Potential employees, for example, should be referred to, and included on, the POVA list if they have abused or harmed vulnerable adults in their care or placed them at risk of harm. These examples provide some protection and support to enable social workers and their managers to minimise some risk.

Other techniques which can be of help in such situations include the use of risk assessment schedules (see Doel and Shardlow [2005] for a discussion). Likewise, social workers who keep up to date with research may also help in identifying risk and opportunity factors in practice situations. But as we have outlined, social workers will continually face situations where their judgement requires them to chart at times an uncertain journey through potentially hazardous situations. One of the more significant challenges to social workers, especially those new to the profession, are the decisions which involve a conflict or dilemma in values which inevitably bring with them issues of hazard and opportunity.

A conflict of values occurs when the social worker is faced with competing imperatives which oppose one another. For example, when we looked at AOP in Chapter 3, we identified the conflict in relation to female circumcision that entailed the social worker respecting the cultural practices of a particular community as against the rights of the individual to choose whether to undergo this particular practice. A dilemma involves the social worker being presented with two equally unpalatable alternatives, again a resolution is required which may not leave the worker with the certainty that they have made the right decision, but one which is the best in minimising harm, given the prevailing circumstances. Examples of a dilemma may be found in relation to assessing an older person who may be in need of residential care. On the one hand, to assess a person as requiring residential care means that the person is likely to lose much personal freedom and autonomy; on the other hand, to leave a person in their own home to face social isolation and to be potentially at risk of physical danger may also be unwelcome. The social worker has to decide which of these two alternatives will produce the least harm. Of course these decisions can be made easier by the social worker acting positively to assess the relative strengths of the situation and deciding how to build on them.

In cases of conflict and dilemma then, the element of risk becomes an important factor in making the right decision. In addressing the difficulties posed by such situations it can be helpful for social workers to reflect upon some basic guidelines which may help in resolving such perplexing decisions. Social workers, it is argued, have to act as if they are impartial in their approach to such decisions. This flows, as Reamer (1990) argues, from the ideas of Adam Smith who argued that individuals are likely to reach agreement about the moral decisions they make only by assuming the position of an impartial observer. Such characteristics would include being knowledgeable and informed about the problem under discussion, and being able to control emotion and act in a dispassionate way. There are two problems with this approach. Firstly it is expecting too much of any individual to suggest that the characteristics outlined can ever to be found in any one individual. Secondly the actual characteristics of impartiality and dispassionate decision-making, for example, are themselves not morally neutral and contain moral judgements in themselves. The implication here is that any decision informed by emotion is therefore of lesser value than that arrived at dispassionately, which of course may not always be the case. For example, coming to a decision regarding the potential dilemmas around our example of residential care assessment may benefit from having an empathic response to the service user. The social worker in this case may very well imagine, on the one hand, engaging with the kinds of emotions and feelings that the service user may be experiencing when confronted with the possibility of losing their home and moving into residential care. On the other they may try and understand the social isolation and fear of living on one's own when you perhaps feel no longer able to support yourself.

Reamer (1990) draws on the work of Gewirth (1978) to provide some alternatives to this impasse. For social workers, conflicts often occur between the duties they have through their statutory role to uphold the law and/or as employees in terms of their employment contract, against their ethical duties to the service user to protect their rights as citizens. Reamer's guidelines will be placed within the context of social work in the UK.

1 Where there is a threat to the physical/mental well-being of a service user (all primary goods) this takes precedence over ethical duties not to lie or reveal confidential information. In addition, welfare which involves physical/mental well-being, takes precedence over such secondary goods such as wealth, education or leisure if one has to make a choice between them in the provision to service users.

2 Basic well-being must take precedence over another individual's right to freedom. Thus where an individual's right to freedom prevents or threatens another's basic well-being, then basic well-being must prevail.
An individual's right to freedom takes precedence over their basic well-being. This involves a person's right to remain in a risky situation as long as they are able to understand the consequences of the dangers that they place themselves in. This must be qualified by the caveat that their dangerous behaviour does not put others at potential or immediate risk.

3 Social workers are obliged to abide by the rules and regulations by which they are employed and by the wider rule of law. However, this is not to say that they should not campaign against unjust laws or seek to ensure the well-being of service users within their understanding of the particular law where it calls for their professional judgement. Neither should they blindly accept unjust policy and guidelines which limit service user's rights to services that their particular employer may have put in place.

4 The obligation to prevent basic harm such as poverty and social exclusion overrides the right to retain property. This refers to the public provision of welfare through taxation and the use of such government money to invest in appropriate welfare services.

These guidelines are general and will need to be applied to the specific cases that you will face as a social worker. You may also wish to think about the usefulness and the truthfulness of the guidelines themselves as a means to help resolve some of the thorny problems you are likely to face. The important thing to note is that by not engaging in this debate and by not having some basic guidelines upon which to think through these dilemmas and conflicts, you will be leaving yourself open to working in an unethical and ineffective way. By a careful consideration of the respective conflicts and dilemmas in any situation you are engaging in principled and competent practice.

Figure 5.1 highlights some common imperatives often found in competition with each other in social work.

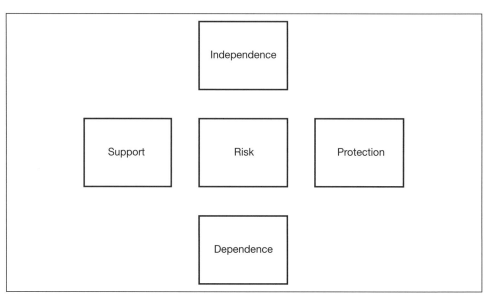

Figure 5.1 *Dependence, independence, protection and support*

ACTIVITY **5.3**

Using the guidelines outlined above, identify what the likely conflicts and dilemmas might be and identify the hazards and the opportunities present in the case study below.

How might you resolve the dilemmas and conflicts that you have identified here?

CASE STUDY

Mr Grey is 85 years old and lives very happily in a supported housing scheme in Wrexham. He values his independence highly. He receives no social service help, refusing any assistance except from his daughter Mrs Williams, who has increasingly been drawn into providing more care for him, for example shopping, handling his money and tidying up around the home. Over the past few years his daughter who lives near by has noticed a gradual decline in her father's memory. Last weekend she was called by the police from Birmingham to request that she collect her father from the central police station, he had been found in the railway station lost and confused. This appears to be last straw for the daughter: the previous week she had been called to her father's flat after he had left the cooker on which caused a small fire in his kitchen. The on-site support workers in the sheltered scheme have also rung you repeatedly over the last few weeks, requesting a social work assessment. They contend that Mr Grey is surly with his fellow residents, even attacking one of his neighbours with his walking stick. He does not join in any of the social activities and tells you quite frankly he needs putting into care. Mr Grey tells you that his neighbours are always abusing him, calling him 'Ignorant' saying he should speak English when he speaks Welsh to them. To compound the situation Mrs Williams's GP has also contacted the office suggesting Mr Grey be considered for residential care. Mrs Williams, although wanting to care for her father, is at the end of her tether and is now being prescribed tranquillisers.

Comment

I will identify here one conflict and one dilemma. There are many more which may be suggested.

Conflict

The most striking conflict here is that facing the social worker in assessing Mr Grey's needs. On the one hand we have an unsatisfactory situation in which the service user is currently coming into conflict with his fellow residents and his care staff and increasingly his daughter. This results in some aggression exerted by Mr Grey against his fellow residents and in the exhaustion of his daughter by his insistence on being cared for by her. On the other hand, Mr Grey is exercising his right to self-determination and autonomy, saying he is happy staying where he is.

In relation to Reamer's guidelines I would suggest we need to consider point 3, which says:

An individual's right to freedom takes precedence over their basic well-being. This involves a person's right to remain in a risky situation as long as they are aware and able to understand the consequences of the dangers that they place themselves in. This must always be tempered by the caveat that their dangerous behaviour does not put others at potential or immediate risk.

Comment

The issue here then becomes how much harm is Mr Grey doing to his fellow residents, the care workers and his daughter? Does this harm outweigh Mr Grey's right to remain in his own home? In addition, we need to consider if Mr Grey is able to understand some of the presenting problems (which may not all be of his making) in his current situation. We could suggest ways that could resolve the situation firstly in favour of Mr Grey by seeking some conflict resolution. Clearly the other residents do not like him speaking Welsh, but as we know if Mr Grey is a first-language Welsh speaker he may well prefer to try and converse in his own language and seek out other residents who may speak Welsh. We also understand that as people get older they may revert to speaking their first language, particularly if the person's short-term memory becomes a problem. If Mr Grey is suffering more pronounced memory problems and he moves into experiencing Alzheimer's disease, then he may revert to his first language more regularly.

Dilemma

One of the key dilemmas here might revolve around Mr Grey's insistence on his daughter caring for him. From research into the nature of gender and caring we know that approximately seven out of ten carers are women. As people live longer it is also increasingly the case that often older daughters in their late 50s and 60s find themselves caring for their much older parents in their 80s and 90s. We also know the extreme difficulty carers face in tending to their family partners which can result in carers experiencing physical exhaustion and mental and physical health problems. The dilemma concerns on the one hand Mrs Williams becoming increasingly exhausted and depressed to the extent that she is now on antidepressants, so that clearly she cannot continue to care for her father in the way that she has. On the other hand is her desire to care for her father. Not to alleviate the caring responsibilities of Mrs Williams is likely to continue her physical and emotional decline, whilst on the other hand to immediately step in to add extra domiciliary care or if appropriate remove Mr Grey into residential care is likely to leave Mrs Williams feeling guilty and responsible for failing to keep her father in his own home.

We also need to consider Reamer's second guideline:

> *Basic well-being must take precedence over another individual's right to freedom. Thus where an individual's right to freedom prevents or threatens another's basic well-being then basic well-being must prevail.*

In order to assess whether intervention may be required it is possible to identify three categories of risk (Stevenson and Parsloe, 1993). You may want to apply this typology of risk to Mr Grey's situation to see if your decision might follow a similar path to that which you used under Reamer's guidelines. The three types of risk are:

Physical risk

Circumstances causing harm to self or others:

- Caused by Mr Grey:
  - Mr Grey is certainly causing some harm to other residents by his use of his walking stick.
  - Mr Grey is causing harm to his daughter by his insistence that she continues to care for him.
- Perpetrated on Mr Grey:
  - Fellow residents of Mr Grey are impatient and abuse him when he converses with them in his first language.

Social risk

Social circumstances where individual's behaviour isolates and alienates them from others. Others' behaviour in marginalising those considered to be outside the social norm.

- Mr Grey should be encouraged to be more patient with his neighbours regarding the use of his language.

- Residents should be more accepting of Mr Grey's use of his first language and attempt greater inclusion in social activities.

Emotional risk

Physical and emotional health put at risk by the role a person occupies.

- Mrs Williams's poor mental and physical health as carer to her father.

Underpinning the management of these risks are values. The tension inherent in a risky situation puts social work values in opposition to one another as the social worker attempts to wrestle with the problem and chart the best course of action. In terms of managing the risks inherent in Mr Grey's situation we can identify the following conflicts:

- Tension between the individual autonomy exercised by Mr Grey to live in his own home, and protecting Mrs Williams from the burden of care and other residents from Mr Grey's current frustration.

- Tension between overreaction and underreaction in response to the multiple pressures from Mrs Williams, her GP, the other residents and the care team supporting Mr Grey

- Too much control may lead to an inappropriate reception into care against Mr Grey's wishes and also perhaps against Mrs Williams's wishes if suitable alternatives can be found in terms of additional support for her. On the other hand, an over-identification with Mr Grey's right to live as he wishes and the perceived need to protect him from the pressure of others may leave him vulnerable – unable to continue to live in his own home, with his relationships with others deteriorating and without any other supports being put in place could lead to an emergency admission to residential care.

So far, in discussing the ethics of risk assessment the voice of the service user has been absent. However, if principles of AOP are to be developed then they must be progressed even in the most challenging of situations. An example of involving service users in risk assessment can be taken in respect of those who use mental health services. From the beginning of the 1990s there has been much focus upon mental health issues, particularly the well publicised cases of some service users who have exhibited violent behaviour and have injured and in some cases killed their fellow citizens. Mental health service users are increasingly stereotyped as being a risk to themselves and the wider community, even though research evidence consistently shows that the exhibition of violent behaviour is negligible. Nevertheless, policy in this area moves towards more control of individuals considered to be a risk to others. As with child protection, assessing and managing risk is now a key requirement for mental health professionals. The problem with this construction of service users as dangerous means that people so defined will be excluded from making decisions about their lives by defensive, risk-averse social work professionals.

It is then incumbent upon social workers working towards AOP to involve service users in their own risk assessments, yet this is not always the case.

> ### RESEARCH SUMMARY
>
> *Langan and Lindow (2004) show how difficult social work and related professionals find it to involve service users in mental health services. Many service users themselves are aware that they may be posing a risk on some occasions and are keen to help reduce the chances of such a risk from developing further. The research found service user involvement in risk assessment and management was variable and depended upon individual professional initiative. More worrying was that few professionals were undertaking any systematic risk assessment or risk management plans. Consultation with service users became almost negligible where the risk in the situation was considered too high. It is worrying given the high sensitisation these professionals had to risk that few professionals undertook systematic risk assessment or constructed risk management plans. To this end the researchers suggest clear procedures are developed to include service users' views about risks.*

C H A P T E R   S U M M A R Y

Values are at the core of social work practice and in the case of risk they become of central importance in enabling practitioners to manage risk. As Kemshall (2002) argues, risk management cannot guarantee to prevent risk. It can attempt to limit the chances of risky situations turning into dangerous ones or reduce the consequences of such situations. As she suggests, *minimization rather than reduction is the key (p128)*. This includes a clear and considered development of procedures to involve service users and carers in risk management. You will experience practice situations where you will be unable to fully protect service users either from the harm of others or the harm they do to themselves. If you are able to justify your practice and show that it was informed by the needs of the service user and the wider community then you may still be criticised for your actions by others, but you will be able to justify your actions in the light of such criticism. What is important here is that you have practised in a way that was informed by your skills, values and knowledge and that you used them in a justifiable, reasonable and principled way.

Social work within the PSS has always been, despite the best efforts of campaigners, a residualised service to the poor. The risks that we have discussed above fall to a much greater extent upon the shoulders of those who are excluded from the material success of the capitalist society that the privileged few now inhabit. To be a service user of the PSS is by definition to be a person living with risks of ill health, poverty and social exclusion. As the social work and social care support for service users has been trimmed, so the language of need has been replaced by a language and practice of risk. This results in further limiting available social work resources to an ever more prioritised group of service users. Such targeting of services barely alleviates the most pressing need but leaves social workers working with people with more severe problems. This in turn requires more complex decision-making involving riskier and therefore potentially more ethically demanding decisions to be made. What must not be lost is the ability of social workers to use their professional judgement, to be confident in the use of their value and knowledge base to enable the best outcome for all the service users they work with.

Kemshall, H (2002) *Risk, social policy and welfare*. Buckingham: Open University Press.
Kemshall's book discusses both the theoretical and practical implications of risk across the public services as a whole.

Webb, S (2006) *Social work in a risk society: social and political perspectives*. Basingstoke: Palgrave.
Webb's book is a more challenging read but is worth persevering with as he delves much deeper into the theoretical issues associated with risk while focusing on social work.

Chapter 6

Advocacy and social work organisations

A C H I E V I N G A S O C I A L W O R K D E G R E E

This chapter will begin to help you to meet the following National Occupational Standards:

Key Role 3 Support individuals to represent their needs, views and circumstances.

Unit 10 – Advocate with, and on behalf of, individuals, families, carers, groups and communities.

- Assess whether you should act as the advocate for the individual, family, carer, group or community.
- Assist individuals, families, carers, groups and communities to access independent advocacy.
- Advocate for, and with, individuals, families, carers, groups and communities.

Unit 11 – Prepare for, and participate in decision making forums

- Prepare reports and documents for decision-making forums.
- Work with individuals, families, carers, groups and communities to select the best form of representation for decision-making forums.
- Present evidence to, and help individuals, families, carers, groups and communities to understand the procedures of and the outcomes from, decision making forums.
- Enable individuals, families, carers, groups and communities to be involved in decision-making forums.

This chapter will also help you to follow the GSSC's Code of Practice for Social Care Workers:

3 As a social care worker, you must promote the independence of service users while protecting them as far as possible from danger or harm.

It will also introduce you to the following academic standards as set out in the social work subject benchmark statement:

3.2.4 Skills in Working with Others

Honours graduates in social work should be able to work effectively with others, i.e. to:

- involve users of social work services in ways that increase their resources, capacity and power to influence factors affecting their lives;
- consult actively with others, including service users, who hold relevant information or expertise;
- act co-operatively with others, liaising and negotiating across differences such as organisational and professional boundaries and differences of identity or language;
- develop effective helping relationships and partnerships with other individuals, groups and organisations that facilitate change.

Advocacy and social work

As an advocate social workers represent the interests of service users when service users are unable to do so. Advocacy work is often the routine of social work, for example telephoning the local benefits office to find out about a person's benefit entitlement or ringing the housing department or the utility companies. All these activities involve representing the service user's interests by negotiating on their behalf. Advocacy only becomes important when and if service users are unable or unwilling to represent themselves. To advocate on behalf of a person is a position of power for the advocate: service users put their trust in advocates to represent them fairly and diligently and it requires social workers to operate in an ethically informed way to ensure their subsequent accountability to service users. Conversely, acting as an advocate is, in a way, also disempowering for service users as they are ceding power to a surrogate who then uses their own power and abilities on behalf of the service user. Ethically it is more empowering to enable service users to develop the skills of self-advocacy but in the short term advocacy on behalf of service users may be a necessary expedient which should only be entered into under specific circumstances.

This chapter is concerned with professional advocacy. Other forms of advocacy are just as valid but this book is about social work ethics and how social workers can act in an ethical way for others.

Ethical issues are inseparable from the principles of advocacy, particularly when you are required to advocate on behalf of someone who may have acted in ways that you find morally repugnant or dangerous to the wider community. This requires a significant engagement and reflection upon your own personal values and how they may clash with the professional imperative to work in the best interests of the service user. Advocacy is inextricably linked with empowerment and partnership in that social workers engage with powerful organisations that confront service users and use their power to achieve positive outcomes for those service users. Advocacy can also engage with wider political processes when social workers involve their trade union or their professional association to contest government policy or organisational practices which inhibit the welfare of service users.

Advocacy on behalf of service users is important, yet this chapter will also consider how social workers should advocate for themselves in relation to their employers and the wider political process. Arguably a social worker unable to advocate for their own interests may lack the insight and commitment to advocate on behalf of others. To advocate for decent pay and working conditions for oneself as a social worker will be of benefit in the longer run to service users. Well paid, well trained and therefore competent and settled workers are able to provide a more effective service for others. The crisis of recruitment to social work in recent years may not be as acute as it is now if social workers were paid, for example, a salary commensurate with that of GPs. In values terms, is it unethical to want to protect your own work and pay even though you may be visiting people who themselves may be experiencing extreme forms of poverty? This issue will be tackled later in the chapter.

A definition of advocacy

- Speaking for someone who has no effective voice of their own – this may include enabling them to express themselves, to make their own decisions and to contribute and be recognised on equal terms with others.

- Informing and enabling people to make choices about, and remain in control of, their own social and health care

Forms of advocacy

- *Citizen advocacy*. This provides a one-to-one partnership between a trained unpaid volunteer and a vulnerable person. This tends to be a long-term relationship.

- *Professional or practitioner advocacy*. Paid professional staff with expert knowledge (legal, health or social care) act as advocates. They tend to work with people on a shorter-term basis than citizen advocates, supporting the person with a particular issue or issues.

- *Collective (or group) self-advocacy*. Support is offered to allow vulnerable people to come together and gain strength from a collective voice.

Advocacy in values and ethics therefore speaks to those aspects of individual and collective empowerment which seek to enhance the autonomy and self-determination of those people unable to speak for themselves because they are either temporarily or permanently excluded from:

- access to key resources;

- access to key services;

- access to social networks;

- access to political process networks.

Advocacy, then, is concerned with the rights of service users. As Bateman (2000) argues:

> *One major advantage of advocacy is that it brings a rights based perspective into individually focused work–work which can otherwise lead to the individual being blamed for the failures of the external world* (p20).

Thus advocacy is significant in developing practice which is anti-oppressive. The process takes on a more inclusive and democratic focus placing the service users' demands for appropriate services at the centre of social work. It implies that service users have rights to services. Increasingly the delivery of services and benefits is being tied to a more conditional approach in which the state requires certain behaviours to be carried out before a service or benefit is delivered. Jobseekers Allowance is a case in point where benefit is paid subject to the claimant proving his or her willingness to seek work, rather than being paid because of their status as unemployed. Similarly, approaches to Incapacity Benefit paid to those who are unable to work due to long-standing health problems or disability are taking a similar path, with payment of such benefit tied to a person's willingness to retrain and take up employment. In addressing rights, then, advocacy seeks to enable service users to achieve their full entitlements as citizens (see Figure 6.1).

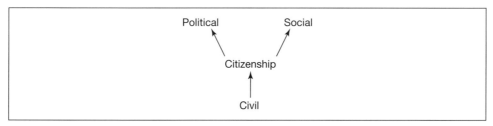

Figure 6.1 *Spheres of citizenship*

- *Political rights* are essential to the idea of citizenship and the extension of the franchise in society, in theory demonstrating the liberal-democratic state's commitment to formal equality.

- *Civil rights* entail in a formal sense 'equality before the law', i.e. equal treatment in law irrespective of income or wealth.

- *Social rights* involve 'equality of opportunity' to educational, medical and welfare services. For example, the establishment of the NHS in 1948 provided health care for all citizens based upon need.

These rights are, of course, theoretical in the sense that the experience of many user groups shows how these rights have in effect been denied. Many disabled people's organisations identify that much service provision for disabled people has been provided by charities. Historically, charities have filled the gaps present in mainstream services provided by the state, thus ensuring that disabled people's social rights to appropriate services is not based upon equality of opportunity but on notions of desert. From a rights perspective, the dominance of charity means that service provision is dependent upon the patronage and goodwill (however misdirected at times) of individuals and philanthropic organisations. Much of the advertising done by charitable groups has also reinforced the dependent stereotype of disabled people, portraying disabled people as objects of pity. The issue then is one of rights, not charity (Swain et al., 2003).

The role of social workers and other professionals should be to challenge these crude stereotypes as an ethical practice to ensure that the formal realisation of rights for all marginalised groups is met through a range of empowering strategies and partnerships, including advocacy. For example, in the case of political rights, many service users with a disability are effectively excluded from political participation and even basic voting rights through their lack of access to transport and community networks. Those service users with a mental health problem who require treatment in hospital can be effectively disenfranchised if they are not helped to register to vote or enabled to exercise a vote by proxy or by post. The concern then to satisfy the rights of service users is therefore an aspect of the ethical underpinning of social work and its commitment to social justice.

Bateman's principles of advocacy

Bateman (2000) has argued that in order for advocacy to be both successful for and respectful of service users then the following principles as outlined in Figure 6.2, need to be employed.

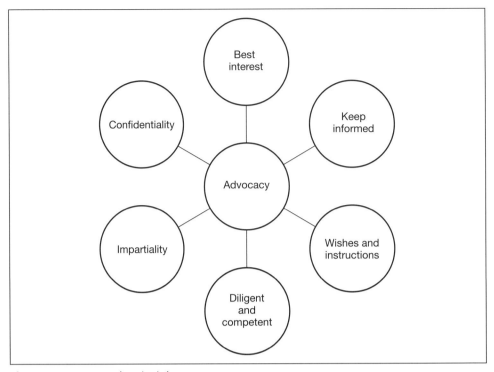

Figure 6.2 *Bateman's principles*

- *Best Interest*. Social workers should act in the best interests of the service user. This is a well understood but sometimes misrepresented principle. In social work there will be many competing interests which will test your resolve to keep the service user's wishes at the core of your practice.

- *Service user's instructions and wishes*. Action undertaken on behalf of the service user starts and finishes with the voice of the service user directing the intervention. This requires constant reflection to ensure that the service user's wishes are being met.

- *Diligent and competent*. In undertaking advocacy, ensure that you have the necessary skills and knowledge to succeed. Preparation means doing your homework to ensure that if you offer your services, you can carry your promises through.

- *Information*. To meet the service user's wishes keep him or her constantly informed so that they can make decisions effectively. Overloading a person with too much information or presenting this in the wrong way by not screening for jargon, for example, is likely to confuse or overwhelm the person.

- *Confidentiality*. Maintaining trust in the process of advocacy is essential and therefore ensuring that the service user can share information with you in confidence secures a more effective practice. Service users who distrust you may hide information which may be crucial to the successful outcome of the process.

- *Impartiality*. Offer independent advice. This means being able to give the service user information they may not want to hear. Likewise, for some workers who may be regularly advocating for a range of people with the same organisation, it is important to keep a professional distance and not become involved in collusive relationships with officials you may be communicating with regularly. You may have to be very assertive with other welfare workers who control resources you may need to access in order to advocate effectively for the service user.

CASE STUDY 6.1

Mr and Mrs Bangara have repeatedly contacted their local housing department to get repairs completed to their front room window. It is now six months since they made their first call, and they must have made at least eight calls in total. They now approach social services as they are concerned that the condensation which collects around the damaged window is now causing a health problem to their children. They have a letter from their GP confirming that the damp and condensation is aggravating their children's breathing problems.

CASE STUDY 6.2

A group of local disabled people have been campaigning to get their local library to stock more appropriate reading materials for the visually impaired as the stock they have is of poor quality and out of date. They decide after unsuccessfully talking to the chief librarian to mount a picket at the front of the library asking people not to use the library until something is done. They call the local newspaper and local television to get publicity for the story.

CASE STUDY 6.3

Brian Fox is a young ex-homeless man who has just been offered his own bedsit by the local housing association. He comes into the duty office asking you to ring the 'social' (Job Centre Plus) about his Jobseekers Allowance as the payment has been delayed. You agree to ring on his behalf.

ACTIVITY 6.1

Identify which of these case studies are examples of:

- *collective self-advocacy;*
- *professional advocacy;*
- *inappropriate advocacy.*

Comment

Ethically it is not appropriate for professionals to immediately handle a person's particular problem without the service user first of all taking some initiative themselves. Self-determination is a fundamental value that entails us to respect the person and encourage that person to act for themselves. Therefore in Case study 6.3 we would encourage Brian to make the call himself, though we might want to go through with him what he thinks he should say when he telephones the relevant office, and we may also provide him with access to a telephone and sit with him when he makes the call to provide support. This becomes more empowering if Brian can make a successful call to progress his benefit payment and therefore realises that you as his professional support have confidence in him to deal with his own matters.

In Case study 6.1, professional advocacy would seem an appropriate way forward to progress Mr and Mrs Bangara's problem. Clearly they have tried everything that they can and have come up against the inertia of the housing authority. However, you must be careful not to compromise Bateman's principles above by ensuring that you progress this case with the consent and knowledge of the service users. You need to maintain their confidentiality and work to their instructions and with their best interests in mind. Above all, you must ensure you are competent to deal with this aspect of housing policy, ensure you know on what and how you can negotiate and be prepared to use appropriate legal pressure to ensure a successful outcome if the housing authority still remains inactive.

Case study 6.2 is an example of collective self-advocacy and can be very effective in providing people who are marginalised by society with the opportunity to experience the power they have as a group. We have already looked at one such group before, i.e. DAN which has engaged in similar actions that have been highly successful both on a local and a national scale.

Government policy

In the last five years, the government has begun to respond to the calls for advocacy on behalf of a number of different groups. The White Paper *Valuing People* (DoH, 2001) is unequivocal in its support for advocacy for people with learning difficulties, highlighting the transformational impact it can have in changing attitudes and services. One of the key objectives of the government's Quality Protects (QP) programme for improving children's services is to promote the participation of children, young people and their families in the planning and delivery of services, and in decisions which affect their day-to-day lives. Recent legislation has highlighted the need for increased participation by service users:

- The Children Act (2004), section 53 requires local authorities to give due consideration to the child's wishes and feelings in child protection and children in need assessments.

- Section 3 of the Disability Discrimination Act 2005 emphasises the need to promote positive attitudes towards disabled people and the need to encourage participation by disabled people in public life.

This gives encouragement to social workers and other local authority workers to develop participation but also to advocate on behalf of service users to ensure their wishes are accounted for. The idea of government-sponsored advocacy raises a number of ethical dilemmas for advocates which are worth pursuing. Inevitably questions arise where a paid employee of an organisation may be advocating on behalf of a service user against his or her employing organisation. Typically this is known as a conflict of interest.

As an example, the case of the recently appointed Children's Commissioner for England will be considered. The first Children's Commissioner appointed in the UK was Peter Clarke who became the Commissioner for Wales in 2001; this was followed by another appointed in Northern Ireland in 2003 and by Aynsley Green's appointment in 2005 for England. The remit and powers of the commissioners in Scotland, Wales and Northern Ireland differ little from one another. They are all responsible for reviewing new laws and policy if they affect or potentially affect children. They can hold public inquiries and subpoena witnesses and must adhere to the United Nations' Convention on the Rights of the Child (UNCRC).

However, the English commissioner has a more circumscribed role. Unlike the other UK commissioners, his brief is limited to promoting the views and interests of children and young people, rather than safeguarding their rights – although he too must adhere to the UNCRC. He is also less independent of government as he can carry out formal investigations only with the approval of the relevant Secretary of State. In contrast, the other UK commissioners can initiate inquiries. The English commissioner has the power to set up an inquiry which focuses on an individual child only if the Secretary of State decides it has wider implications for children generally. The problem in ethical terms then surrounds the powers of government to limit the remit of the Children's Commissioner in England as compared to the Commissioner for Wales, for example.

The extent to which government is concerned by the power of the Welsh Commissioner comes from the criticism placed upon Clarke by government ministers. The Children's Minister, Margaret Hodge, criticised Clarke, claiming he paid too much attention to individual cases and not enough to policy. Mr Clarke hit back, accusing her of taking a *narrow and bureaucratic* view of his role. His achievements to date include winning £700,000 in funding for mental health services for children, after he claimed that the service was in crisis. He also influenced the Welsh Assembly in its decision to develop a strategy for child poverty.

A comparison of the respective powers of the English Commissioner and those of Wales, Northern Ireland and Scotland shows the limitations of the role in England.

- In England the Commissioner is not allowed to investigate individual cases unless it is the Secretary of State's view that the case raises issues that are relevant to other children, yet it was the death of Victoria Climbié that led to the Children Act 2004 and the new Commissioner's post.

- In Wales, Northern Ireland and Scotland the Commissioners can respond to children's individual complaints; this is not so in England.

- Unlike in the other three countries, the principal aim of the Children's Commissioner' post in England has been diluted to promoting awareness of children's views and interests rather than promoting their rights and welfare outright.

- Estimates put the running costs in England at £2.5m per annum. This is relatively low in comparison to the £1.4m allocated by the Welsh Assembly which has a population of just 662,779 under-18s.

Ethical dilemmas

To put the ethical dilemmas of professional advocates into the realm of more direct social work practice let us consider the following case study.

CASE STUDY 6.4

Janet is a qualified social worker who is employed as an advocate by Parents Advice, a voluntary organisation set up to advocate on behalf of parents who are being investigated by social services in respect of child protection procedures. Janet sees her role as ensuring that the child's safety is paramount so that she should:

- *empower parents to be informed about the child protection process and to be enabled to speak up for themselves whenever feasible;*

- *to keep lines of communication open between the local authority and the parents, and to promote a constructive working relationship between the two parties.*

She is currently supporting Mr and Mrs Davies who are the subject of an investigation; concerns were raised at their youngest child's school about some unexplained bruises on her legs.

As part of the social work investigation the social workers seek a meeting with Janet in confidence and ask her directly for information upon the parenting skills of Mr and Mrs Davies and ask her to report any further information she might collect on the parent's behaviour which may affect the investigation. Janet's manager is also very concerned about this case as the local authority provides a significant grant of money each year to support Parents Advice and asks Janet to 'tread carefully'.

ACTIVITY 6.2

What ethical challenges should Janet recognise and how should she respond?

Comment

It is important that Janet is not directly employed by the local authority and that she is seen by the parents to be independent. The local authority is statutorily responsible for protecting children who are suspected of suffering significant harm. Thus to avoid any conflicts of interest between the rights of parents and the rights of children, an independent advocate for the parents is vital. How could the parents trust Janet unless her independence is clear? Developing independence as a principle involves a conscious and ongoing effort by Janet to ensure her independence from the local authority social workers. This independence is crucial to developing a trusting working relationship. Janet must therefore:

- be aware of the reasons why she must maintain her independence and understand the principles informing this;

- be aware that her independence could be compromised or be perceived to be compromised, for example if the advocacy organisation she works for receives funding from the local authority.

Janet must maintain an assertive attitude and vigorously challenge the local authority. She should be prepared to make a complaint on behalf of a parent and recognise that she may experience pressure to keep silent.

How should Janet respond to the social workers' request?

Janet should clarify to Mr and Mrs Davies and the local authority that where she suspects any significant harm done to the children, she will report any evidence she might have.

But

She must show her intervention is on behalf of the parent, refuse to express a personal judgement about the level of risk to the child and decline to give an opinion about registration in a child protection conference if invited to do so.

The importance of confidentiality

Janet's work in Case Study 6.4 must be informed by confidentiality. This is crucial to maintain parental trust. Parents are more likely to feel secure enabling them to explore issues of parenting and possible resolutions to the concerns raised by the local authority. However, Janet must inform the parents that there is a limit to her confidentiality. She is under no statutory duty to report information regarding harm to the child but has an ethical duty to communicate information likely to protect the child from harm.

Balancing parents' rights and children's safety

Initially there is no balance to be struck here, Janet is advocating on behalf of the parents and must support them as her first priority. However, she must adhere to the principle of controlled emotional involvement and be aware of any emotional challenges in this case. This means:

- helping the parent to understand any child protection concerns;
- avoiding any false expectations by challenging the parent's wishes if they are likely to compromise their child's safety;
- avoiding collusion with the parents;
- acting on evidence suggesting the child is at risk.

Ethics, the self and others

Recent writing on ethics has addressed the ethics of the self in social work (Beckett and Maynard, 2005; Hugman 2005; Banks, 2004). In Chapter 3 we introduced the idea of virtue ethics and in this part of the book we will be developing these ideas further. These can be very complex arguments to engage with in an introductory text but it is worthwhile because it asks you to consider the importance of developing the use of self. Professional integrity is central to valuing yourself as a social worker, as it enables you to defend yourself in the light of the increasing pressures on social workers. For example, you may be asked to carry more cases than is appropriate for you to deal with. Thus your professional integrity to provide a valued service will be undermined if you are too overburdened to give each case its due regard.

Supervision

Supervision is an important medium through which your professional self can be developed. There are three kinds of supervision:

- *administrative* – the promotion and maintenance of good standards of work, coordination of practice with policies of administration, the assurance of an efficient and smooth-running office;
- *educational* – the educational development of each individual worker on the staff in a manner calculated to evoke their maximum potential;
- *supportive* – the maintenance of harmonious working relationships, the cultivation of esprit de corps (Kadushin, 1992 p293).

For social workers all three aspects are important in supervision from your immediate line manager. Each element of supervision has important ethical content. The purpose which should inform all aspects of supervision is the interests of the service user and the delivery of the best service possible. Supervision, then, should seek to protect the interests of the service user and promote his or her welfare while at the same time enabling the professional development of the worker.

Administrative supervision

Administrative supervision ensures that you as an employee maintain good standards of work and that your decisions are in accord with the policies and procedures of the organisation you work for ensuring accountability.

Educational supervision

Educational supervision should be about the development of the skills and attributes of the social worker so that as a professional worker he or she can reach the highest standards possible. It is also important in the development of the social worker as a human being in encouraging self-development through identifying the individual strengths and needs of the worker. It should also encourage a reflexive attitude towards the worker's organisation where encouragement to think critically about the employing organisation can contribute to more progressive policies and procedures.

Supportive supervision

Supportive supervision encourages social workers to see themselves as part of a team with a common purpose. Thus the development of self is also dependent upon the development of other workers in the team to work together. It also contributes to positive and creative practice whereby workers can spark ideas off one another and develop innovative methods of working. Supervision then should be about developing the confidence as well as the competence of workers.

It is important, however, to recognise that not all agree with the emphasis upon administration. Lishman (1994) argues that supervision is about sharing ideas between equal professionals rather than manager to worker. Milner and O'Byrne (1998) emphasise the importance of review and the discussion of cases to explore the appropriateness of workers' decisions. Good supervision needs to be planned by both worker and manager so that a creative and supportive environment can be achieved. Often supervision becomes difficult to organise when teams are under pressure, but of course this is exactly the time that supervision is most important when serious challenges face the social worker and his or her team.

The importance of good and regular supervision was given prominence by the Climbié Inquiry (Laming, 2003). The report argues that while inadequate supervision was not the only reason for the poor practice that took place, it was one of the contributing factors. Ms Baptiste was one of the managers involved in this case and Ms Arthurworrey was the social worker responsible in Haringey Social Services for Victoria Climbié.

ACTIVITY *6.3*

Read the extract below identifying the problems that the social worker faced in accessing regular supervision. But first read what Lord Laming had to say about the social context within which Haringey Social Services was embedded.

Haringey is an outer London borough with many of the characteristics and problems of an inner city area. In its 1998 position statement to the Joint Review of Social Services in Haringey Council, Haringey noted that it is the thirteenth most deprived authority in England. A large proportion of its residents were described as experiencing 'severe poverty, unemployment and deprivation, which manifests itself in all areas of their lives, such as the lack of adequate affordable housing, poor levels of educational attainment, poor health and high numbers of children in need'. I heard evidence that Haringey has one of the most diverse populations in the country, with 160 different languages spoken locally, a long tradition of travellers settling in the borough and a high proportion of asylum seeking families (nine per cent of the total population). The pressure this places on all departments within the local authority is inevitable – none less so than for the children and families' services. (Lamming, 2003 6.4–6.5)

The atmosphere within the North Tottenham Initial Assessment Teams (IATs) was hectic in 1999. Shanthi Jacob spoke of the 'bombardment factor' and Mary Richardson, director of social services in Haringey at the time, stated:

'Undoubtedly North Tottenham was the busiest social work office. As a consequence of that, by definition staff probably held, on average, slightly more cases than their Hornsey counterparts … there was regular and fairly unremitting pressure on the north Tottenham office.' It was an issue recognised by the Joint Review team in early 1999, who referred in their report to potential staff 'burn out', which needed to be addressed quickly. Ms Arthurworrey told the Inquiry that initially her caseload at Haringey was manageable, but it slowly increased. By the end of August 1999 she was responsible for 19 cases (of which half were child protection). This is seven more cases than the maximum laid out in the Duty Investigation and Assessment Team Procedures devised by Ms Mairs. Mr Duncan argued that it was hard to imagine how a social worker could work on more than 12 cases at a time. Yet Ms Arthurworrey said she was unaware of the guidance, and during 1999 Mr Duncan said he knew, though Ms Wilson said she did not, that staff in the IATs were dealing with a high number of cases and that the average caseload was in excess of the recommended maximum. (6.13–6.15.)

Now read the section on supervision:

The tensions that had featured during Ms Baptiste's time in the children and families' team began to resurface in IAT B. As a result, according to Ms Baptiste, she found it hard to engage some social workers, Ms Arthurworrey included, in the regular supervision so fundamental to good practice. Although Ms Arthurworrey has denied ever refusing supervision when it was offered, there clearly was an issue about the quality and timeliness of the supervision that was provided in Ms Baptiste's team. This was confirmed by the director of social services at the time, Mary Richardson. Ms Arthurworrey understood she would get supervision every two to three weeks, 'but this never happened'. In practice she received supervision about once every seven weeks. 'When I asked about drawing up a supervision contract Carole [Baptiste] told me that I was responsible for doing that.' Ms Arthurworrey said she experienced serious problems in arranging supervision sessions with Ms Baptiste because of her continued unavailability. Often Ms Baptiste would cancel or rearrange sessions or simply not appear without an explanation. Of equal concern, Ms Arthurworrey said she found supervision with Ms Baptiste frustrating because, more often than not, they would start discussing cases and then Ms Baptiste would go off on a tangent. Ms Arthurworrey stated that Ms Baptiste often talked about her experiences as a black woman and her relationship with God. The result was that they would not have time to finish discussing the cases. Ms Arthurworrey said she just tried to manage. Generally it was Ms Baptiste's practice to agree with whatever suggestions Ms Arthurworrey put in front of her. Ms Arthurworrey found this disturbing in the sense that it led her to question Ms Baptiste's knowledge base. (6.38–6.40)

Comment

There is a number of issues here that hindered the supervision process, linked with issues raised in the report:

- *Cancellation of supervision.* Ms Arthurworrey said she experienced serious problems in arranging supervision sessions with Ms Baptiste because of her continued unavailability. Often Ms Baptiste would cancel or rearrange sessions or simply not appear without an explanation

- *Lack of clarity about the nature of supervision and inappropriate issues raised by the manager unrelated to Ms Arthurworrey's caseload.* Ms Arthurworrey said she found supervision with Ms Baptiste frustrating because, more often than not, they would start discussing cases and then Ms Baptiste would go off on a tangent. Ms Arthurworrey stated that Ms Baptiste often talked about her experiences as a black woman and her relationship with God. The result was that they would not have time to finish discussing the cases

- *Infrequent supervision.* Ms Arthurworrey understood she would get supervision every two to three weeks, *but this never happened*. In practice she received supervision about once every seven weeks.

- *Responsibility for supervision placed only onto workers shoulders. When I asked about drawing up a supervision contract Carole [Baptiste] told me that I was responsible for doing that.*

- *Lack of trust in professional competence of the supervisor.* Generally it was Ms Baptiste's practice to agree with whatever suggestions Ms Arthurworrey put in front of her. Ms Arthurworrey found this disturbing in the sense that it led her to question Ms Baptiste's knowledge base.

It is worth reinforcing the ethical reasons as to why supervision is important and to place this within the wider ethical responsibilities that social workers have towards service users and the wider community.

Service users

The supervisor's main objective must be to secure the best possible service for the service user. It also involves protecting the interests of the service user, particularly in relation to their own welfare

The wider community

Social workers not only work with individual problems but when these individual problems are shared by many then they become social problems which require social and individual social work intervention. Social workers have to consider that their work with individuals may then impact on the wider society. It may very well be the case that sometimes the individual needs of service users clash with the concerns of the wider community. These tensions are reflected in what Banks (2006) argues are the four first-order principles central to social work:

Bank's first-order principles

1 Respect for and promotion of individuals' rights to self-determination.

2 Promotion of welfare or well-being.

3 Equality.

4 Distributive justice.

In supervision, interaction between supervisor and supervisee will circle around these issues. For example, supervisors may have to remind supervisees of the requirement to consider how a course of action they are pursuing leads to promoting the autonomy of service users, or that they are providing services and resources which are distributed according to agreed principles of fairness and need. Supervisees on the other hand may well identify inappropriate and exclusionary procedures within their organisations which may inhibit meeting the needs of service users.

Being part of a professional community

It is necessary for individual social workers to understand that they belong to a wider professional community. Individual actions should fit with the broader professional viewpoint encapsulated in codes of ethics. This is important because the authority to engage in these arguments comes from membership of a professional body (BASW) or a statutory body (the Care Council) which requires social workers and their supervisors to account for their decisions in the light of these codes of ethics and of practice (Smith, 1996).

Assertiveness and caring for self

In any advocacy situation the advocate has to show assertiveness in promoting the rights of the service user. This is no different when advocating for oneself either in supervision or in drawing support from broader political forums such as trade unions. McBride (1998) argues that social workers have been poor in promoting their rights. She argues that believing in your rights is important to giving social workers the confidence to tackle situations likely to create conflicts of interest. Bateman (2000) argues that assertiveness becomes more important where there are fewer structures and procedures to which individuals can refer, what he calls an unbounded problem.

If we refer to the Climbé example, we can see there was a number of barriers blocking the social worker's access to supervision. This is not to assume that the social worker involved did not try and assert herself or that she was ineffective. What I am suggesting is that social workers, in accessing supervision, need to be very clear why supervision is so crucial for professional development and act assertively to achieve it (see Figure 6.3). This is essential in protecting service users and social workers' abilities to be effective practitioners. It may require the social worker to use the management hierarchy by going above their immediate supervisor if supervision is not happening. It is in supervision that social workers can actively develop their professional capacity to carry out social work.

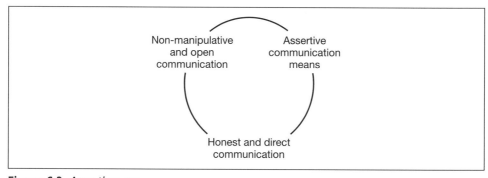

Figure 6.3 *Assertiveness*

Assertive behaviour can be developed. Assertive social workers are confident social workers, their confidence coming from their considered use of the knowledge base of social work, their purposeful application of the skills and methods of social work and their reflective application of the values and ethics of social work. The active application of knowledge, skills and values ensures that they will be highly regarded by their colleagues for their professional integrity (Bateman, 2000). In terms of self-advocacy then, social workers must engage with the organisation in which they work, understand the organisational structures and hierarchies, and access relevant information to intervene in an assertive manner when their professional integrity is threatened by poor management practice. In advocating for the self, it can be useful to outline to your immediate supervisor what consequences may follow if your needs as a worker are not accounted for. You could in a clear and factual way suggest that a formal complaint will be made and that this will be put in writing to the relevant manager above the supervisor in the hierarchy. It is important that on some aspects of your position you can negotiate where it is less clear that a formal process has been breached, but where there may be a clear breach of practice then a formal process is much more appropriate. In this regard, putting a complaint in writing is a very good idea in that this creates a record of the event and then requires those in authority to respond.

Trade unions and social work

For the generation of young people in Britain coming to adulthood at the beginning of the twenty-first century, their experiences of labour history are very different from their parents' generation. They may have had no personal experience or knowledge of trade unionism and their world view has been partly shaped by the anti-collectivist discourse of the Thatcher period. (Lawrence, 2005, p140).

Joining a trade union is an ethical practice. Social workers may find difficulties comprehending this if, as younger professionals, they have been brought up in an atmosphere of distrust for the collective values of trade unionism. As Lawrence (2005) suggests, the image of trade unions is more aligned with blue collar, i.e. manual, workers who experience problems at work than with white collar (non-manual) workers who have opportunities for career advancement and relatively comfortable working conditions. Yet trade unions are of relevance for all paid employees, including social workers.

Trade unions have a wider social role in achieving social benefits for all working people in which a wider political struggle to achieve social justice is paramount. They also have a more limited yet important function by providing services for members such as low-cost insurance, free legal advice and support if a member is involved in an accident at work, and of course bargaining over pay and conditions. Trade unions are to be distinguished from a professional organisation such as the BASW, which attempts to influence and control the content of social work and does not involve itself with bargaining over pay and conditions.

From an AOP perspective, trade unions can be an effective voice in progressing equality issues. The Trades Union Congress, which represents the bulk of unions in the UK, campaigns against discrimination at work and in the wider society. UNISON, which represents the majority of social workers, and social care workers, is a useful case study. Look at the box below taken from UNISON's website for women workers:

UNISON has almost one million women members – more than two-thirds of our union. Women still earn a lot less than men and face sex discrimination and harassment at work. Our members also juggle work and home commitments. Many have caring responsibilities and almost half work part-time. This is why UNISON takes a lead on negotiating and campaigning on women's rights at work and in the community. (**www.unison.org.uk/women/index.asp**)

UNISON runs a series of campaigns focused upon specific groups of people such as equal rights for part-time workers, equality for black workers, and lesbian and gay rights. Trade unions are currently campaigning in favour of maintaining a woman's right to choose an abortion (see **www.unison.org.uk/file/B2139.pdfn**). Other campaigns involving UNISON include a campaign against domestic violence (**www.unison.org.uk**). These two brief examples show how trade unions are involved in much broader struggles which are of direct relevance for social workers and service users.

CASE STUDY 6.5

For nine months Debbie has been working as a childcare social worker. The team in which Debbie works has for the past six months never had more than half its total complement of staff. This has led to some social workers leaving rather than carrying on with the pressurised workload. One of Debbie's colleagues has recently taken extended sick leave with stress and is likely to be absent from work for the foreseeable future. Her immediate manager has also experienced periodic bouts of stress and she has been off work leaving the team with little or no appropriate supervision. Debbie in her role as the local UNISON steward has had repeated discussions with the area manager regarding the problems of staff shortages and the burdens that this is placing on the existing staff, i.e. working above normal contracted hours, increased levels of stress and high sickness rates. The area manager is sympathetic to her argument but he says little can be done at the moment as the local council have frozen any recruitment until the next financial year which is in three months' time. Debbie decides that the situation is too dangerous to carry on and calls a local meeting of union members to discuss the problem. She will propose taking strike action.

ACTIVITY 6.4

What is your response to this situation?

Do you think Debbie is acting ethically in arguing for strike action?

Comment

Debbie argues that both social workers and service users will benefit from strike action. She argues that by calling for more staff to be appointed the quality of service to service users will be improved and the reduction in stress and extra hours working will benefit the social workers and their families and friends. Alice (one of Debbie's colleagues) recounts her own experience which is echoed by other members in the meeting in that she repeatedly finds herself in situations where she can provide only a substandard service to the families and children that she is working with because of the pressure of having to juggle so many cases.

Deciding to strike is a serious issue; social workers will feel uncomfortable with this proposal, given their general ethical concern to work for the benefit of service users. In the area of child support and protection, by striking they may potentially cause harm to the very people they are trying to help. Ethically is it justified to cause distress to service users as a lever to pressurise employers into meeting the striker's demands?

What are the ethical arguments?

Three different ethical approaches will be considered:

- consequentialist;
- duty-based;
- rights-based (Benjamin and Curtis, 1992).

Consequentialist

This approach considers if strike action will on balance lead to a greater number of positive over negative consequences.

One approach to increasing the likelihood of the positive over the negative is to:

- not withdraw services to priority cases (such as those on the child protection register);
- give advance warning of an impending strike (something which by law must happen, in that a ballot for strike action must be taken if workers wish to operate inside the law under the Trade Union Act 1984).

In arguing for the benefits of strike action then more long-term concerns are of relevance here. Social workers might focus upon the long-term benefits of having qualified social workers who have time to work with service users, rather than having to fill in the gaps made by absent, sick or non-recruited staff. Creating supportive conditions of employment, it can be argued, will lead to the retention of staff and reduce those who are unhappy and who eventually leave. All of these arguments will be of direct benefit to service users in the long term.

From this brief synopsis it can be argued that consequentialist arguments do have some force here. However, although this may be the case, Debbie must also consider the short-term negative consequences which are immediate and more pressing. Some social workers may feel that they have certain duties which override these utilitarian arguments and they may also consider that service users have rights to a service in the present which may also override any long-term considerations.

Duty-based

In respect of BASW's Code of Ethics and the GSCC's Code of Practice it is clear that justifying strike action does pose serious problems. For example, the General Care Council's statements could all be interpreted as compromising the idea of strike action.

- Protect the rights and promote the interests of service users and carers.
- Strive to establish and maintain the trust and confidence of service users and carers.
- Promote the independence of service users while protecting them as far as possible from danger or harm.
- Respect the rights of service users while seeking to ensure that their behaviour does not harm themselves or other people.

115

- Uphold public trust and confidence in social care services.

- Be accountable for the quality of their work and take responsibility for maintaining and improving their knowledge and skills.

How would protecting the rights and promoting the interests of service users be justified in terms of the strike? If the point of the strike is to hold out the threat that the interests and rights of service users would be damaged then the strike would be illegitimate. The fundamental principle here from the code would therefore be violated. Likewise, the BASW's (2002) Code of Ethics is clear:

4.1.1 Priority of service users' interest

Social workers will:

Give priority to maintaining the best interests of service users, with due regard to the interests of others;

Or:

4.1.3 Self-determination by service users

Social workers will help service users to reach informed decisions about their lives and promote their autonomy, provided that this does not conflict with their safety or with the rights of others. They will endeavour to minimise the use of legal or other compulsion. Any action which diminishes service users' civil or legal rights must be ethically, professionally and legally justifiable.

However, the strength of such arguments depends upon two assumptions which may not necessarily be valid.

The first assumption is that the current service which is being withdrawn does meet service users' interests and enables their rights to be met. Debbie and the managers she has consulted recognise that the current situation does not meet the interests of either service users or social workers, so this first assumption is clearly contestable. Thus if, under the existing situation, children and parents are receiving significantly poorer services which already compromise the safety of children and families, then social workers would not appear to be violating their duties to service users.

The second assumption is that those presently harmed by strike action will not be those who may benefit in the future if the strike was successful. Many children and families are long-term users of the service and as such are more likely to benefit by strike action if it is successful. Thus we can argue here that, on balance, there is not necessarily a current group of service users who would be sacrificed for the future benefit of a different group of service users.

By investigating the two meanings of a duty-based approach it is possible to argue from a duties perspective the validity of engaging in strike action.

Rights based

Social workers and service users have rights. On the one hand social workers, like any other people, have rights and if these are violated by employers then they have the right to protect them. It is surely unacceptable that social workers should be so pressurised in their employment that they suffer from stress and ill health. Therefore in the final instance they have a right to strike. On the other hand, the social workers' right to strike conflicts with service users' right to a social work service. Children's rights to freedom from the dangers of material, physical or emotional abuse are not given a voice in pressing their claims to a service. It would appear that their rights should take precedence over that of the social workers.

Benjamin and Curtis, (1992), in assessing the validity of these claims, make a distinction between what they describe as special and general rights; as follows.

Special rights

These are limited in extent and remain conditional; they depend upon a special relationship. A special right occurs when a social worker promises to do something on behalf of a service user, thus the service user has a special right. Such rights are conditional. They are limited to the person who receives the promise; therefore they have a right to it being fulfilled. They are also limited and depend on the special relationship between the promiser and the promisee.

General rights

These are unconditional and have validity purely on the basis of being a human being. They have much in common with human rights and involve such rights as the right to life or the right to freedom. No conditions are therefore set on their fulfilment. They apply without restriction to everyone and therefore require everyone to respect them. We would not wish to place any conditions upon the right of people not to be killed or imprisoned, whereas a social worker who makes a promise does so under the special conditions of his or her relationship with the service user.

If we return to the case study then, we need to identify if the provision of social work services relates to a special or general right. When a social worker assumes care for a service user it is grounded in the special relationship between particular social workers and particular service users. Once work is undertaken, then a service user has a right to expect that service to be fulfilled. If a strike is called then the service user's rights to a service have been violated. However, once the service has been fulfilled then the rights of the service user cease and the obligations of the social worker have been fulfilled. If Debbie wins her argument about strike action as long as the social workers involved meet their existing obligations, give warning about their intention to strike, and cover any emergency situations, then the extent to which special rights have been violated has been reduced.

The case of general rights is more problematic and depends upon whether a right to a social work service is a general right. Some commentators argue that general rights occur only in relation to non-interference. These are called negative rights and as such require from others merely not to interfere with another person's life in order for those rights of life and liberty to be fulfilled. This argument has been associated with those who believe in the freedom of the individual to be able to say and do what they choose as long as this does not interfere with others' rights to do the same (Hayek, 1944). From this point of view, then, for a social work service to be met requires a positive action or a positive right to be in place. In order for this to happen it will require others to provide time or money through taxation, for example, to meet that right. This is an infringement, so Hayek would argue, of others' rights, as you are taking their time and money in order to provide this for others. This view has been challenged by those who see positive rights as essential in order to meet those negative rights of life and personal liberty (Marshall, 1950). Children's services provide an interesting example as in many cases where social workers work with the most excluded and poorest of children and their families, not to provide such a service would result in loss of liberty and life, for example not engaging in child abuse investigations. However, if, as noted above, emergency measures were put in place to cover such issues of life and liberty then again the ethical arguments against the strike are reduced.

C H A P T E R   S U M M A R Y

This chapter has explored the importance of advocacy for social work. It has highlighted the important role that social workers have in advocating for service users and has shown how this can be justified ethically. It has looked at advocacy from the perspective of professional social work and its use of professional advocacy. It has emphasised that professional advocacy may always be necessary in order to provide some service users with a more effective social work service. Nonetheless, advocacy which enables service users to gain their own confidence and then develop their own advocacy with other service users is the preferable alternative. Collective advocacy truly empowers service users as they take responsibility for and define their own goals. Finally, we have investigated the necessity of social workers advocating for themselves both on an individual basis and from a collective point of view through their engagement with trade unions.

FURTHER READING

Bateman, N (2000) *Advocacy skills for health and social care professionals*. London: Jessica Kingsley.
For those wishing to develop their advocacy skills further Bateman's book is the key text in this regard.

Laming, Lord (2003) *The Victoria Climbié Inquiry*. London: Stationery Office.
All social workers should read this inquiry and in particular should reflect upon the problems which the social workers and managers grappled with while striving to deliver effective children's services in an overstretched inner London social service department.

Todd, M and Taylor, G (ed) (2005) *Democracy and participation*. London: Merlin Press.
Provide an interesting discussion in the chapters on the relevance of social and political action in relation to trade unions and wider social movements.

Chapter 7
The ethics of partnership working

A C H I E V I N G   A   S O C I A L   W O R K   D E G R E E

This chapter will begin to help you to meet the following National Occupational Standards:

Key Role 5 Manage and be accountable, with supervision and support, for your own social work practice within your organisation.

Unit 17 – Work within multi-disciplinary and multi-organisational teams, networks and systems.

- Develop and maintain effective working relationships.
- Contribute to identifying and agreeing the goals, objectives and lifespan of the team, network or system.
- Contribute to evaluating the effectiveness of the team, network or system.
- Deal constructively with disagreements and conflict within relationships.

This chapter will also help you to follow the GSCC's Code of Practice for Social Care Workers:

6 As a social care worker, you must be accountable for the quality of your work and take responsibility for maintaining and improving your knowledge and skills.

This includes:

- Recognising and respecting the roles and expertise of workers from other agencies and working in partnership with them.

It will also introduce you to the following academic standards as set out in the social work subject benchmark statement:

3.1.1 Social work services and service users

The relationship between agency policies, legal requirements and professional boundaries in shaping the nature of services provided in inter-disciplinary contexts and the issues associated with working across professional boundaries and within different disciplinary groups.

3.1.2 The service delivery context

The significance of interrelationships with other social services, especially education, housing, health, income maintenance and criminal justice.

3.1.3 Values and ethics

The conceptual links between codes defining ethical practice, the regulation of professional conduct and the management of potential conflicts generated by the codes held by different professional groups.

3.1.5 The nature of social work practice

The factors and processes that facilitate effective inter-disciplinary, inter-professional and inter-agency collaboration and partnership.

3.2.4 Skills in working with others

- Act co-operatively with others, liaising and negotiating across differences such as organisational and professional boundaries and differences of identity or language;
- Develop effective helping relationships and partnerships with other individuals, groups and organisations that facilitate change;
- Act with others to increase social justice by identifying and responding to prejudice, institutional discrimination and structural inequality;

Partnership and social work

Social workers in recent years have witnessed a significant transformation in the organisational structures in which they work. The election of a Labour government in 1997 heralded a distinctive change in the delivery of welfare services to the population. A discourse of partnership became widespread in which terms such as 'joined-up government' gained currency in reflecting ideas of partnership which Labour argued were essential for their aim of modernising public services (Parrott, 2005). The White Paper *Modernising Social Services* (Department of Health, 1998) outlined this modernising agenda for the PSS. It criticised previous approaches to delivering social work and health care services. The White Paper argued that:

- the existing configuration of health and social care was contributing to service users failing to access appropriate services;

- service users' needs did not fit into existing organisational frameworks;

- organisations delivering health and social care should consider partnership working to prevent such service failures.

In order to deliver its partnership agenda, the Labour government targeted the reduction in professional and organisational autonomy when it considered that these arrangements frustrated the effective delivery of services to service users (Malin et al., 2002).

Partnership working is now firmly established as one of the core features of social work practice both in children's services as outlined within the Children Act 2004 and in adult services with the NHS and Social Care Act 2001. This process has been given added impetus with the White Paper *Our health, Our care, Our say* (2005).

Joined-up care

You told us ...

There should be more co-ordination between the health service, social care and the local authority. There needs to be more communication between them.

Here's what we're doing ...

One of our main aims for the future is to make sure that health and social services will work together and share information to give 'joined-up' care to the people they work for. Services will share information about the people in their care so that health, housing, benefits and other needs are considered together. By 2008, anyone with long-term health and social care needs should have an integrated Personal Health and Social Care Plan, if they want one. All Primary Care Trusts and local authorities should have joint health and social care managed networks and/or teams for people with complex needs. We will also be building modern NHS community hospitals, which will offer integrated health and social services (Department of Health, 2005, p10).

The modernisation agenda, then, gives little room for different professional groups to remain fixed within their own organisational structures. The policy-changes instituted require different professional groups to be involved in a wider mission in which they, as the constituent parts, combine to create something of greater benefit to service users. The benefits of partnership can be conceptualised as creating a 'synergy' which is intended to eradicate departmental, organisational and philosophical differences to create 'seamless' services. Unsurprisingly, as different professions come together to deliver services, their different ethical approaches have to be reconciled.

Partnership and professionals

At any one time social workers can find themselves working in partnership with professionals such as police officers, nurses, probation officers, Connections staff and teachers. Given this array of different professions it is clear that the business of partnership becomes a complex problem. As Bates (2005) argues, partnership working is often misunderstood:

> *Simply assuming that various partners share common aims and that conflict is a matter of a failure to align the aims misunderstands the issues* (p52).

Key areas of conflict in partnership working involve different ideologies, values, ethics and different cultures of working, all conspiring to make partnership problematic.

In considering the ethical issues involved in partnership working it is important to define what is meant by the term partnership (see Figure 7.1). As Carnwell and Carson (2005) argue, discussion in health and social care, for example, *is replete with synonyms referring to the need ... to 'work together' more effectively in 'partnership' and in 'collaboration'* (p3). It is important to distinguish the relationship between agencies as a partnership, along with what the protagonists are supposed to do, which is collaborate or work together.

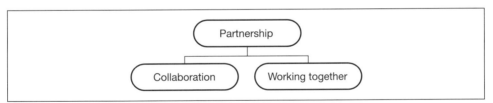

Figure 7.1 *Partnership*

The Improvement Network website sponsored by the government to enable better management of public services in local government defines partnership as:

> *Simply put, a partnership is an agreement to work collectively between two or more independent bodies to achieve a common objective.* (**www.improvementnetwork.gov.uk**)

This relatively simple definition may help clarify, but may also hide, other meanings of partnership which are also relevant when considering ethical issues. For example, partnership also implies an equal and a willing commitment by those wishing to become partners. It implies notions of shared responsibility for the enterprise which is to be undertaken (see *Collins English Dictionary* (1991) and *The Concise Oxford Dictionary* (1992).

Thus partnership may be problematic if the partners are ambivalent about its benefits or have little say in its development. This point is made by Beresford (2006) in his critique of *Our health, our care, our say*, where he argues for a separate White Paper for social care rather than one which is subsumed under health, giving it a privileged position in which social care contributes to a health-oriented agenda.

Effective partnerships

Effective partnerships require sustained relationships, shared agendas built over time and a commitment to shared problem-solving. The government's drive to improve public services is not assisted by rapid change largely imposed from above. This concern with the way partnership has been promoted between health and social care has been highlighted by Jones (2005), who argues that the frequency and pace of change is causing disruption between health and social care partners, echoing Beresford's concern that partnership between health and social care is being promoted more as an integration of social care into the health service.

Partnership therefore does not mean merger or takeover of one group by another, yet much of the current drive for partnership, particularly within adult care, appears to be moving in this direction. When different professional groupings come together in collaboration then they bring with them their own ways of working, organisational cultures and attitudes, their particular practice-experience and their own ethical codes. For professionals who may feel unsure of their own professional standing this can be threatening as they may feel that their own ethical codes of practice may have to be suspended in order to achieve partnership.

CASE STUDY 7.1

Aileen is a social worker who works in a Child Protection Unit with police colleagues. Aileen receives a referral to visit a family well known to both social services and the police. She feels that a police officer will be needed to accompany her as the allegations are serious and therefore may require police intervention. She tells Bill her police colleague that they are visiting the family and he responds with 'Not those bloody gyppos again'.

ACTIVITY 7.1

How might you respond to such a situation and what do you think is being challenged here?

Comment

Social work's ethical commitment to anti-oppressive practice is clearly challenged by the inappropriate comments made by the police officer. Much has been made of the 'canteen culture' which permeates the police force, and evidence suggests that this culture certainly reinforces stereotypical and racist attitudes towards minorities (Macpherson, 1999). The social worker may have met such attitudes before, she may shrug her shoulders and rationalise this as just part of the canteen culture which may not necessarily be discriminatory once the police officer is working alongside the social worker. However, if she does take that line then there are significant issues which she may feel are being lost in order to get along with her partner.

To avoid collusion with this culture, it is clearly in order for the social worker to question her police partner's attitudes and request he refrain from such language. She may wish to engage him in a discussion about the use of such stereotypical language. She may also suggest that if she does not receive an appropriate response then she will take this further and may consult with her line manager who could make a formal complaint. There is no appropriate way that the social worker can condone such language, and even if it were to be argued that this may undermine partnership working, then the social worker needs to be clear what the point of partnership working is. In other words, it is not to form a workable relationship with fellow professionals which results in the dilution of the social worker's value base and the demeaning of service users. The point of partnership working is not to deliver appropriate services to service users only to have them undermined by some partners exhibiting discriminatory attitudes.

RESEARCH SUMMARY

Garrett (2004) in his study of partnership working between social workers and the police found some social work respondents seemed to accept some aspects of their partner's racist language in order to prioritise working together over their ethical principles. Garrett argues it requires secure and confident social workers to work in these challenging environments and to be able then to challenge their partners when required.

Lymbery (2005), in addressing collaborative working between social workers and health professionals, suggests there are key knowledge, values and skills that social workers can bring to inter-professional working. These key attributes are not just appropriate for work between social services and health, but may usefully be a starting point from which social workers can develop security within their own professional role. In addition they can play an effective role within collaboration and joint working with other professionals, Lymbery (2005) suggests, with some additional comments:

1 *Social workers' values and ethical stance are a key element of an inter-professional team as these highlight the real differences between social workers and other professionals. Of value here is the critical role of challenge and questioning of existing practice that can be developed within a multidisciplinary team.*

2 *Social workers as 'social' workers bring with them their expertise and knowledge of the social factors which can influence the behaviour of service users and the operation of the team itself. This holistic approach places the individual within a broader community and social context which other professionals may not share to the same extent. This can be particularly strong in professions which have a narrower remit such as the nursing profession who may in the main operate from a medical model rather than a social model.*

3 *The administrative role of social workers in coordinating care packages for example may give them a strategic position within partnerships with health. They can operate between the different organisations involved to link together various professions into focusing upon the intervention. This connects in many ways to one of the traditional roles of social workers as enablers of service networks, which can be transferred into multidisciplinary teams.*

Given social workers' potential to operate at more strategic levels it becomes possible to develop interpersonal relationships with other professionals in a way that other members of the team would be unable to do given their narrower service focus. The more privileged position then of social workers has the potential to provide for an effective enabling role in binding the multi-professional team together.

Codes of conduct

It is interesting to note that the Nursing and Midwifery Council code of conduct has a specific standard requirement for nurses to work collaboratively:

The NMC code of professional conduct: standards for conduct, performance and ethics

4 As a registered nurse, midwife or specialist community public health nurse, you must co-operate with others in the team

   4.1 The team includes the patient or client, the patient's or client's family, informal carers and health and social care professionals in the National Health Service, independent and voluntary sectors.

For many years nurses have worked alongside different occupational and professional groups within hospitals on a regular basis. By comparison the Social Care Council Code of Practice for Social Care Workers does make specific mention of working with others in partnership:

Recognising and respecting the roles and expertise of workers from other agencies and working in partnership with them …

But this statement is included under the general prescription to:

6 *As a social care worker, you must be accountable for the quality of your work and take responsibility for maintaining and improving your knowledge and skills*

This statement is a much weaker recognition of partnership working than that found in the nursing and midwifery code. Does this reflect the relative autonomy of social work which has until recently had a greater degree of professional freedom to act compared with the more subscribed role of nurses, particularly within the hospital setting?

Although both codes in respect of health workers and social care workers identify that working with others in partnership is important, they do not specify how professionals should work together. In partnership working some of the more general ethical concepts are also important, i.e. trust, respect, honesty; yet for collaborative work the importance of reciprocity is vital. In studies of partnership working the core of success involves the sense in which partners feel that their professional identity is respected. Where partnership becomes problematic therefore is where different professional groupings feel that their particular professional identity is under threat or that it does not receive the same status as others within the team.

RESEARCH SUMMARY

Glendinning (2003) argues that although management systems have integrated partnership working successfully, at lower organisational levels, professional domains and identities continue to be barriers to successful partnership outcomes. This is echoed by Carpenter et al. (2003) who suggest in relation to partnership within community mental health teams that social workers experienced greater degrees of role conflict than their nurse partners which requires in their view more support and supervision for social work-

---

Codes of ethics

Codes of ethics have a crucial role to play here as they define the principles upon which the professional role is carried forward with service users, and delineate one profession's practice from another. A central concern then for respective partners is that they feel that respect for and trust in their partner's ethical practice is reciprocated. As we noted at the beginning of this chapter, social workers and social care workers do not have any choice in whether they work within multidisciplinary teams. Therefore it becomes incumbent upon them to derive effective working relationships within these organisational arrangements. In ethical terms there is a problem. As professional values have often been translated into how individual workers can behave ethically with service users, there has been little or no need to develop ethics which require different professionals in a team to come together to provide a service. As Shardlow et al. (2004) have identified in relation to inter-agency working to safeguard children, there are no specific standards for inter-agency training used by any of the occupational groups involved. Even where standards exist, few refer specifically to inter-agency work issues in relation to safeguarding children. It is important therefore to think about how different professionals can operate in ways which enable them to cooperate together for the benefit of service users. To date there have been few developments which have considered ethical issues within multi-professional teams. One such approach, which was influenced by the Climbié inquiry and was given funding to pursue some of these questions, has come from Shardlow et al. (2004). This project, funded by the Department of Health, has set about developing standards for both multi-agency education and training and practice. Within its brief it has considered the ethical implications for working in multi-professional teams:

FIVE – OPERATIONAL STANDARD: ETHICS AND CONFIDENTIALITY

Use and communicate relevant information with due regard for the preservation of the client's confidentiality as is appropriate.

Practitioners should know the ethical position of their own profession/occupation in relation to maintaining the confidentiality of information that is given to them and act accordingly.

However, information should be shared with other practitioners when it is clear that not to do so may place the child or vulnerable adult at risk. In addition, practitioners should have due regard for, and seek to understand the ethical position of other occupational and professional groups which may be different to their own (Shardlow et al. 2004, p23).

ACTIVITY **7.2**

Look at the statement above. What aspects of the ethics of partnership contained in the box are the most challenging?

Comment

As with all attempts to provide ethical statements, those above are qualified and rely upon you as a social work professional to exercise your judgement, for example when to share information. Therefore those statements which are qualified will provide an element of challenge in that your partner professional may not understand your interpretation of the following ethical statements:

- preservation of the client's confidentiality as is appropriate;

- information should be shared with other practitioners when it is clear that not to do so may place the child or vulnerable adult at risk.

Both these statements require you to decide what information is appropriate to share and when to share it. In relation to service users, the main justification in breaching confidentiality would be where a child or vulnerable adult is at risk. However, it is likely that different professionals' thresholds of what constitutes risk may vary. For example, a community nurse finding an adult living in relatively unsanitary and unkempt surroundings may interpret this as a risky situation to health, yet from a social worker's perspective it may be tolerable if they are maintaining their independence and not posing any immediate risk to themselves. Likewise, a teacher who finds a child's behaviour intolerable and disruptive in class may be more keen to share information about that child's family than a social worker who may see disruption as a lower priority than keeping that child in school away from his or her disruptive home life.

What needs to be considered here is that both workers are coming from their own ethical codes of practice and, whereas there are some similarities, it is perhaps difficult to see how different professionals can work in an ethically sensitive way if they do not share some elements of a common ethical base. The importance of values for social workers when faced with the possibility of working in partnership has been highlighted by Peck and Norman (1999) where social workers felt their values could be threatened by a more outcome-oriented culture evident in the NHS. For social workers, outcomes are important but the process of engaging with service users and the quality of the relationships forged are of equal importance. Thus social work practice is as much concerned with process as with outcome. This focus upon process has been outlined previously in relation to service users and there is ample evidence that process as much as outcome is valued by service users (Aldgate and Statham, 2001). It is relevant here then to think of ethics within multi-disciplinary teams as operating on two levels. The first is where individual workers use their particular codes to engage with service users. The second would be to develop shared ethical principles in working with one another. These principles should be the sub-ject of dialogue and discussion in which the different professions come to an agreement on certain basic principles around which they will work together.

ACTIVITY **7.3**

Think of some key ethical principles or values which go beyond ideas of individually based ethics that you could develop to enable some first principles of joint working.

Comment

As you are thinking of developing relationship-based ethics then those principles based upon individual responsibility may be important but do not encapsulate how partners should work together. Individually based decision-making in respect to values assumes that the choices made align with our values as professionals, but those choices which are appropriate in work with service users may not align with other professionals' value choices. Individually based professional ethics therefore ignore the reality of the connect-edness between different professionals and their values and code of ethics within multidisciplinary teams.

Communicative reason

One approach which has gained increasing purchase in social work is to look at the work of Jürgen Habermas who has developed ideas on democratic communication between individuals which could be adapted for multi-professional working. Habermas (see Spratt and Houston, 1999) argues that we need to find new ways of organising the social world in which we live which should be informed by what he calls 'communicative reason'. This means that the way in which we communicate with one another must involve an ability to be understood and to construct shared meanings. This ought to be ensured by all those involved in joint communication enabling:

- all to be allowed to speak;
- all to be required to listen;
- all to have the capacity to question.

This process must be democratic, taking place on a fair and equal basis. This is potentially significant for partnership working as it seeks to develop a basis upon which different pro-fessional groups can begin to interact and communicate.

> *In communicative action participants are not primarily oriented to their own individual success; they pursue their own individual goals under the conditions that they can harmonize their plans of action on the basis of common situation definitions. In this respect the negotiation of definitions of the situation is an essential element of the interpretive accomplishments required for communicative action* (Habermas, 1984 p285–6).

As this quote suggests, communicative action invites different parties to negotiate their understanding of their particular goals of action based upon agreed definitions of the situation in which their goals develop. What Habermas is suggesting is that communicative action must be based upon reasoned argument which seeks to construct a valid case upon which mutual understanding can lead to a consensus which is agreed upon by the parties to the communication. Communicative action builds upon those interactions by which people are motivated to understand others so that they can share their lives together. This is the opposite of what Habermas calls strategic action where interaction is oriented towards 'success' which in his case means getting others to do or to believe what one wants them to, regardless of their subjective needs or experience. The underlying logic of communicative action suggests that mutual understanding is possible. Those engaged in interaction have reached a background consensus with respect to four types of validity claims: comprehensibility, truth, rightness and sincerity. As Outhwaite (1994) suggests, the background consensus between speaker and hearer is concerned to enable a claim that the speaker is making to be justified. Thus the speaker can be questioned on the basis of:

- what do you mean?, i.e. comprehensibility;

- is what you say true?, i.e. truth;

- are you entitled to say that?, i.e. rightness;

- do you really mean it?, i.e. sincerity.

A consensus constructed in this way is only valid if as a matter of principle we presuppose the possibility of an unrestrained dialogue where all have access to the dialogue and where the logic of the better argument is validated. This process is called an ideal speech situation. As Habermas concedes, the actual ways in which argument occurs is often contrary to this but he is arguing for an ethics by which an open and fair dialogue should and can take place.

As Milley (2002) has argued, this theory can be used to understand that organisations can be moral communities. This can be achieved through a rationally agreed consensus which marginalises individual or small group preferences or particular traditions and ideologies in order to validate just principles to guide action. From the point of view of partnership working this theory can be utilised to develop the new multi-agency teams as moral communities rather than separate inter-professional communities.

Partnership projects

One way to build an underlying consensus can be to develop a shared approach to anti-oppressive practices which seeks to develop social justice. There are many partnership projects which bring different professionals together to work towards social justice or at least to develop social inclusion of marginalised individuals and communities. This has been a core approach developed by the Labour government since their election in 1997.

Policies towards communities have been developed to tackle the problems of disadvantaged areas through a 'joined up' approach at national and local levels.

The National Strategy for Neighbourhood Renewal has put in place Local Strategic Partnerships with additional resources through the Neighbourhood Renewal Fund to focus on the 88 most deprived local authority areas. The New Deal for Communities, neighbourhood wardens and Neighbourhood Management Pathfinders are key community-based approaches to deliver the strategy. Working in partnership the government's new approach to tackling social exclusion emphasised the importance of joined-up working at all levels, together with a more client-centred approach to designing and delivering services. This has been reflected in closer working between central government departments, local government and the voluntary and community sector, and communities (Social Exclusion Unit, 2004, p11).

Thus the experience and expertise designed to tackle social exclusion has focused upon partnership working. This approach is designed to achieve some measure of social justice and therefore has the potential to be transferred across to the personal social services such as children's services and adult care. The recognition that oppression is often multiple and therefore requires a team with a range of different skills is potentially advantageous. The manifestations of multiple injustice can often overwhelm individually placed professionals working out of their own separate teams. Thus teams could collaborate around the principles of embracing diversity to achieve social justice within and through their partnership arrangements.

CASE STUDY **7.2**

The multidisciplinary learning disabilities team in which you are one of the social workers has undergone a rapid reorganisation. The team in which you work is being joined by your partner team from the other half of the city. In essence the team is now doubling in size. As a result there have been significant problems in developing working relationships between the new team members. Managers have tried to counter these problems by outlining what support each of the respective professionals would get in terms of supervision, and have clarified the management arrangements of the new team. Nevertheless, despite these extensive arrangements, members of the new team have not worked well together. Both teams tend to distrust the other and there has been a number of arguments between individual members regarding the style of work. It appears that this is not necessarily to do with different professional cultures but that in your team, the working relationships were well founded and partnership working tended to develop well. Unfortunately, in merging with the other team their working arrangements were not so well progressed towards partnership, and as such their lack of co-operative working has undermined the new team arrangements. This has affected a number of service users where different members of the team have not communicated effectively over different cases, leaving service users confused about what service they should be in receipt of and from whom.

ACTIVITY 7.4

Using the approach suggested by Habermas to develop communicative action within the team, what suggestions would you make to develop partnership working?

Comment

A useful starting point in developing an ethics of partnership would be to take the principles:

- comprehensibility

- truth

- rightness

- sincerity.

These can be applied to the idea of partnership, i.e. using comprehensibility as a starting point:

- How can we speak of partnership?

- What do the different professionals understand by the term?

- Can they agree on what it means in the newly formed team?

Secondly, it implies that when we agree to partnership working we are prepared to act truthfully and diligently upon this agreement. Finally, we affirm that our definition of partnership is one on which we can agree, ensuring that it meets what the different professional groupings want from partnership. We may then talk about what the partnership wants to achieve in delivering social justice to the service users it serves. This will require a further exploration using the above principles to agree upon how social justice is then understood, and how it is seen as appropriate for the team to use as its overall objective.

Although Habermas's ideas have been criticised for his belief in the possibility of a shared understanding of truth through democratic dialogue, potentially it can enable different partners to engage in a democratic process designed to provide some basic principles through which 'right actions' can be developed. For Habermas, only when everyone in a particular society who has the capacity to make a contribution to what constitutes 'right action' has participated and given their agreement, can a particular course of action be said to be universal. If certain norms have been only partially agreed upon then this represents a sectional interest. For social work this has many implications in relation to partnership working. It means that a democratic dialogue is a prerequisite of partnership. In turn this requires that service users have access to the dialogue, for example in identifying what they require from partnership working. If service users are not given a voice to determine the ethical codes of partnership work then partnership ethics represent a sectional interest (Hugman, 2005).

This approach has been called a discourse ethics approach. What this means is that knowledge is built upon consensus or a general agreement. This is achieved through open communication in which knowledge is developed as a public understanding and is not the property of any particular individual or sectional interest (Outhwaite, 1994).

As Milley (2002) shows in relation to organisations, discourse ethics can potentially develop beyond individual or sectional interests to achieve a shared understanding of what the organisation, or in our case the multi-agency partnership, is trying to achieve ethically and practically. In relation to partnership working we can distinguish between a partial or subjectivist approach to working together which looks at the implications of actions and ideas from a particular professional or individualistic viewpoint, or we can identify a discourse approach which takes a more universal and generalised position looking at the different interests and seeking a consensual view of the actions or ideas under consideration.

RESEARCH SUMMARY

Banks (2004) in her research has identified the following as most challenging to practitioners wishing to work in partnership:

- *Professional identity. This refers to how the professional integrates him or herself into the professional role and how the professional role influences how they see themselves. This is often developed through initial training in the education process which socialises the student and encourages them to see themselves in a certain way.*

- *Professional values. Used broadly to refer to general principles which inform the profession to think and act in a particular way. It can refer to those principles within different codes of professional practice. It can also refer to more generalised belief systems or ideologies which are said to encompass what certain professionals think, i.e. social workers are seen to work from a social model.*

- *Professional culture. This refers to a professional way of doing and speaking about things, identifying those within the profession from those outside. Cultures often become visible when they conflict with other professional or non-professional cultures. For example, the development of the service users' movement has brought into sharp distinction the conflict between professional culture to construct service users as passive receivers of service in contrast to the proactive and independent culture of service user groups.*

ACTIVITY 7.5

How would a subjectivist approach look at professional identity, culture and values? We will then look at the approach of a discourse ethics.

Comment

Professional identity

Identity from a subjectivist approach helps us to understand the importance of individual professional identity and its different manifestations among professional groups. A discourse ethics will highlight the importance of a shared identity within the team that will accommodate individual identities as a process of the mutual exploration of uncovering those aspects which can be shared within the team.

Professional values

A subjectivist view helps us to understand the particular sets of values and their meanings which the different professionals in the multi-agency team hold. A discourse ethics provides a means to understand the paradoxes of the particular notions of ethical professional conduct and the importance of identifying commonalities between different codes of conduct for a broader based ethics within the team.

Professional culture

Subjectivist views will identify the particular differences between professional cultures and how these inform the particular models of practice while a discourse ethics will emphasise the importance of a shared understanding, which includes different conceptions as a model for a shared understanding to enable the recognition and accommodation of such different professional cultures.

ACTIVITY 7.6

Look at the following two statements. The first comes from the code of practice for social care workers, the second from the nursing and midwifery code of professional conduct. Identify from each list those statements which both nurses and social work and social care workers have in common.

Code of practice for social care workers

- Protect the rights and promote the interests of service users and carers.

- Strive to establish and maintain the trust and confidence of service users and carers.

- Promote the independence of service users while protecting them as far as possible from danger or harm.

- Respect the rights of service users while seeking to ensure that their behaviour does not harm themselves or other people.

- Uphold public trust and confidence in social care services.

- Be accountable for the quality of their work and take responsibility for maintaining and improving their knowledge and skills.

The NMC code of professional conduct:

- Obtain consent before you give any treatment or care.

- Protect confidential information.

- Cooperate with others in the team.

- Maintain your professional knowledge and competence.

- Be trustworthy.

- Act to identify and minimise risk to patients and clients.

Comment

If we compare the two lists, both professional groups share many value and ethical principles which can provide the foundation for partnership work. From an ethics of discourse perspective in assessing the respective lists, it is important to identify that it is no easy matter to develop partnership working. For example, the principle of confidentiality is a principle shared by both groups. In terms of their partnership working then it would be necessary for the different professionals to share what they understood confidentiality to mean and to agree under what circumstances they would share information and under what circumstances they would keep confidentiality.

ACTIVITY 7.7

If you were the nurse in Case study 7.3 below, would you feel it appropriate to share this information? Should Neil share this with the other members of the team who are working on this young man's offending behaviour.

CASE STUDY 7.3

Neil is a community nurse working within a youth offending team. He is working with a young man who has contracted a sexually transmitted disease and has provided the appropriate initial advice before referring him for treatment.

Comment

The rules of confidentiality here are very pertinent. Do we as professionals relax our ethical principles for an imagined belief in partnership work or do we uphold our own professional values while working within the team? Does partnership come with a complete derogation of our own professional ethics or should partnership allow us as professionals to develop those within the context of partnership working?

Within the Youth Justice team the focus is upon preventing offending behaviour, so the question then needs to be posed whether this young man's problems have anything to do with his offending behaviour. If we can answer that the issue is unrelated, then Neil has a perfect right and duty to maintain confidentiality. If, however, the problem was related to his offending behaviour, then Neil should share the information. Indeed, under section 115 of the Crime and Disorder Act 1998, information pertinent to criminal activity can be shared between agencies (see Banks, 2004).

Thus for the team to move forward, some general principles developed from pertinent examples to give context to the ethical problem could be used by the team to reach agreement as to how and if information will be shared.

C H A P T E R   S U M M A R Y

This chapter has explored the meaning of partnership working from an ethical standpoint. It has discussed some of the barriers to partnership working and emphasised the importance of culture, identity and value as key concerns for professionals within multi-agency teams. These concerns go to the heart of the problems professionals face in working in partnership. This chapter has identified the priority given in partnership working to management and resource systems which provide the structure to partnership. While these are essential, unless the particular professional identities are then addressed by reconciling different professional cultures that flow from this then partnership will be problematic. In addressing these problems the work of Habermas and the relevance of discourse ethics have been considered as a possible way forward in bringing different professional groupings together to work effectively within a multi-agency team.

FURTHER READING

Quinney, A (2006) *Collaborative Social Work Practice*. Exeter: Learning Matters.
This is an excellent introduction for social workers to the different contexts in which partnership working is now taking place.

Carnwell, R and Buchanan, J (2005) *Effective practice in health and social care: A partnership approach*. Maidenhead: Open University.
Provides a wide-ranging discussion of the different aspects of partnership working drawing upon a range of perspectives to inform the debate.

Chapter 8
Ethics in social work organisations

ACHIEVING A SOCIAL WORK DEGREE

This will begin to help you to meet the following National Occupational Standards:
Key Role 5 Manage and be accountable, with supervision and support, for your own social work practice within your organisation.

This chapter will also help you to follow the GSCC's Code of Practice for Social Care Workers:
2 As a social care worker, you must strive to establish and maintain the trust and confidence of service users and carers.
This includes:
- Honouring work commitments, agreements and arrangements and, when it is not possible to do so, explaining why to service users and carers.
- Declaring issues that might create conflicts of interest and making sure that they do not influence your judgement or practice.
- Adhering to policies and procedures about accepting gifts and money from service users and carers.

3 As a social care worker, you must promote the independence of service users while protecting them as far as possible from danger or harm.
This includes:
- Using established processes and procedures to challenge and report dangerous, abusive, discriminatory or exploitative behaviour and practice.
- Bringing to the attention of your employer or the appropriate authority resource or operational difficulties that might get in the way of the delivery of safe care.
- Following practice and procedures designed to keep you and other people safe from violent and abusive behaviour at work.
- Informing your employer or an appropriate authority where the practice of colleagues may be unsafe or adversely affecting standards of care.
- Helping service users and carers to make complaints, taking complaints seriously and responding to them or passing them to the appropriate person.

5 As a social care worker, you must uphold public trust and confidence in social care services.
In particular you must not:
- Abuse, neglect or harm service users, carers or colleagues.
- Exploit service users, carers or colleagues in any way.
- Discriminate unlawfully or unjustifiably against service users, carers or colleagues.
- Condone any unlawful or unjustifiable discrimination by service users, carers or colleagues.
- Put yourself or other people at unnecessary risk.

5.8 Behave in a way, in work or outside work, which would call into question your suitability to work in social care services.

It will also introduce you to the following academic standards as set out in the social work subject benchmark statement:

3.2.5 Skills in personal and professional development
Honours graduates in social work should be able to:

- reflect on and modify their behaviour in the light of experience;
- identify and keep under review their own personal and professional boundaries;
- manage uncertainty, change and stress in work situations;
- handle inter-personal and intra-personal conflict constructively;
- understand and manage changing situations and respond in a flexible manner;
- challenge unacceptable practices in a responsible manner.

Ethics and organisations

Social workers and their employers have an ethical duty to ensure that the organisations they work for operate in a just manner. A just social work organisation must convince those it employs and those whom it serves that social work is something worth upholding as good in itself, and that the operation of social work organisations will lead to good and just outcomes. Social workers and their employers therefore have to act in a way which shows those who contribute through paying taxes that their organisation operates in a fair way treating all with equal respect. It must enable citizens to contribute to how the service is planned, organised and delivered to them. At an organisational level this process enables citizens to give legitimacy to social work organisations and recognise that social work's aims are to achieve social justice for those whom it serves (Rothstein, 1998).

Public bodies now have a number of legal duties relating to social justice matters. For example, equal opportunities legislation requires public bodies like local authority social service departments to operate in a manner which does not discriminate on the grounds of physical ability, gender and race, and is soon to include age. The Race Relations (Amendment) Act 2001 requires all public authorities in carrying out their work not to commit any act constituting discrimination, although some public bodies are excluded, for example the security services and military units. Local authority social service departments must act to eliminate unlawful discrimination and to promote equality of opportunity and good relations between persons of different racial groups.

In respect of the treatment of social work and social care employees, the code for social care employers (**www.gscc.org.uk**) expects employers' organisations to operate in a way that enables social workers and social care workers to work according to their own code of practice. Point 2 of the employers code is clear in this regard:

> *2 As a social care employer, you must have written policies and procedures in place to enable social care workers to meet the GSCC's Code of Practice for Social Care Workers.*

This includes:

Implementing and monitoring written policies on: confidentiality; equal opportunities; risk assessment; substance abuse; record keeping; and the acceptance of money or personal gifts from service users or carers.

2.2 Effectively managing and supervising staff to support effective practice and good conduct and supporting staff to address deficiencies in their performance;

Having systems in place to enable social care workers to report inadequate resources or operational difficulties which might impede the delivery of safe care and working with them and relevant authorities to address those issues; and

Supporting social care workers to meet the GSCC's Code of Practice for Social Care Workers and not requiring them to do anything that would put their compliance with that code at risk.

To enable social work institutions to operate in a just way there are two basic assumptions which underpin this principle. Firstly, service users, social work employees and their managers should be able to influence the social work processes and organisational practices in their employing organisations. Secondly, these organisations must take responsibility to ensure that they can respond and reshape those processes and practices in response to all legitimate demands (see Miller, 1987).

If social workers are to work in an ethical manner then they will have to engage with the ways in which their organisation:

- organises their work;

- resources their work;

- supervises their work;

- enables service users' participation.

This means that social workers need to consider the nature of the managerial and organisational contexts which shape their working lives. In particular, they need to ensure that their professional autonomy is enhanced appropriately and, where it is constrained by policy and procedure, that this is exercised fairly and for the benefit of service users. The problems social workers face in their employing organisations is often translated into issues around professional discretion, in which some anti-managerialist discourses see any imposition of rules and procedures on social workers as necessarily a bad thing. As Evans and Harris (2004) argue, the increase in guidance, procedures and rules should not immediately be equated with greater control over professional discretion; excessive rule-making may create more discretion, which in itself may not be positive either. This can be the case where a proliferation of rules which may be contradictory or which become overly complex, leaves social workers to use their discretion, by default creating rules of thumb through the thicket of bureaucratic control. Rules and procedures can operate positively or negatively. In a positive sense, they can clarify and enhance social workers' ability to access services and enable service user's social justice, by ensuring that services are delivered fairly according to agreed criteria which are open and transparent. In a negative sense, poorly conceived rules and procedures can enable managers and professionals to hide behind them, to use them as an excuse for inaction or to create the opportunity for professional abuse of power.

Social workers, if they work for local authority social service departments, find themselves part of an organisation which is organised bureaucratically. To work effectively to deliver services to large groups of service users, work has to be delivered in a rational and transparent way. This form of working is often best suited to bureaucratic styles of organisation. Let as define what we mean by an organisation and then what is meant by bureaucracy through an internet search for definitions.

An organisation:

- describes a group of people acting to achieve a common goal (**www.wikipedia.org/wiki/Organisation**);

- group of people who work together toward a common goal; for example, a sporting club, business, government department, professional body (**www.mckinnons.vic.edu. au**);

- deliberate arrangement of people to achieve a particular purpose (**www.wordnet. princeton**).

The definitions above describe both a way of working together to achieve a common goal and the actual disposition of people into different roles and responsibilities to achieve the most efficient outcome. Roles and responsibilities have been formally organised and managed to achieve a particular purpose.

A bureaucracy

- a form of organisation marked by division of labour, hierarchy, rules and regulations and impersonal relationships (**www.crfonline.org**);

- a system in which people are expected to follow precisely defined rules and procedures rather than to use personal judgement (**www.wps.prenhall.com**);

- rule by bureaus of appointed officials. Group of agencies marked by a clear hierarchy of authority in charge of implementing collective choices made through political institutions. Formal organisations that carry out policy through written rules and standardised procedures based on the specialisation of duties and striving for the efficient attainment of organisational goals (**www.elissetche.org**);

- a sociological concept of government and its institutions as an organisational structure characterised by regularised procedure, division of responsibility, hierarchy and impersonal relationships (**www.wikipedia.org/wiki/Bureaucracy**).

A bureaucracy such as that found within a social services department divides activities between different people with an identified hierarchy of responsibilities, so that in theory each person in the organisation knows who has which responsibility. Authority for completing activities comes from the top down, so that power is designated down through each level of the hierarchy.

The abuse of professional power in the form of the damage that can be done by a bureaucracy, within which those entwined in its grasp come to inhabit a nightmare world of contradictory and self-defeating rules, has been closely associated with the writing of Franz Kafka and the adjective Kafkaesque. Kafka's book *The Trial* begins with the protagonist Joseph K. waking one morning to find himself under arrest. He has not been previously informed that he has done wrong, and no one can tell him what charges have been brought against him. Even the officials who have come to arrest him don't know – they're just doing their jobs. Joseph K. spends the rest of the novel trying to discover these charges, attempting to outwit the excessively bureaucratic system that has put him under arrest, while at the same time trying to maintain a hold on his fragmenting personal life. As the forces against Joseph K. steadily grow stronger, he slowly comes to the revelation that the entire world may be under control of the court that is trying to condemn him (Kafka, 2004).

Another associated term which describes some of the essence of bureaucratic thinking is the term from the book and film *Catch-22* (Heller 2005). The story concerns bomber crews in the Second World War where the chances of survival were slim. We have all come up against certain circumstances where no matter what we try and do to chart a way forward, we are confronted with a Catch-22 situation:

> *There was only one catch and that was Catch-22, which specified that a concern for one's own safety in the face of dangers that were real and immediate was the process of a rational mind. Orr was crazy and could be grounded. All he had to do was ask; and as soon as he did, he would no longer be crazy and would have to fly more missions. Orr would be crazy to fly more missions and sane if he didn't, but if he was sane he had to fly them. If he flew them he was crazy and didn't have to; but if he didn't want to he was sane and had to. Yossarian was moved very deeply by the absolute simplicity of this clause of Catch-22 and let out a respectful whistle* (Heller, 2005, p55).

This catch keeps the hero of the book Yossarian in the war because a concern for one's own life proved that he is not really crazy, and to get out of combat you have to be crazy. The catch is used by the superior powers to uphold and increase their power, and yet it is harmful to those who do not have power in the first place.

This frame of thinking describes the way in which an organisation is able to live inside people's heads so that their ability to act is neutralised through the way their thoughts and behaviour are influenced by these organisational and bureaucratic imperatives. A useful analysis of the impact of welfare institutions upon individuals has been provided by Foucault (1977) who investigated the procedures to control and punish criminals in the nineteenth century through the idea of a Panopticon, a prison designed by the utilitarian Jeremy Bentham. The prisoners were subject to constant surveillance through the architectural design of the prison where all prisoners could be watched from a central point. The surveyed prisoner was induced to be obedient because he or she did not know when they were being watched. Although they may not be being observed, they must behave if they are and therefore control is achieved even when the observation by the guards may be absent. This results in the prisoner controlling their own behaviour almost automatically (Prado, 2000). A more commonplace example concerns police speed cameras placed by the roadside which may or may not be switched on, thus the motorist does not know if he or she will be caught speeding by the camera and therefore adjusts the speed of their car accordingly. Ultimately the motorist responds almost immediately as a speed camera sign is observed and adjusts their speed. This deliberate and largely unconscious response can also be evidenced in how some people are socialised into an inflexible bureaucratic mindset. Thus the operation of a bureaucracy which requires the utmost conformity to rules has two effects:

- It converts deliberate obedience of regulations into habitual compliance with rules and norms. In this they become 'mores' reflecting a strong moral imperative for workers feeling they 'ought' to comply. A failure to conform to rules will result in a much stronger social response from your colleagues who resent your failure to behave appropriately.

- The habitual compliance itself converts to adoption or internalisation of these norms.

This rather pessimistic description of bureaucratic forms of organisation has been further reinforced through the work of Bauman (1989, 1994) who suggests that the bureaucratic way of working divorces ethics from the organisation of the work that the bureaucracy processes, so that people become bodies to be processed rather than human beings to be respected.

> Now this ideal model can work properly only on the condition that all people involved in the work of the organization follow the commands they receive and are guided only by them (their actions are, as it is said sometimes, 'rule-guided'). And that means that people should not be diverted by their personal beliefs and convictions or by emotions – sympathy or antipathy – to fellow workers or to individual clients or objects of action (Bauman, 1994, p11).

For Bauman (1994) bureaucracies encourage moral ambivalence and ethical blindness, defending themselves and their employees against troublesome ethical criticism in two ways:

- the phenomenon of 'floating responsibility' – which suggests that as long as the employee followed the rules faithfully and did what was asked by his or her superiors, no responsibility can be placed upon the worker for the effects of such allegiance that this may have on the objects worked on;

- ethical indifference – which neutralises and then exempts members of a bureaucracy from any moral judgement. Thus people are merely following the agreed principles and procedures which are neither good nor bad, but merely requirements to achieve the smooth running of the bureaucracy.

CASE STUDY 8.1

Mrs Williams is a single parent living with her 14-year-old daughter Melanie who is both physically and learning disabled. Two years ago Melanie was a passenger in her uncle's car when it was involved in an accident killing her uncle and leaving her with serious body and head injuries. Melanie's behaviour can be very difficult for Mrs Williams to handle and the physical demands of caring for Melanie often leave Mrs Williams exhausted. Melanie, in order to give her mother a break, goes four times a year to a respite care facility. This is a very over-subscribed service and the social services department has limited the use of the facility to four times a year. As you are Mrs Williams's social worker, you are now faced with a problem in that Mrs Williams is asking for an extra respite care break, even though she has already received her allocated breaks. In supervision, your team manager points out that Mrs Williams can be very demanding and that there is no possibility for Mrs Williams to receive more than her fair share of respite care, as the resource panel which decides such issues has already refused other carers who have made similar demands.

ACTIVITY 8.1

What is your response in this case?

Comment

You will need to assess the circumstances leading to Mrs Williams seeking extra help. If you feel that there are special circumstances which has led Mrs Williams to require a further break and you assess her need is justified, then you may find yourself in conflict with the organisational imperative to ration care breaks in this way. Alternatively, you may agree that the social services department decision to ration services is justified to enable other carers to access some services. Or you may feel sympathy for both positions, in that Mrs Williams does have a pressing need which requires some action on your part but you also feel that, imperfect as it is, the social service department does need to ration services in order to spread a limited resource fairly around other carers.

On the face of it there are two initial responses that have been identified by writers such as Banks (2006) and Payne (2000). These can be characterised as a flexible or reflective response in contrast to a bureaucratic or procedural response.

Bureaucratic/procedural approach

This approach encourages the social worker to follow the rules. If procedures are in place and they have been arrived at impartially then ethically nothing else can be done. If Mrs Williams feels aggrieved and angry at you because you have reported back that no more care is available, then you do not bear any responsibility and no blame attaches to you. The idea of responsibility means in this case that you have done your duty. You have made a case for extra help but Mrs Williams does not meet the criteria.

Flexible/reflective approach

This approach asks you to recognise and critically reflect upon the dilemmas and conflicts which are inherent in social work and social care, rather than taking an 'either/or' approach in which as a social worker you argue against the injustice to Mrs Williams in having her needs ignored or alternatively follow procedures. If you recognise that Mrs Williams has a legitimate need but it is necessary to uphold the impartiality of the procedures to ration services fairly, then you may be able to develop a more flexible approach. You may achieve a solution for Mrs Williams and uphold the integrity of the procedures. As Banks (2001) argues, social workers have a duty to make ethical choices where the needs of the agency and individuals are in conflict and develop a practical way forward.

Flexible action

Just because your team manager asserts that other applications have been refused if carers have already had their maximum allocation of respite care, this should not prevent a case being made to the resource panel if it is justified. Thus all rules and procedures operate from general cases and cannot by definition cover all aspects and differences between carers' needs. You might argue that this is a special case requiring Mrs Williams accessing this extra break, you may be successful. More pragmatically, you might inquire if any carers have not used their full compliment of care and on this basis query whether you could use the resource so that places do not go to waste.

You may feel that in the long run the only way this problem may be resolved is for carers to take action. Clearly other carers have been in the same position as Mrs Williams and may feel similarly that the overall level of provision is inadequate. Rationing services does not reflect the absolute need of individual carers, but is a relative judgement based upon the numbers of carers with a need and the availability of resources to meet that need. The department's rationing procedure may be necessary in the short run to manage inadequate supply of respite care, but in the long run the problem will remain. Carers may wish to be enabled to pressurise the social service department for a review of the procedure. In this event you may advise them on how to progress this further, while being aware that you are an employee of the organisation.

Social service departments as bureaucracies are concerned therefore to provide services which are delivered in an impartial way and require their employees to reflect this value. But this brings them into conflict with their employees who are given the duty of administering these procedures, in which they experience the struggles and pains of the service users in trying to meet their welfare needs. The impartiality of the worker is sorely tested and rightly so. To engage in a soulless assessment of need without recourse to the humanity and context of the situation would be impossible except for a robot. This conflict has been characterised by Clark (2006) as one between the instrumental and the moral.

Instrumental relationship

This limits an employee to a narrow focus upon the business in hand, often to a single transaction or event, for example buying and selling goods, or when a civil servant processes a passport application. In these examples neither party to the relationship has any interest or need to be concerned about the character of the other as long as the procedures are adhered to. The quality of the social interaction in the relationship is not intertwined with the transaction. As long as the exchange of goods occurs or the application is processed, then the quality of the relationship between the provider and receiver of the service is incidental to the outcome.

Moral relationship

On the other hand, there are professional–client relationships which are imbued with moral purpose. The social worker–service user relationship is one in which the moral qualities of the persons involved have a significant effect on the quality of the work done. Professional relationships mix both the instrumental and the moral. Social workers may deal with fairly routine assessments for services, which require little beyond a technical competence in assessment and knowledge of the appropriate services. However, on other occasions he or she may engage with service users over fundamental moral choices relating to a person's autonomy and independence.

The moral elements of the working relationships in social work become more personalised, as Clark (2006) argues, when social workers work alongside service users in more informal ways. As residential social workers find out very swiftly, they are continually compelled to work out what is 'normal' or morally acceptable in respect of the behaviour that they come into contact with when caring for children and young people. In effect, they become surrogate parents who have to provide some moral guidance as to how those children should live their lives. These elements are rarely experienced by the managers and administrators of social service departments, whose concerns take on a more utilitarian mode in deciding what is in the best interests of the many that they have responsibility for. What social workers are continually required to do then, is to reconcile the broader policy and guidance statements that form the boundaries of their work, with the particular problems which service users face which do not necessarily fit easily with these general policy statements. It requires social workers to judge the particular situation in the light of the general rules and find an acceptable way through for service users, reconciling their particular needs with the universal rules governing access to services. In reconciling these concerns, ethical codes of practice can provide guides to action, as can a recourse to policy and procedures, but ultimately it requires the judgement of the social worker to assess their relative weight and significance and make a decision accordingly.

The recent critiques of bureaucracy have in part come from the New Right and their restructuring of the welfare state by the Conservative governments of the 1980s and early 1990s. The critique, aimed at state bureaucracies rather than the big and nonetheless bureaucratic capitalist multinational corporations, charged government bureaucracies with being inefficient and inflexible with regard to the needs of modern citizens, who increasingly saw themselves as consumers of services rather than beneficiaries of what was argued were paternalistic state services. This analysis also maligned the professionals staffing these bureaucracies as essentially self-interested, with a vested interest in building unwieldy organisations to accrue greater power and personal gain (Marsland, 1996). This critique of bureaucracy was not limited to the political right, but the caricature which it portrayed was particularly effective in playing a part in the restructuring of welfare state services.

The old-style bureaucratic social services have not been replaced wholesale with supposedly more efficient privatised forms of service but with a hybrid. This hybrid – known as a quasi-market – has introduced market-like competition with a reduction in the provision of local authority social services, replaced in theory by private and voluntary providers competing for contracts to provide services, for example in domiciliary/residential care, family support and children's residential care. Control over the organisation, management, assessment and commissioning of services remains with the local authority social services department. Enthusiasts for such an approach argue this has injected much dynamism and flexibility into social services. For critics such as Bauman (1996), it has brought the worst of both worlds – a bureaucratically-managed service with the inequities of competition between providers, leading to a concern with cost efficiency rather than service effectiveness. For some writers, the pressure to develop standardised services within a managed market replicates some of the worst features of the mass consumer market (James, 2004).

An example of such a merger of the rational bureaucratic organisation of services within a fiercely marketised and competitive industry is that of the fast food chain McDonald's. This has led Ritzer (1993) to suggest that this form of organisation has far reaching consequences. Rationalisation reaches into all areas of everyday life. Ways of thinking are colonised by self-interested concern with efficiency and formal social control. The supreme manifestation of this is the bureaucracy, representing the process of rationalisation. This has a knock-on effect in which human interaction is controlled and then developed further into a rationalist framework.

Ritzer suggests that the fast food restaurant and the processes of rationalisation and bureaucratic control encapsulated within it, i.e. McDonaldisation, has become so powerful that its rationalising logic has permeated everyday interaction and individual identity.

> *McDonaldization is the process by which the principles of the fast food restaurant are coming to dominate more and more sectors of American society as well as of the rest of the world* (Ritzer, 1993, p1).

Ritzer outlines five dominant themes within McDonaldisation: efficiency, calculability, predictability, increased control, and the replacement of human by non-human technology.

Efficiency

Efficiency develops systems which produce the maximum output for the least cost. In McDonald's this is sold to the consumer as being of benefit to them – fast food delivered quickly and cheaply. Much of the cost for this efficiency is placed onto the consumer, for example in queuing to order their food, placing their empty food cartons and trays into the waste bin.

Calculability

All actions in the restaurant are calculated and quantified so that the consumer is given the choice of an array of differently sized meals, the bigger the better. Thus quantity is valued over the quality of the product.

Predictability

Consumers of a 'Big Mac Meal' know exactly what to expect. A 'Big Mac' will be the same whether it is served in Wrexham or Reykjavik – it will be the same size, taste the same and be served in the same environment. Thus the 'Golden Arches' of the McDonald's logo becomes the universal sign to attract you from a car driving on a motorway or strolling in a shopping mall. The experience of eating a meal is repeated endlessly across the globe or repetitively each time you buy a 'Big Mac'.

Control through the substitution of non-human for human technology

> *... these two elements are closely linked. Specifically, replacement of human by non-human technology is often oriented towards greater control. The great source of uncertainty and unpredictability in a rationalizing system are people – either the people who work within those systems or the people who are served by them* (Ritzer, 1993, p148).

Each employee in McDonald's is drilled in what to say and how to say it. The production process which brings the Big Mac onto your tray is pre-packaged, pre-measured, automatically controlled. Both the employee who serves the meal and to an increasing extent the consumer are not required to think, just follow the instructions or see what others do in the queue.

This process therefore is ethically problematic as our skills and capabilities are diminished and powers of judgement dulled. Our identities are moulded by our dependence upon and subordination to the rational bureaucratic processes evidenced in the McDonald's experience. Ritzer argues the process of McDonaldisation shows the ultimate irrationality of a system that does not meet human need but rather does more to damage it.

> *Most specifically, irrationality means that rational systems are unreasonable systems. By that I mean that they deny the basic humanity, the human reason, of the people who work within or are served by them* (Ritzer 1993, p154).

In the USA this has had a damaging effect with an increase in diagnoses of Type 2 diabetes. Critser (2004) argues that Type 2 diabetes has increased dramatically since the early 1990s, quoting figures from paediatric diabetes centres as showing Type 2 now making up 45 per cent of new diabetes cases, particularly in the poorer parts of the USA. These figures can be repeated for the UK where diabetes in general is on the increase.

RESEARCH SUMMARY

As in many countries worldwide, diabetes is increasing in England. Since 1991, the prevalence of diagnosed diabetes has more than doubled in men and increased by 80 per cent in women. It is estimated there will be about 3 million people with diagnosed diabetes in the UK by the year 2010 (Department of Health, 2005).

Critser lays the blame for this increase in diabetes mainly at the doors of fast food chains and government. As fast food has become cheaper, eating out no longer becomes a treat but more the norm. The servings of giant portions are replete with fat, sugar and salt, leading to a huge increase in calorie intake. The US government has not restricted the operations of the fast food companies, but at the same time has cut back on money available to schools for PE and other organised exercise activities.

ACTIVITY 8.2

When you are on placement, look at how the service in the agency in which you are placed reflects the concerns of:

- *efficiency;*
- *calculability;*
- *predictability;*
- *control through the substitution of non-human for human technology.*

Comment

Applying these concepts across the general provision of social services you may be able to draw some interesting parallels with developments in social work. James (2004) argues that the processes below have become increasingly important in the organisation of local authority social service departments.

- *Efficiency*. The focus on Best Value requires local authorities to develop and improve services on a continuous basis, informed by the principles of efficiency, effectiveness and economy. However, this has led to an increased concern with efficiency which predominates in the guidance literature on Best Value (Boyne, 2000).

- *Calculability*. The National Occupational Standards are used to assess the competence of social work students so that the actions of the students are broken down into discrete areas for assessment. Evidence-based practice is being introduced, which then assesses and calculates the effectiveness of practice based upon outcome rather than process.

- *Predictability*. There is a drive for standardisation through, for example, National Standards for Adoption and national assessment frameworks such as Quality Protects in children's services.

- *Control through the substitution of non-human for human technology*. One-stop centres have been developed on the internet where service users can tap into their local authority website to access different claim forms and information.

James (2004) suggests that the McDonaldisation of social work will lead to a lack of creativity and innovation, as services and access to them become standardised. From an ethical standpoint, social workers who are required to follow sets of mechanistic procedures will find that their role in engaging in the moral and practical concerns of service users becomes neutered. If values are to remain central to social work practice then reducing social work to a set of discrete and unrelated actions becomes formulaic and therefore insensitive to the contexts and moral uncertainties of practice.

McDonaldisation represents a powerful critique of modern society. However, this anti-bureaucratic discourse has been contested by Du Gay (2000) who argues that bureaucracies can embody ethical practices. Du Gay suggests that bureaucracies have their own ethical practices, and should be judged by these standards and not by a generalised ethical perspective which has little relevance to the accomplishments of bureaucracies. In a democratic society, bureaucracies should involve mediation and compromise between conflicting interests. Thus the bureaucrat embodies or should embody ethically an impartial spirit which is crucial for running publicly-funded state bureaucracies. For social workers, this means that they ethically embody this form of impartiality and should ensure that services that they are responsible for operate with equity. This requires making tough and difficult decisions between different groups with equal claims to resources. It also requires social workers to act with equity where some groups have been excluded from services, and requires them to work in a positive way to restore equity in an anti-discriminatory framework.

> ... *while we may sometimes experience a sense of personal frustration in our dealings with state bureaux, we might learn to see such frustration as largely the inevitable by-product of the achievement of other objectives that we also value highly: such as the desire to ensure fairness, justice and equality in the treatment of citizens* (Du Gay, 2000, p2).

Accountability

For social workers it is important that their actions are open to public and professional scrutiny, and therefore they are required to keep scrupulous records to ensure that the information upon which accountability depends is made available and accessible to those who wish to ensure that social workers' actions have been undertaken with fairness. Payne (2000) argues that a professional social worker working within a bureaucracy does have to be accountable, and as such has to explain their actions and justify them, usually on records and files kept by the organisation. This process requires that the worker has a duty to be accountable which can be expressed in a number of ways (see Figure 8.1):

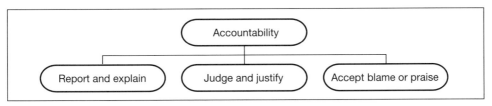

Figure 8.1 *Duties of accountability*

- *Report and explain* – involves accounting for one's actions by telling someone what has happened, for example in supervision or writing a report for a case conference. We must also not merely account for but also show why we acted in the way that we did, so explaining our actions.

- *Judge and justify* – social workers need to judge a situation and make a decision based upon the evidence they have gathered. This is mostly found in social work assessments. Once we have presented the evidence and made our decision, we need to be able to justify that our decision was the right one.

- *Accept blame or praise* – as a consequence, social workers have a duty to accept blame if they have done something wrong which may lead to their dismissal. They also have a duty to accept praise which may lead to promotion if we choose it or extra pay.

The codes of practice for employers and social work and social care workers are central in developing accountability. As Clark (2006) argues, there has been a shift in the use of language and the responsibilities that this requires. The new standards contain duties to be fulfilled, but also qualities to be met in terms of trustworthiness and honesty, which extend into all aspects of their work and also how social workers behave in private.

The codes of practice are important for social workers because this requires for the first time that employers have a duty to ensure that they support workers to do their jobs well. It is not enough to leave this to employers, as we saw in the previous chapter on advocacy. Workers have to engage with organisational issues to assess how far their organisation acts as an enabler or a barrier to effective social work and social care practice.

Whistle-blowing

One of the key developments over the past few years highlighting the negative aspects of public organisations has been the issue of 'whistle-blowing'. This has become important, for example, since the events outlined in the North Wales Tribunal (see Waterhouse, 2000).

The issue of 'whistle-blowing' deals directly with the moral character of social workers. It requires of them, as we shall see below, courage, motivation and commitment to seek justice when, for example, their employing organisation or their superiors act in a dangerous or unjust fashion.

Whistle-blowing–a definition

The disclosure by an employee, in a government agency or private enterprise, to the public or to those in authority, of mismanagement, corruption, illegality, or some other wrongdoing.

To highlight this an example will be taken from outside social work.

Katharine Gun, a British civil servant, faced two years' imprisonment in England for the 'crime' of leaking an embarrassing US intelligence memo indicating that the US had mounted a spying 'surge' against UN delegations in early 2003, in an effort to win approval of the Iraq war resolution. In early March 2003, the *Observer* newspaper in Britain published a US National Security Agency memo describing a 'surge' in UN spying aimed at winning authorization for war on Iraq – targeted 'against' delegations from swing countries on the Security Council.

The British government eventually decided not to proceed with this case and Katherine Gunn was allowed her freedom.

The provisions introduced by the Public Interest Disclosure Act 1998 protect most workers from being subjected to a detriment by their employer. Detriment may take a number of forms, such as denial of promotion, facilities or training opportunities which the employer would otherwise have offered. Employees who are protected by the provisions may make a claim for unfair dismissal if they are dismissed for making a protected disclosure.

Qualifying disclosures

Certain kinds of disclosures qualify for protection ('qualifying disclosures'). Qualifying disclosures are disclosures of information which the worker reasonably believes tend to show one or more of the following matters is either happening now, took place in the past or is likely to happen in the future:

- a criminal offence;

- the breach of a legal obligation;

- a miscarriage of justice;

- a danger to the health or safety of any individual;

- damage to the environment;

- deliberate covering up of information tending to show any of the above five matters.

It should be noted that in making a disclosure, the worker must have reasonable belief that the information disclosed tends to show one or more of the offences or breaches listed above ('a relevant failure'). The belief need not be correct – it might be discovered subsequently that the worker was in fact wrong – but the worker must show that he or she held the belief and that it was a reasonable belief in the circumstances at the time of disclosure.

Making a qualifying disclosure to the employer or via internal procedures

A qualifying disclosure will be a protected disclosure where it is made:

- to the worker's employer, either directly to the employer or by procedures authorised by the employer for that purpose; or

- to another person whom the worker reasonably believes to be solely or mainly responsible for the relevant failure.

The only additional requirement on the worker is that he or she should act in good faith. No other requirement is necessary to qualify for protection. Disclosure to the employer will in most cases ensure that concerns are dealt with quickly and by the person who is best placed to resolve the problem (**www.dti.gov.uk/er/individual/pidguide**).

In Chapter 1, we looked at the case of Alison Taylor and her attempts to reveal serious child abuse inside a number of children's care homes in North Wales. We will now use her example as a case study on whistle-blowing in social work and social care.

CASE STUDY 8.2

Alison Taylor, a residential care worker in a children's home in North Wales, became concerned in 1989 about the abusive and aggressive behaviour of her manager at the time, Nefyn Dodd, who later had overall responsibility for all the residential child care services in Gwynedd, North Wales. Her allegations were not proved at the time and she was dismissed from her job. She continued to make her claims, and told of other abuses across children's homes in North Wales. When a former child care worker, Stephen Norris, was convicted of the sexual abuse of boys at a community home in Wrexham Bryn Esten, it was found that Dodd had also worked there. Taylor, with two local politicians and the newly appointed director of social services in Clwyd, joined together and unearthed previous allegations of child abuse in homes across North Wales, which had not been investigated properly. After much pressure from Taylor and her colleagues a tribunal (Waterhouse, 2000) was eventually set up to look into the allegations leading to a final report in 2000.

ACTIVITY 8.3

Look at the guidance presented by the DTI on the Public Interest Disclosure Act 1998 – remember Alison Taylor's case predates this act.

Do Alison Taylor's actions make a qualified disclosure?

If Alison Taylor believed this was happening but events prove her wrong, is she still covered by the act?

What ethical issues in relation to both the employer's code of practice and the code of practice for social care workers are present here?

Comment

Under the Public Interest Disclosure Act 1998, Alison Taylor's claims make a qualified disclosure: it involves a criminal offence and a threat to health. As a result of her dismissal, ,there is at least the suspicion that someone was covering up the issue and removing Alison Taylor might solve the problem.

As the legislation makes clear, as long as Alison Taylor was acting in good faith and felt she had genuinely good grounds for her complaint then she would still be covered by the act.

What is important is that workers are supported if they are forced to 'whistle-blow'. This requires that the process be made easier for workers, and that supportive institutions such as employers, professional bodies and trade unions all provide the assistance needed. To blow the whistle can have a number of consequences for the worker, who can be faced with many challenges which need to be recognised. Alison Taylor (1998) has spoken powerfully about the obstacles she found in addressing her complaint to those in authority:

> *Often you are blowing the whistle on powerful figures within a local authority who are able if they so choose to mobilise their power to discredit you.*

Fellow practitioners through a sense of loyalty to their colleagues may see you as a trouble maker.

Often the service users on whose behalf action is taken are not listened to and seen as less credible because of their stigmatised status as service users (Taylor, 1998, p72).

This requires then a degree of courage and bravery on the part of the whistle-blower which relates to our discussion of virtue ethics (see Chapter 3). For Alison Taylor the costs of her actions were profound.

I made myself unacceptable to employers and colleagues, some of whom shared my disquiet to the extent that they had taken their own concerns to management. However, I was the only one to break out of the institutional edifice, to commit 'professional suicide', while others apparently relegated individual and collective ethics sidestepped the mess I was creating on behalf of children who were generally regarded as intrinsically worthless (Taylor, 1998, pp58–59).

In material and emotional terms whistle-blowing has a cost – the danger of losing one's job and income, and the pressure placed on those close to you, i.e. family and friends. As Doel and Shardlow (2005) argue, there are many countervailing social pressures which will militate against taking action. Thus a whistle-blower needs commitment, motivation, personal strength and support.

It is to be welcomed then that the Government has introduced a number of supports to the whistle-blower in respect of children. As noted previously, Children's Commissioners can act to investigate suspected areas of abuse to children, although with variable powers between the different Commissioners in the UK.

C H A P T E R   S U M M A R Y

This chapter has identified the importance of social workers understanding the organisations that employ them. Organisational policies and procedures are important in defining the boundaries within which social workers practice. Where policies operate in ways which limit service users' fair access to services, this chapter has argued for the ethical necessity for social workers to challenge such injustice. Whistle-blowing represents one important response if the social worker's organisation operates in an unethical manner, or powerful individuals within the hierarchy act illegally. Whistle-blowing presents an ethical test to social workers in highlighting dangerous or illegal practices which they believe have been covered up. Whistle-blowing, because of the powerful consequences that can develop, must not be undertaken lightly or with naivety. Likewise there are many supportive organisations such as BASW and UNISON who can provide important support and protection to individual workers.

This returns us to the opening chapter of this book where we began to explore the reasons why social workers behave in an ethical way. The motivation to become a social worker cannot be divorced from the ethical reasons which inform that motivation. Vague feelings of wanting to help people will not suffice within the challenging environments in which social workers now find themselves. Social workers need to practise a sustained commitment to social justice underpinned by a dedicated application of personal and professional integrity and compassion. These qualities when used in conjunction with both professional codes of ethics as well as the GSCC codes of practice will enable social workers to meet the challenges which await them over the coming years.

We have argued that values and ethics are at the core of social work practice. When we apply our ethics to practice situations we are doing so in order to enhance our practice with service users and seek effective personal and social change. Social work is a tough profession and it can take its toll emotionally and physically. A recent Social Work Manifeso (Jones et al., 2006) has highlighted the serious malaise in which social workers find themselves. In some ways the Manifesto is a rather bleak document which would not encourage new workers into the profession, although from a different perspective it is also rather encouraging. The authors point to a number of significant changes, both within and outside social work, which gives hope for the future, in particular working in partnership with service users and linking this work to wider social and political movements both nationally and globally. This book in a number of ways has also drawn upon these hopeful currents showing the possibilities for social workers to work ethically.

There is a positive future for social work and social workers as long as they are prepared to defend and develop the principles which first encouraged them to become social workers.

FURTHER READING

Jones, C, Lavalette, M and Penketh, L (2006) *Social Work Manifesto*, at **www.liv.ac.uk/sspsw/Social_Work_Manifesto.html** accessed 04/04/06.
Read this manifesto and if you agree with the arguments, sign up!

Payne, M (2000) *Anti-bureaucratic social work*. Birmingham: Venture Press.
Provides a sound analysis of the ways in which social workers can recognise their duties as social workers but also to work within these duties in a creative and non-bureaucratic way.

References

Abbott, A (1998) *The system of professionals: An essay on the division of expert labor.* Chicago University of Chicago Press.

Adams, R (2003) *Social work and empowerment.* Basingstoke: Palgrave.

Aldgate , J and Statham, D (2001) *The Children Act now.* The Stationery Office, Department of Health.

Allan, K (2001) *Communication and consultation: Exploring ways for staff to involve people with dementia in developing services.* Bristol: Policy Press and the Joseph Rowntree Foundation.

Asquith, S, Clark, S and Waterhouse, L (2005) The role of the social worker in the 21st century – a literature review. *Insight 25.* Scottish Executive Education Department.

Banks, S (2004) *Ethics, accountabilty and the social profession.* London: Palgrave.

Banks, S (2006) *Ethics and values in social work.* 3rd edition. Basingstoke: Palgrave.

Banks, S and Williams, R (2005) Accounting for ethical difficulties in social welfare work. *British Journal of Social Work*, 35 (7), 1055–1022.

Bateman, N (2000) *Advocacy skills for health and social care professionals.* London: Jessica Kingsley.

Bates, J (2005) Embracing diversity and working in partnership in R. Carnwell and J.Buchanan (eds) *Effective Practice in Health and Social Care: A Partnership Approach.* Maidenhead: Open University.

Bauman, Z (1989) *Modernity and the Holocaust.* Cambridge: Polity.

Bauman, Z (1994) *Alone again: Ethics after certainty.* London: Demos.

Beck, U (1992) *Risk society: Towards a new modernity.* London: Sage.

Becker, S (1997) *Responding to poverty; the politics of cash and care.* London: Longman.

Beckett, C and Maynard, A (2005) *Values and ethics in social work: An introduction.* London: Sage.

Benjamin, M and Curtis, J (1992) *Ethics in nursing.* 3rd edition. Oxford: Oxford University Press.

Beresford, P (2006) Social care leaders must seize chance. *Community Care Magazine*, 9 February.

Beresford, P and Croft, S (2001) Service user' knowledges and the social construction of social work. *Journal of Social Work*, 3, 295–316.

Biestek, FP (1974) *The casework relationship.* London: Allen Unwin.

Billington, R, Hockey, J and Strawbridge, S (1998) *Exploring self and society.* Basingstoke: Macmillian.

Bochel, H, Bochel, C, Page R and Sykes, R (2005) *Social policy: Issues and development.* Harlow: Pearson.

Boyne, G (1999) *Managing Local Services: from CCT to Best Value.* Ilford: Frank Cass.

Brayne, H and Carr, H (2005) *Law for social workers 2005.* 9th edition. Oxford:Oxford University Press.

Brearley, C (1982) *Risk and social work.* London: Routledge Kegan & Paul.

British Association of Social Workers (2002) *Code of ethics for social work*. Birmingham: BASW.

Butler-Sloss, Baroness E (1988) *Report of the inquiry into child abuse in Cleveland*. London: HMSO.

Butrym, Z (1976) *The nature of social work*. London: Macmillan.

Charnwell, R and Buchanan, J (2005) *Effective practice in health and social care: A partnership approach*. Maidenhead: Open University.

Carnwell, R and Carson, A (2005) Understanding partnerships and collaboration. In R Carnwell and J Buchanan (eds) *Effective practice in health and social care: A partnership approach*. Maidenhead: Open University.

Carpenter, J, Schneider, J, Brandon, T and Wooff, D (2003) Working in multi-disciplinary community health teams: The impact on social workers and health professionals of integrated mental health care. *British Journal of Social Work*, 3, 1081–103.

Chahal, K (2004) *Experiencing ethnicity:Discrimination and service provision*. York: Joseph Rowntree Foundation.

Chang, J (1991) *Wild swans: three daughters of China*. London: Flamingo.

Clark, C (2000) *Social work ethics: Politics, principles and practice*. Palgrave: Basingstoke.

Clark, C (2005) The deprofessionalisation thesis. *Social Work and Society*, 3 (2), 182–90.

Clark, C (2006) Moral Character in Social Work. *British Journal of Social Work*, 36(1), 75–89.

Clarke, J (2004) *Changing welfare changing states: New directions in social policy*. London: Sage.

Cohen, M (2003) *101 ethical dilemmas*. London: Routledge.

Critser, G (2004) *Fatland: How Americans became the fattest people in the world*. London: Penguin.

Crouch, C (2003) *Commercialisation or citizenship education policy and the future of public services*. Fabian Ideas No. 606. London: Fabian Society.

Crown Prosecution Service (2005) *Racist incident monitoring annual report 2004 – 2005 (including report for religiously aggravated crime 2004–2005)*. London: CPS.

Dalrymple, J and Burke, B (1995) *Anti-oppressive practice*. Buckingham: Open University Press.

Dean, H (2004) Human rights and welfare rights: Contextualising dependency and responsibility. In H. Dean (ed) *The ethics of welfare*. Bristol: Policy Press.

Dench, G, Garvon, K and Young, M (2006) *The new East End: Kinship, race and conflict*. London: Profile Books.

Department for Education and Science (2004) Local Authority Social Services Letter LASSL (2004) 4.

Department for Education and Skills (2004) *Every child matters: Change for children in social care*. London: DfES.

Department of Health (1995) *Messages from research*. London: HMSO.

Department of Health (1998) *Modernising Social Services*. London: HMSO.

Department of Health (2000) *Framework for the assessment of children in need and their families*. London: Stationery Office.

Department of Health (2001) *Valuing people: A new strategy for learning disability for the 21st century*. London: Stationery Office.

Department of Health (2003) *No secrets: Guidance on developing and implementing multi-agency policies and procedures to protect vulnerable adults from abuse*. London: Stationery Office.

Department of Health (2005a) *Health survey for England*. London: Stationery Office.

Department of Health (2005b) *Our health, our care, our say*. London: Stationery Office.

Devaney, J (2004) Relating outcomes to objectives in child protection. *Child and Family Social Work*, 9, 1365–2206.

Doel, M and Shardlow, SM (2005) *Modern social work practice: Teaching and learning in practice settings*. Aldershot: Ashgate.

Dominelli, L (2002) *Anti-oppressive social work theory and practice*. London: Palgrave Macmillian.

Douglas, M (1992) *Risk and blame: Essays in cultural theory*. London: Routledge.

Du Gay, P (2000) *In praise of bureaucracy: Weber – organization – ethics*. London: Sage.

Dunkerley, D, Scourfield, J, Maegusuku-Hewett, T and Smalley, N (2005) The experiences of front-line staff working with children, seeking asylum. *Social Policy and Administration*, 39 (6), 640–52.

Evans, T and Harris, J (2004) Street-level bureaucracy, social work and the (exaggerated) death of discretion. *British Journal of Social Work*, 34, 871–96.

Everitt, A, Hardiker, P, Littlewood, J and Mullender, A (1992) *Applied research for better practice*. London: Macmillian/BASW.

Farmer, E and Owen, M (1995) *Child protection practice, private risks and public remedies: Decision making intervention and outcome in child protection work*. London: HMSO.

Farnworth, C (1997) *Development education in the community*. London: Development Education Association.

Ferguson, H (1997) Protecting children in new times: child protection and the risk society. *Child and Family Social Work*, 2 (4), 221–34.

Ferguson, I, Lavalette, M and Mooney, G (2002) *Rethinking welfare: A critical perspective*. London: Sage.

Fook, J (2002) *Social work: Critical theory and practice*. London: Sage.

Foucault, M (1977) *Discipline and punish: The birth of the prison*. Harmondsworth: Allen Lane.

Franklin, B (ed) (1999) *Social policy, the media and misrepresentation*. London: Routledge.

Friedson, E (2001) *Professionalism: The third logic*. Cambridge: Polity.

Froggett, L (2002) *Love, hate and welfare: Psychosocial approaches to policy and practice*. Bristol: Policy Press.

Garrett, P (2004) Talking child protection: The police and social workers 'working together'. *Journal of Social Work*, 4 (1), 77–97.

Gatrad, A R and Sheikh, A (2002) Palliative care for Muslims and issues before death. *International Journal of Palliative Nursing*, 8, 526–31.

Gatrad, AR and Sheik, A (2003) Editorial: Palliative care needs of minorities: Understanding their needs is the key. *British Medical Journal*, 327, 176–7.

Gewirth, A (1978) *Reason and morality*. Chicago: Chicago University Press.

Gibbons, J, Conroy, S and Bell, C (1995) *A study of child protection practices in English local authorities*. London: HMSO.

Giddens, A (1994) *Beyond left and right: The future of radical politics*. Cambridge: Polity.

Giddens, A (2006) *Sociology*. 5th edition. Cambridge: Polity.

Gilligan, C (1982) *In a different voice: psychological theory and women's development*. Cambridge, MA: Harvard University Press.

Glendinning, C (2003) Breaking down barriers: Integrating health and care services for older people in England. *Health policy*, 65, 139–54.

Goldhagan, DJ (1996) *Hitler's willing executioners: ordinary Germans and the holocaust*. New York: Knopf.

Graham, M (2002) *Social work and African-centred worldviews*. Birmingham: Venture Press.

Gupta, A (2004) *Involving families living in poverty in the training of social workers*. Royal Holloway: University of London.

Habermas, J (1984) *The theory of communicative action, vol.1*. Cambridge: Polity.

Hacking, I (1990) *The taming of chance*. Cambridge: Cambridge University Press.

Harris, J (2003a) *The social work business*. London: Routledge.

Harris, J (2003b) Let's talk business. *Community Care*, 21 August, 211–13.

Hayek, F (1944) *The road to serfdom*. London: Routledge & Keegan Paul.

Healey, K (2005) *Social work theories in context: Creating frameworks for practice*. Basingstoke: Palgrave.

Heller, J (2005) *Catch-22*. London: Vintage

Hewett, T, Smalley, N, Dunkerley, D and Scourfield, J (2005) *Uncertain futures: Children seeking asylum in Wales*. Cardiff: Save the Children. Available at: **www.savethechildren.org.uk**

Horne, M (1999) *Values in social work*. 2nd edition. Aldershot: Ashgate.

Houston, S (2003) Establishing virtue in social work: A response to McBeath and Webb. *British Journal of Social Work*, 33, 819–24.

Hugman, R (2005) *New approaches in ethics for the caring professions*. London: Palgrave.

Humphries, B (2004), An unacceptable role for social work: Implementing immigration policy. *British Journal of Social Work*, 34, 93–107.

James, D (2004)The McDonaldization of social work – or come back Florence Hollis, all is (or should be) forgiven. In R Lovelock, K Lyons and J Powell (eds) *Reflecting on social work: Discipline and profession*. Dartford: Ashgate.

Johns, R (2005) *Using the law in social work*. 2nd edition. Exeter: Learning Matters.

Jones, C (2001) Voices from the frontline: Social workers and New Labour. *British Journal of Social Work*, 31 (4), 547–62.

Jones, C Lavalette, M and Penketh, L (2006) *Social work manifesto*. At **liv.ac.uk/sspsw/Social_ Work_Manifesto.html** Accessed 04/04/06.

Jones, R (2005) Disruptive change. *Guardian Newspaper*, 17 October.

Kadushin, A (1992) *Supervision in social work*. 3rd edition. New York: Columbia University Press.

Kafka, F (2004) *The trial*. London: Vintage.

Kemshall, H (2002) Risk assessment and management. In M Davies (ed) *The Blackwell companion of social work*. Oxford: Blackwell.

Kemshall, H (2002) *Risk, social policy and welfare*. Buckingham: Open University Press.

Kohlberg, L (1984) *The psychology of moral development*. New York: Harper & Row.

Laming, Lord (2003) *The Victoria Climbié inquiry*. London: Stationery Office.

Langan, J and Lyndow, V (2004) *Living with risk: Mental health service user involvement in risk assessment and management*. Bristol:The Policy Press.

Larson, M (1977) *The rise of professionalism*. Berkeley, CA: University of California Press.

Lawrence, E (2005) Trade unions. In M Todd and G Taylor (eds) *Democracy and participation*. London: Merlin Press.

Leigh, S and Miller, L (2004) Is the third way the best way? Social work intervention with children and families. *Journal of Social Work*, 4 (3), 245–67.

Lindley, B and Richards, M (2002) *Protocol on advice and advocacy for parents (child protection)*. University of Cambridge: Centre for Family Research.

Lishman, J (1994) *Communication in social work*. Basingstoke: Macmillan.

Lister, R (1997) *Citizenship: Feminist perspectives*. Basingstoke: Macmillan.

Lister, R (2003) *Citizenship: Feminist perspectives*. 2nd edition. Basingstoke: Palgrave.

Little, M (2004) *Refocusing children's services towards prevention: Lessons from the literature*. Dartington: Dartington Social Research Unit.

Local Government Association (2006) *Social services finance 2005/06: A survey of local authorities*. Research Briefing 1.06. London: LGA Publishing.

Lownsborough, H and O'Leary, D (2005) *The leadership imperative: Reforming children's services from the ground up*. London: Demos.

Lymbery, M (2005) *Social work with older people*. London: Sage.

Mcbeath, G and Webb, SA (2002) Virtue ethics and social work: being lucky, realistic and not doing one's duty. *British Journal of Social Work*, 32, December, 1015–36.

McBride, P (1998) *The assertive social worker*. Aldershot: Ashgate.

Mcdonald, C (2002) *A guide to maoral decision making*. At: **www.ethicsweb.ca/guide** Accessed 14/04/06.

McLaughlin, K (2005) From ridicule to institutionalisation: Anti-oppression, the state and social work. *Critical Social Policy*, 25 (3), 283–305.

Macpherson, W (1999) *The Stephen Lawrence inquiry*, Cmd 4262-1. London: Stationery Office.

Malin, N, Wilmott, S and Manthorpe, J (2002) *Key concepts and debates in health and social care*. Birmingham: Open University.

Marshall, TH (1950) *Citizenship and social class*. Cambridge: Cambridge University Press.

Marsland, D (1996) *Contradictions and dilemas in social policy*. New York: St. Martin's Press.

Martin, G, Phelps, K and Katbamna, S (2004) Human motivation and professional practice: Of knights, knaves and social workers. *Social Policy and Administration*, 38 (5), 470–87.

Mayer, J and Timms, N (1970) *The client speaks*. London: Routledge.

Miller, D (1987) Justice. In D Miller (ed) *The Blackwell encyclopedia of political thought*. London: Blackwell.

Milley, P (2002) Imagining good organizations: Moral orders or moral communities? *Educational Management & Administration*, 30 (1), 47–64.

Milner, J and O'Byrne, P (1998) *Assessment in social work*. Basingstoke: Macmillan.

Mullaly, B (2002) *Challenging oppression: A critical social work approach*. Oxford: Oxford University Press.

Norward, J (2002) *Teaching social policy from a Black South African perspective*. BPD Update Online, Winter. Online at: **www.bpdonline.org/**

Noyce, P (2002) *Rabbit-proof Fence*. Buena Vista Home Entertainment.

Older People's Steering Group (2004) *Older people shaping policy and practice*. York: Joseph Rowntree Foundation.

Outhwaite, W (1994) *Habermas: A critical introduction*. Cambridge: Polity Press.

Parekh, B (2000) *Rethinking multiculturalism: Cultural diversity and political theory*. London: Macmillan.

Parker, S, Fook, J and Pease, B (1999) Empowerment: The modernist social work concept par excellence. In B Pease, and J Fook (eds), *Transforming social work practice: Postmodern critical perspectives*. London: Routledge.

Parrott, L (2003) *Social work and social care*. London: Routledge.

Parrott, L (2005) The political drivers of partnership. In R Carnwell and J Buchanan (eds) *Effective practice in health and social care: A partnership approach*. Maidenhead: Open University Press.

Parton, N (1998) Risk, advanced liberalism and child welfare: The need to recover uncertainty and ambiguity. *British Journal of Social Work*. 28 (1), 5–27.

Parton, N and O'Byrne, P (2000) *Constructive social work: Towards a new practice*. Basingstoke: Macmillan.

Payne, M (2000) *Anti-bureaucratic social work*. Birmingham: Venture Press.

Payne, M (2005) *Modern social work theory*. 5th edition. Basingstoke: Palgrave.

Peck, E and Norman, I (1999). Working together in adult community mental health services: exploring inter-professional role relations. *Journal of Mental Health*, 8 (3), 231–42.

Penna, S and O'Brien, M (1998) *Theorising welfare: Enlightenment and modern society*. London: Sage.

Phinney, JS (1990) Ethnic identity in adolescents and adults: Review of research. *Psychological Bulletin*, 108 (3), 499–514.

Porter, E (1999) *Feminist perspectives on ethics*. London: Longman.

Porter, R (2000) *Enlightenment: Britain and the creation of the modern world*. London: Allen Lane.

Prado, CG (2000) *Starting with Foucault: An introduction to genealogy*. New York: Westview.

Proctor, R N (1988) *Racial hygiene: Medicine under the Nazis*. London: Harvard University Press.

Quinney, A (2006) *Collaborative Social Work Practice*. Exeter: Learning Matters.

Reamer, F (1990) *Ethical dilemmas in social services: A guide for social workers*. New York: Columbia University Press.

Rees, S (1978) *Social work face to face*. London: Edward Arnold.

Ritzer, G (1993) *The McDonaldization of society*. New York: Pine Forge Press.

Rothstein, B (1998) *Just institutions matter: The moral and political logic of the universal welfare state*. Cambridge: Cambridge University Press.

Rowland, M (2003) *The philosopher at the end of the universe*. London: Ebury Press.

Schön, D (1987) *Educating the reflective practitioner*. San Fransisco: Jossey-Bass.

Sevenhuijsen, S (1998) *Citizenship and the ethics of care: Feminist considerations on justice, morality and politics*. London: Routledge.

Shakespeare, T (2000) *Help*. Birmingham: Venture Press.

Shardlow, S, Davis, C, Johnson, M, Long, T, Murphy, M and Race, D (2004) *Education and training for inter-agency working: New standards*. Salford Centre for Social Work Research: University of Salford.

Silvers, A, Wasserman, D and Mahowald, M (afterword by L Becker) (1998) *Disability, difference, discrimination: perspectives on justice in bioethics and public policy*. Lanham, MD: Rowman & Littlefield.

Smith, M K (1996) *The functions of supervision. Encyclopedia of informal education*, Last update 28/01/05. Online at: **www.infed.org/biblio/functions_of_supervision.htm**

Social Exclusion Unit (2004) *Tackling social exclusion: Taking stock and looking to the future: Emerging findings*. Office of the Deputy Prime Minster: Stationery Office.

Spratt, T and Houston, S (1999) Developing critical social work in theory and in practice: Child protection and communicative reason. *European Journal of Social Work*, 4 (4), 15–324.

Stanley, N and Manthorpe, J (2004) *The age of the inquiry: Learning and blaming in health and social care*. London: Routledge.

Stevenson, O and Parsloe, P (1993) *Community care and empowerment*. York: Rowntree Foundation with Community Care.

Strinati, D (1995) *An introduction to theories of popular culture*. London: Routledge.

Swain, J, French, S and Cameron, C (2003) *Controversial issues in a disabling society*. Buckingham: Open University.

Tarleton, B, Ward, L and Howarth, J (2006) *Finding the right support?* Norah Fry Research Centre: Bristol University.

Taylor, A (1998) Hostages to fortune: the abuse of children in care. In G Hunt (ed) *Whistleblowing in the social services*. London: Arnold.

Thompson, N (2001) *Anti-discriminatory practice*. Basingstoke: Palgrave Macmillan.

Timms, N (1983) *Social work values ... An enquiry*. London: Routledge & Kegan Paul.

Todd, M and Taylor, G (eds) (2005) *Democracy and participation*. London: Merlin Press.

Tronto, J (1993) *Moral boundaries: a political argument for an ethic of care*. New York: Routledge.

Waterhouse, R (2000) *Lost in care: report of the tribunal of inquiry into the abuse of children in care in the former county council areas of Gwynedd and Clwyd since 1974*. London: Stationery Office.

Waterson J (1999) Redefining community care social work: Needs or risks led? *Health and Social Care in the Community*, 7 (4), 276–9.

Webb, S (2006) *Social work in a risk: society social and political perspectives*. Basingstoke: Palgrave.

White, C, Wiggins, R, Blane, D, Whitworth, A and Glickman,M (2005) Person, place or time? The effect of individual circumstance. *Health Statistics Quarterly*, Winter, 18–28.

Williams, R (1977), *Marxism and literature*. Oxford: Oxford University Press.

Winefield, H and Barlow, J (1995) Client and worker satisfaction in a child protection agency. *Child Abuse and Neglect*, 19 (8), 897–905.

Internet

Department of Trade and Industry, guide to the Public Disclosure Act 1998:

- **www.dti.gov.uk/er/individual/pidguide**

Gateshead Council, Child Protection Investigations:

- **www.gateshead.gov.uk/CareandHealth/ChildrenandFamilies/ChildreninNeed/Investigations.aspx**

Social Policy and Social Work (SWAP), subject centre of the Higher Education Academy:

- **www.swap.ac.uk/**

- **www.swap.ac.uk/about/miniproject7.asp** (SWAP Report: Anna Gupta (2004) *Involving famiies living in poverty in the training of social workers*. Royal Holloway: University of London)

Unison campaign on abortion

- **unison.org.uk/acrobat/1295.pdf**

Unison campaign on domestic violence

- **www.unison.org.uk/file/B2139.pdf**

Index

Added to a page number 'f' denotes a figure and 't' denotes a table.

A
Aborigines Act 27
absolutism, cultural 32
accountability 65–81
  case studies 71, 80–1
  duties 147–8
  ethics 76–8
  law 72–6
  personal level 70–1
  practical reason 78–80
  and trust 12–13
administrative supervision 108
adult abuse 90
advocacy
  assertiveness and caring for self 112–13
  Bateman's principles of 101–7
  case studies 103, 104, 106–7, 114–15
  confidentiality 107
  definition 100
  ethics, self and others 107–11
  first-order principles 111
  forms of 100–1
  social work 99
    and trade unions 113–15
anger 55
anti-bureaucratic discourse 147
anti-discriminatory practice 1, 24
anti-oppressive practice 23–43
  advocacy 100
  commitment to 5
  competing models 25
  critical reflection 79
  culture, values and relativism 30–7
  empowerment 38–9, 40–1
  minimal intervention 42–3
  orientation and values 23–30
  partnership 39–40
  service users 37–8
  social justice 128
  social work values 1, 20
  trade unions 113
Anti-Terrorism, Crime and Security Act (2001) 19
approval seeking 58
Aristotle 55
assertiveness 112–13
assessment 5, 26, 28, 39, 72
autonomy 45, 51, 87, 120

B
Bank's first-order principles 111
Bateman's principles of advocacy 101–7
Bentham, Jeremy 51, 140
best interest 102
Best Value 146
British Association of Social Workers (BASW) 76
bureaucracy 138–40, 143
bureaucratic social services 144
bureaucratic/procedural approach 141
business-speak 4
Butler Sloss report (1988) 70

C
calculability 144, 146
canteen culture 122–3
care *see* ethic of care; joined-up care
Care Standards Act (2000) 12–13, 76
case studies xvi
  accountability 71, 80–1
  advocacy 103, 104, 106–7, 114–15
  ethics 141
  managing risk 92–3
  partnership 122, 129, 133
  principles and consequences 44–5, 48, 51
  social work values 10
  whistle-blowing 150
Catch-22 139
categorical imperative 48

charities 101
child abuse, diagnosis of 70
child care, partnership in 40
child protection
   inter-agency working 125
   minimal intervention 42–3
   panel conferences 86
   parents' rights 107
   risk 88
children, whistle-blowing in respect of 151
Children Act (2004) 89, 104, 120
Children's Commissioners 105, 151
children's rights 117
Children's Trusts 67
citizen advocacy 100
citizenship, spheres of 101f
civil rights 101
Clarke, Peter 105
class conflict 20–1
Climbié/Laming Inquiry 109, 112, 125
Code of Conduct (NMC) 124–5, 132
Code of Ethics (BASW) 84, 115, 116
Code of Practice (GSCC) xi–xii, xvii, 76, 115,
    124–5, 132, 137
codes of ethics 77, 125
codes of practice 77
collective advocacy 100, 104
common sense 16
communication, democratic 127–8, 130
communicative action 128
compassion 57
competence 68, 102
competition 2, 3
comprehensibility, ethics of partnership 130
confidentiality 54, 102, 107, 133
conflicts
   managing risk 89–96
   in partnership 121
   see also class conflict; ethical conflicts
consensus, in communication 128
consequentialist approaches 45, 46–7
   importance of 54
   strike action 115
   utilitarian 51–3
constitutive approach 6
consultation, with service users 37, 41
consumerist approach, empowerment 41
contracts 2, 3

control 145–8
core values 34
courage 55, 56
Crime and Disorder Act (1998) 19, 133
critical self-reflection 79, 81
cultural absolutism 32
cultural relativism 32
culture
   professional 131, 132
   values and relativism 18, 30–7
   see also canteen culture; outcome-
      oriented culture; professional culture;
      reflexive culture

D
death/dying, cultural practices 31–2
deceit 5–6
decision-making
   child protection panel conferences 86
   ethical 58, 61–2
   impartial and dispassionate 90–1
   partnership 41
democratic approach, empowerment 41
democratic communication 127–8, 130
deontology 47–51
dependence 92f, 101
   see also independence
diabetes (type 2) 145–6
dialogue principle 34
difference 27–8, 31–2
diligence 102
Disability Action Network (DAN) 28, 29
Disability Discrimination Act (2005) 104
disability movement 70
disabled people
   assessment against norms of non-
      disabled world 28–9
   independence 63–4
   service provision 101
disclosures, qualifying 149–51
discourse ethics 130–1
discourse(s)
   anti-bureaucratic 147
   challenging dominant 80f
   povertyism 81
   power relations 16
   social work practice 79
discrimination 25, 27, 29

see also anti-discriminatory practice
Dodd, Nefyn 13
dominant discourses, challenging 80f
dominant groups, acceptance of values
    15–16
domination 27
duty-based approach, strike action 115–17
duty/duties 19, 49, 50, 54, 60, 136

E
educational supervision 108
effectiveness 2
efficiency 2, 144, 146
emotional risk 95
emotions 57
empathy 29, 39
empowerment 38–9
  advocacy and 99
  democratic and consumerist approaches
    40–1
England, Children's Commissioner 105
Enlightenment 47, 84
equal opportunities legislation 136
ethic of care
  problems 62–4
  see also feminist ethic of care
ethical choices 9
ethical conflicts/dilemmas 5, 56, 75, 104–5
ethical content, reflection 79
ethical indifference 140
ethical manner 17–20
ethical preferences 20
ethical principles 21, 56
ethical truth 32
ethics
  accountability 76–8
  case study 141
  government-sponsored advocacy 104–5
  Kantian and utilitarian 54
  partnership working 119–34
  self and others 107–11
  see also relationship-based ethics; virtue
    ethics
ethnic cleansing 28
ethnic minorities
  needs research 30–1
  stereotypical and racist attitudes towards
    122–3

evaluation, partnership in 39
extermination 27, 28

F
fast-food chains, diabetes 145–6
'fateful moment' 88
female voice 59f
feminist ethic of care 57–62, 63–4
first-order principles 111
flexible action 142
flexible/reflective approach 142
'floating responsibility' 140
Foucault, Michel 16, 139
freedom, individuals right to 91

G
general principles 77, 78
general rights 117–18
General Social Care Council (GSCC) xi, xvii
general statements 77
genocides 28
'golden mean' 55
Goldilocks test 55
good life 55
government pressure 2
government-sponsored advocacy 104–5
Gramsci, Antonio 15
Greenwood, Jeffrey 70

H
Habermas, Jürgen 127–8
half-cast aborigines, plan to eliminate 27–8
happiness 51, 52, 53
hegemony 15–16
helping relationship 57
Hitler's willing executioners 49
Hodge, Margaret 105
Human Rights Act (2000) 34
human rights principle 34
human technology, replaced by non-human
    technology 145–8
hybrid social services 144

I
'identification by proxy' 32
identity, professional 67, 125, 131
ideology 15, 66
immoral community 8

impartiality 102
imperialism 32
increased scrutiny 3
independence 63–4, 92f
   see also dependence
individual empowerment 38
individualism 15
inequality 26
information, and advocacy 102
information technology systems 3
injustice 129
instrumental relationship 142–3
inter-professional working 123
intermediate approach 6
intervention 36f, 39, 42–3

J
joined-up care 120–1
Joseph Rowntree Foundation 31, 66
judgement
   exercise of 54
   see also sound judgement
justice
   link between care and 64
   objectification of human beings 60
   see also injustice; principle of justice;
      social justice

K
Kafka/Kafkaesque 139
Kant, Emmanuel 47, 50
knowledge 16
Kohlberg's classification, moral
   development 58–9

L
Laming Inquiry 109, 112, 125
law(s)
   accountability 72–6
   campaigning against unjust 91
legal duties, social justice 136
legal powers, justifications for exercising 72
Lisicki, Barbara 28, 29
local authorities, law and accountability 72
Local Safeguarding Children Boards (LSCBs)
   89–90
Local Strategic Partnerships 129
lying 47–8

M
McDonaldisation 144, 145, 146, 147
male dominance, moral concepts 59–60
male voice 59f
management and business cycle 3f
managerial ethos 2
Marxists 15
media, process of accountability 12
media pressure 2
Mill, J.S. 51
minimal intervention 42–3
modernisation 2, 38, 120, 121
Modernising Social Services 120
moral ambivalence 140
moral code 13
moral communities 128
moral considerations 49
moral decisions 90–1
moral development 58–9
moral duty 19
moral relationship 143–4
moral relativism 32, 33
moral sensitivity 56
moral theory 47–8
moral thinking 58
morality 8, 14, 18–19, 49
mortality risk 27

N
narrative, as legitimate 39
National Health Service and Community
   Care Act (1990) 2, 37, 72, 120
National Occupational Standards (NOS) xi
   accountability 65
   advocacy 98
   anti-oppressive practice 23
   ethics in social work organisations 135
   managing risk 83
   preparing for social work 1
   principles and consequences 44
National Strategy for Neighbourhood
   Renewal 129
negative rights 117–18
neighbourhood deprivation 27
Neighbourhood Renewal Fund 129
Neville, A.O. 27
New Deal for Communities 129
New Right 143

no harm principle 34
non-human technology, replacement of
human technology by 145–8
normality 28
Norris, Stephen 13
Northern Ireland, Children's Commissioner
105
Nursing and Midwifery Council Code of
Conduct 124

O
objectification, of human beings 60
'obligation to care' 60
Older People's Steering Group (2004) 66
oppression 25, 29, 129
see also anti-oppressive practice
organisational autonomy 120
organisations see social work organisations
'othering' 29
Our health, Our care, Our Say (2004)
120–1, 122
outcome-oriented culture 127
overprotection, risk assessment 88

P
Panopticon 139–40
parents' rights, children's safety and 107
participation
legislation for increased 104
pyramid of 40f
partnership 119–34
advocacy 99
anti-oppressive practice 39–40
case studies 122, 129, 133
empowerment 41
social work 120–33
social work organisations 67
patronage 101
performance indicators 3
philanthropy 101
physical risk 94
planning, partnership in 39
pleasure/pain balance 51, 52
police force 122
political attributes, professions 68
political correctness 70
political rights 101
positive rights 118

povertyism 81
power
differences 25
hierarchies 26, 67
relations 16
sharing 29, 38
see also legal powers; professional power
practical moral social work 3, 4t
practical reason, and accountability 78–80
practitioner advocacy 100
predictability 145, 146
primary level, intervention 42
'principle of justice' 51
'principle of utility' 51
principled approaches 45, 46
deontology 47–51
importance of 53–4
professional advocacy 100
professional autonomy 45, 120
professional community 111
professional culture 131, 132
professional development xvi–xvii
professional identity 67, 125, 131
professional power, abuse of 139
professional relationships 143
professional values 131, 132
professionalism 67
professions
competence and political attributes 68
state and market 69f
protection
in social work 92f
see also child protection; overprotection
Protection of Vulnerable Adults (POVA) 90
prudential reason 19
Psy discourse 16
Public Interest Disclosure Act (1998) 150

Q
qualifying disclosures 149–51
qualities, social workers 57t
Quality Protects programme 104
quasi-market 144

R
R v Gloucestershire County Council, ex
parte Barry [1997] 72, 73
Rabbit-proof fence 27, 32

Race Relations (Amendment) Act (2001)
136
racial hostility 19, 30, 122–3
radical model, anti-oppressive practice 25
radical social work movement 20–1
rational technical social work 2, 4t, 57
rationalisation 19, 144
rationality 47–8, 49, 50–1
   see also practical reason
reflective practice xvi–xvii, 79, 81, 142
reflexive culture 88
reformist model, anti-oppressive practice
   25
relationship-based ethics 58, 127
relativism 32, 33
respect 32, 50, 55
responsibility 15, 85, 88
right action 130
right(s)
   advocacy and 100
   of citizenship 101
   'othering' and the denial of 29
   service users 117
   social workers 12, 117
   to freedom 91
   see also general rights; parents' rights;
      special rights
risk analysis 87
risk assessment 88, 95
risk assessment schedules 90
risk averse society 85, 89
risk avoidance 85, 87
risk management 83–96
   case study 92–3
   community care assessment 5
   conflicts and dilemmas 89–96
   in social work 84–9
risk orientation 89t
risk sharing 86
risk society 84
rules
   bureaucracy and conformity to 140
   see also specific rules

S
Scotland, Children's Commissioner 105
scrutiny, increased 3
secondary level, intervention 42

self
   caring for 112–13
   ethics and others 107–11
self-advocacy 100, 104
self-determination 104, 116
self-governance 88
self-interest 19, 50, 144
self-reflection, critical 79, 81
sensitivity 29–30
separatist approach 5–6
service provision, disabled people 101
service user movements 1–2
service users
   action undertaken on behalf of 102
   anti-oppressive practice 37–43
   criticisms of social workers 70
   difficulties in thinking rationally 50
   expectations xii–xiii
   involvement in mental health services 96
   legislation for increased participation by
      104
   local authorities' duty to provide
      information to 72
   nature of conflicts with 75t
   priority of interests 116
   rights 117
   self-determination 116
   social justice 24
   what they value 66–71
   see also social worker-service user
      relationship
service withdrawal, local authorities'
   powers 72
shared values 18–19
siege mentality 5
sincerity 130
skills, inter-professional working 123–4
Smith, Adam 90
social class
   mortality risk 27
   see also class conflict
social conduct, regulation of 87–8
social differentiation 26
social exclusion 129
social insurance 84
social justice
   anti-oppressive practice 24, 128
   duty to maintain 12

public bodies, legal duties 136
values 20, 38f
social mandate, social work 69–70
social rights 101
social risk 94–5
social services
hybrid 144
percentage spend, support needs 88
see also service provision; service users;
service withdrawal
social work
advocacy 99
controlling 3f
definitions ix, 74
educational requirements ix–xiii
partnership 120–33
risk and 84–9
social mandate 69–70
and trade unions 113–15
values see values
virtue-based 55–6
wider community 111
social work organisations 135–51
alienation from 5
as moral communities 128
need for in present form 67
and risk 89
social worker-service user relationship 21,
143
social workers
assertive 112
developing empowering practice 39
educational requirements ix–xiii
importance of values 126–7
legal protection of title 12–13
obligations 12
professional identity 67, 125, 131
qualities 57t
responsibilities 11f
rights 12, 117
service users' criticisms of 70
siege mentality 5
as street-level bureaucrats 45
what service users value 66
socially acceptable behaviour 58
sound judgement 55, 56
special rights 117
specific rules 77, 78

standardised practice 2
state control 68, 69f, 70
strategic action 128
street-level bureaucrats 45
subject skills x–xi
supervision 108–11, 112
support, in social work 92f
support needs, percentage spend on 88
supportive supervision 108

T
tacit knowledge 79
Taylor, Alison 13
telling the truth 48, 49
tertiary level, intervention 42
The Trial 139
three-stage approach, intervention 42
toleration, cultural 32
trade unions, and social work 113–15
traditional values 20–2
trust 12–13
truth
ethics of partnership 130
see also ethical truth; telling the truth
turn-taking 59
type 2 diabetes 145–6

U
UNISON 113–14
universality 48
utilitarian consequentialism 51–3

V
validity claims, consensus 128
value systems 14, 19, 21
values
anti-oppressive practice 23–30
case study 10
conflict of 90
cultural relativism 30–7
defined 13–14
importance for social workers 126–7
inter-professional working 123
political and social context 1–12
process of acquiring 15–16
professional 131, 132
purpose of 17
risk management 96

social justice 38f
traditional 20–2
Valuing People (DoH) 104
virtue ethics 55–7, 58
virtue theory 55

W
Wales, Children's Commissioner 105
welfare state 84–5, 143
welfarism 67, 70
well-being 91

well-being orientation 89t
whistle-blowing 148–51
  case study 150
  definition 148
  qualifying disclosures 149–51
white culture 30
wider community, social work 111
Wild Swans 49
wisdom 55
women, moral development 59
Working in Partnership 129

Transforming Social Work Practice – titles in the series

Applied Psychology for Social Work	ISBN: 978 1 84445 071 8
Collaborative Social Work Practice	ISBN: 978 1 84445 014 5
Communication and Interpersonal Skills in Social Work	ISBN: 978 1 84445 019 0
Courtroom Skills for Social Workers	ISBN: 978 1 84445 123 4
Effective Practice Learning in Social Work	ISBN: 978 1 84445 015 2
Groupwork Practice in Social Work	ISBN: 978 1 84445 086 2
Introducing International Social Work	ISBN: 978 1 84445 132 6
Loss and Social Work	ISBN: 978 1 84445 088 6
Management and Organisations in Social Work	ISBN: 978 1 84445 044 2
New Directions in Social Work Practice	ISBN: 978 1 84445 079 4
Practical Computer Skills for Social Work	ISBN: 978 1 84445 031 2
Proactive Child Protection and Social Work	ISBN: 978 1 84445 131 9
Reflective Practice in Social Work	ISBN: 978 1 84445 082 4
Research Skills for Social Work	ISBN: 978 1 84445 179 1
Safeguarding Adults	ISBN: 878 1 84445 148 7
Service User and Carer Participation in Social Work	ISBN: 978 1 84445 074 9
Sexuality and Social Work	ISBN: 978 1 84445 085 5
Social Work and Human Development (second edition)	ISBN: 978 1 84445 112 8
Social Work and Mental Health (third edition)	ISBN: 978 1 84445 154 8
Social Work and Mental Health in Scotland	ISBN: 978 1 84445 130 2
Social Work in Education and Children's Services	ISBN: 978 1 84445 045 9
Social Work Practice: Assessment, Planning, Intervention and Review (second edition)	ISBN: 978 1 84445 113 5
Social Work with Children and Families (second edition)	ISBN: 978 1 84445 144 9
Social Work with Children, Young People and their Families in Scotland (second edition)	ISBN: 978 1 84445 156 2
Social Work with Drug and Substance Misusers	ISBN: 978 1 84445 058 9
Social Work with Looked After Children	ISBN: 978 1 84445 103 6
Social Work with Older People (second edition)	ISBN: 978 1 84445 155 5
Social Work with People with Learning Difficulties	ISBN: 978 1 84445 042 8
Sociology and Social Work	ISBN: 978 1 84445 087 9
Studying for Your Social Work Degree	ISBN: 978 1 84445 174 9
Thriving and Surviving in Social Work	ISBN: 978 1 84445 080 0
Understanding and Using Theory in Social Work	ISBN: 978 1 84445 139 5
Using the Law in Social Work (third edition)	ISBN: 978 1 84445 114 2
Values and Ethics in Social Work	ISBN: 978 1 84445 067 1
What is Social Work? Context and Perspectives (second edition)	ISBN: 978 1 84445 055 1
Youth Justice and Social Work	ISBN: 978 1 84445 066 4

To order, please contact our distributor: BEBC Distribution, Albion Close, Parkstone, Poole, BH12 3LL. Telephone: 0845 230 9000, email: **learningmatters@bebc.co.uk**. You can also find more information on each of these titles and our other learning resources at www.learningmatters.co.uk.